MADNESS

The Ten Most Memorable NCAA Basketball Finals

Mark Mehler and Charles Paikert

SPORTS PUBLISHING

Copyright © 2018 by Mark Mehler and Charles Paikert

All rights reserved. No part of this book may be reproduced in any manner without the express written consent of the publisher, except in the case of brief excerpts in critical reviews or articles. All inquiries should be addressed to Sports Publishing, 307 West 36th Street, 11th Floor, New York, NY 10018.

Sports Publishing books may be purchased in bulk at special discounts for sales promotion, corporate gifts, fund-raising, or educational purposes. Special editions can also be created to specifications. For details, contact the Special Sales Department, Sports Publishing, 307 West 36th Street, 11th Floor, New York, NY 10018 or sportspubbooks@skyhorsepublishing.com.

Sports Publishing® is a registered trademark of Skyhorse Publishing, Inc.®, a Delaware corporation.

Visit our website at www.sportspubbooks.com.

10 9 8 7 6 5 4 3 2 1

Library of Congress Cataloging-in-Publication Data is available on file.

Cover design by Tom Lau
Cover photo credit: AP Images
All interior photos courtesy of AP Images

ISBN: 978-1-61321-993-5
Ebook ISBN: 978-1-61321-994-2

Printed in the United States of America

CONTENTS

Acknowledgments v

Introduction—Why We Care vii

Chapter 1: The Hunters: Duke vs. Butler, 2010 1

Chapter 2: The Improbable Game: Michigan vs. Seton Hall, 1989 23

Chapter 3: A Perfect Game from an Imperfect Team: Villanova vs. Georgetown, 1985 43

Chapter 4: Hope Is a Thing with Leather (or Rubber): North Carolina State vs. Houston, 1983 65

Chapter 5: Dean, Redeemed: North Carolina vs. Georgetown, 1982 89

Chapter 6: Too Much, the Magic/Bird Show: Michigan State vs. Indiana State, 1979 109

Chapter 7: The Wiz Waves Goodbye: UCLA vs. Kentucky, 1975 133

Chapter 8: What Price, Glory?: Texas Western vs. Kentucky, 1966 155

Chapter 9: The Contrast Contest: Loyola vs. Cincinnati, 1963 177

Chapter 10: The Slickers vs. the Hicks ... and Wilt: North Carolina vs. Kansas, 1957 199

Chapter 11: The Consolation Games (2016, 2008, 2003, 1993, and 1987) 223

Sources 231

Index 237

Acknowledgments

I would like to thank the following:

My friend and coauthor, Charlie Paikert, who came up with the idea for this book. Charlie's all Orange (Syracuse), and I'm all Red (St. John's), but we make it work.

Our editor, Ken Samelson, for his encouragement and support throughout the editorial process.

My friend, Greg Prince, for making this book possible by introducing us to Ken. Greg also reintroduced me to the New York Mets, for which I am less inclined to thank him.

My junior high school friend, Michael Klahr, for getting me hooked on St. John's University basketball (and college basketball in general) fifty-four years ago.

My late friend, Bill Brookman, another college basketball fanatic, who taught me how one can ride the bench and still be the coolest guy on the team.

My father, Irving Mehler, who throughout my professional life urged me to write about the things I love.

And, finally, my wife, Phyllis, who could care less about college basketball or any other sport but who is the best sport I've ever known.

—Mark Mehler

Thanks to my coauthor Mark Mehler for shouldering a heavy load; my wife, Bernice Napach, for her patience and encouragement; my friend, M. C. Antil, for timely assists, and my daughter, Anna Paikert, for being a fan. And in memory of my father, Géza Paikert, who shared his love of college basketball with me on cold winter nights in Syracuse.

—Charles Paikert

Introduction

Why We Care

"If you make every game a life and death proposition, you're going to have problems. For one thing, you'll be dead a lot."
—Dean Smith, former head basketball coach
of the North Carolina University Tar Heels

Sports Psychology 101:
We watch sports and root for our favorite teams out of our fundamental human desire to connect with one another and with something bigger than ourselves. As the institutional pillars of society that once served that function—governments, churches, schools—crumble and fall (don't take our word, watch *The Simpsons*), we gravitate to the one remaining institution that never fails to remind us that we are one.

For many of us, the act of rooting follows a progression that looks something like this: strong interest, turning into mild obsession, then into the homicidal Robert DeNiro character in *The Fan*, and, ultimately, to a Duke University Cameron Crazy, the apogee of rooting fanaticism.

Among all the viewing options in the vast universe of televised sports that inspire fan devotion of this magnitude, the NCAA Final Four holds a unique and indelible place. The American college football championship entails a mere four-team playoff; the NFL, a twelve-team roundelay leading to Super Bowl Sunday. Paltry stuff, indeed. The two-week countdown to the Final Four, by contrast, is a basketball smorgasbord, a veritable hardcourt feast, offering a delectable array of sixty-four games (the tournament field as of this writing comprises sixty-eight teams and growing). These games are contested in nearly every nook and cranny of the American landscape.

And with all these tournament games come the kind of wild and crazy goings-on that are found in no other team sport. They do not call it "March Madness" for nothing. You won't witness Princeton besting UCLA on the gridiron, but back in March of 1996, the mighty Bruins, coming off their eleventh national championship season, were thoroughly upended, if not humiliated, by a group of skinny Ivy Leaguers from New Jersey.

Siena over Stanford, Bucknell over Kansas, little Hampton University over Iowa State, Middle Tennessee over Michigan State, and most impressive of all, George Mason over North Carolina, Michigan State, and UConn—in one fortnight, no less. These nearly impossible to comprehend, monumental upsets are among the hundreds of sporting miracles that have defined the early rounds of the championship for years. If you truly wish to celebrate the magic and the mania of big-time sports, the NCAA basketball tournament is the place to park your keister every March.

But March Madness is about more than the games themselves. There's bracketology, the ever-popular pseudo-science of selecting the sixty-eight teams, matching them up against each other in four regional brackets, and picking the winners of each game. Anyone can play bracketology—the math whizzes who gave us the algorithms that crashed the global economy back in '08 seem to perform particularly well at this pursuit. Likewise, everyone can share in the annual "Selection Sunday" ritual of complaining about the qualified "bubble" teams that should have made the cut. And, of course, there are the office betting pools, the beer bashes, the alumni pissing contests, and the over-the-top media hype that would lead one to believe that each NCAA tournament is the most important event of its century.

"I don't believe I'm a better coach now than I was two and a half hours ago."
—Dean Smith, in the minutes after winning his first NCAA championship in 1982

Leave it to the late, great coach Dean Smith to inject a little homespun common sense and wisdom into all this mayhem.

The NCAA tournament, suffice it to say, was not always a round-the-clock whirligig of must-see TV. Its humble roots go back to 1939, when, as the new kid on the block, it vied for supremacy with the more prestigious National Invitation Tournament (NIT) held at Madison Square Garden in New York. In its first decade, the NCAA played a very distant second fiddle to the well-established NIT. All that began to change in 1951 when City College of New York (winner of both the NIT and NCAA) became embroiled in a point-shaving scandal that severely tarnished the image of the Big Apple and, by extension, its Broadway baby, the NIT. New York, to be sure, remains a basketball mecca, but worshippers of the game are more likely to encounter transcendence on the rough and tumble playground courts of the Bronx and Brooklyn than they are in midtown Manhattan.

The NCAAs, originally an eight-team tournament, expanded to sixteen by the early 1950s, grew to between twenty-two and twenty-five teams from the mid 1950s to early 1970s, thirty-two in 1975, forty in 1979, forty-eight in 1980, and sixty-four in 1985. The field was further expanded to sixty-eight in 2011.

The accomplishment of gaining selection into a widely expanded NCAA field has surely been devalued to a degree. On the other hand, as compared to college football, where losing teams participate in an absurdly bloated bowl system, the NCAA tourney can appear as exclusive as a Palm Beach golf club. And with its expanded roster, the ultimate goal of winning the whole shebang now requires a grueling six-game slog. Win and advance. Lose and go home. It's no easy ride to college basketball's summit.

By the time this two-week traveling basketball circus wends its way to the Final Four, fans and non-fans alike are primed for maximum excitation. The Bucknells, Sienas, and Hamptons are generally long gone by this point (but not always—more on this in subsequent chapters). Still, the madness these pint-sized Davids have engendered on the journey somehow carries over to the final reckoning with the Goliaths.

While the Final Fours themselves may be less likely to provide those shocking jolts, they retain the extraordinary ability to amaze. Over the first ten chapters, you'll read about ten iconic championship games. You'll read a bit about history, strategies, matchups, all the Xs & Os stuff. But more important, you'll read about the memories of grown men, reliving their glory and reflecting upon their youthful dreams. All these years later, we found that Dean Smith's observation about the relative unimportance of winning and losing holds true, more often than not. Over time, the won-loss distinction has a way of becoming blurred, if not forgotten. A grandfather, taking a break from watching daytime TV on the chaise to chat with a reporter about a game he played as a kid fifty years ago, is less likely to recall the sting of a loss than the camaraderie of his teammates and coaches and the exhilaration of playing a game he loved on college basketball's biggest stage.

We acknowledge in advance that the selection process we employed was highly subjective, and we make no claims of infallibility. Indeed, we welcome the brickbats with big, warm smiles, because we had such a good time researching and writing this tome—traversing the country (by phone; our travel budget was quite limited) and talking basketball with dozens of ballplayers, coaches, referees, and courtside wags. And we got to rummage and cull through mounds of fascinating archival material, sports history as told by America's keenest observers of the great game of roundball. For two lifelong college basketball junkies like us, this was a thoroughly enjoyable way to spend several months.

As regards our selection process, we employed four basic criteria.

- What went on between the lines—the quality of play, the level of excitement, tension and drama displayed over a forty-minute span;
- The influence of those games on the future development and popularity of college and professional basketball;
- The social, cultural, and economic significance of the games;
- And last, but hardly not least, the outsized personalities who played and coached in those games, leaving behind their imprints on college basketball history.

Of course, there are more than ten NCAA finals that meet one or more of these criteria, and rather than ignore them, we've included a chapter at the end touching on five classic games that narrowly missed the cut.

And finally, just a word about what we learned as fans in researching this book. It was a rare experience for us to watch these marvelous games streaming on our PCs with total, unimpeded concentration. We're all used to viewing games, whether live or on TV, while engaging in conversation with others, periodically running to the fridge for a beer, or conducting some other unrelated activity. Drilling down to focus on every possession forces a viewer to recognize a fundamental truth about basketball. There are hundreds, if not thousands, of things, large and small, that occur in the course of a game that contribute to the outcome—a flick of a wrist, a head fake, the tip of a sneaker that nips the sideline. It is never one shot, one pass, or one missed opportunity which determines the end result. The game ebbs and flows for forty minutes, offering a glorious mixture of power, finesse, strategy, and the human conquest over fatigue. When the stakes are as high as they are in the NCAA final, that constant ebb and flow can be positively sublime.

All that being said, we are not oblivious to big-time college basketball's dark web. As of this writing, the US Justice Department is engaged in a sweeping criminal investigation of corruption that has already ensnared several Division I assistant coaches, apparel reps, and financial advisers. The initial charges involved payoffs to the coaches to steer their players toward those companies. But those accusations appear to be the tip of the iceberg.

This kind of news should surprise no one. College basketball is a big money operation, and big corruption tends to follow big money.

But, for now, we ask you to put all that negativity aside, set your focus squarely on the game itself, and join us in luxuriating in a timeless sporting ritual.

Let the Madness begin.

Chapter 1

The Hunters: Duke vs. Butler, 2010

Time, as Einstein taught us, is a relative construct.

Practically speaking, it takes a basketball, launched into the air from just over midcourt, between one and two seconds to arrive at the basket, carom off the glass backboard, ricochet off the front rim, and descend harmlessly to the floor.

That's how long this journey lasted for millions of TV viewers of the 2010 NCAA final, contested by the Bulldogs of Butler University and the Duke University Blue Devils at Indianapolis's Lucas Oil Stadium on April 3. Those were the millions with no particular rooting interest in the outcome of the game.

But for the nearly 71,000 fans in the arena, the coaches and players, and the millions more at home who did care, the time between the launching of Gordon Hayward's last-ditch, forty-six-foot desperation shot and the arrival of the ball at its final resting place seemed just shy of an eternity. When net and ball failed to connect, history recorded a 61–59 victory for Duke (their fourth NCAA title). That's basketball history, but not the monumental, silver-screen-ready history that would have been made had the ball bounced through the net, giving Butler the 62–61 victory.

A Butler win would have been considered by many the greatest upset in NCAA finals history and would have closed the perfect loop on a vintage, pre-packaged Cinderella story line. For this is Indiana, where basketball fables have a way of bypassing fiction and going straight to historical fact.

Historical fact: in 1954, tiny Milan High School, with a total student enrollment of 161, led by a kid named Bobby Plump, won the state championship in miracle fashion over powerhouse Muncie Central. It was Plump who made the winning basket as time expired. The game was played at Butler Fieldhouse (now Hinkle Fieldhouse). Milan's triumph ultimately begat the film *Hoosiers* and its Plump stand-in, Jimmy Chitwood. It will surprise no one to learn that *Hoosiers* has been consistently voted by film viewers among the most popular sports flicks of all time. As we've noted, Americans like their underdogs victorious, slathered in mustard and relish. So, fifty-six years later, in rides Butler, out of the lightly-regarded Horizon League, playing less than seven miles from its home court, going against the mighty Blue Devils (emphasis on Devils) in a stadium located not far from "Plump's Last Shot," Bobby Plump's own sports bar. And here goes Hayward's desperation heave, traveling in slow motion through the thick, Lucas Oil air, with 71,000 looking on in total silence toward a rendezvous with history and a movie theatre near you.

And, then, just like that, the Plump balloon popped, and Indiana went from being a spot where fairytales come to life to just another red state.

Of course, the story line, upon closer examination, doesn't hold up. For one thing, Butler was no Cinderella, coming into the season ranked 10th in the country in the coaches' poll, and eighth entering the NCAA tournament. The matchup with Duke was hardly a mismatch. Both teams were deep and talented and extremely well coached—Duke by everybody's Hall of Famer Mike Krzyzewski, and Butler by the boy genius Brad Stevens—and especially strong on the defensive end. Both sides entered the action fully expecting an intensely played, back-and-forth defensive struggle, which is precisely what they got.

On the other hand, the Cinderella angle made better copy and was way cooler. Butler wanted to play this angle for all it was worth.

"Some of our board members asked us before the game to measure the height of the basket, just like Gene Hackman and his team did it in the movie, so they could get a cool photo op," recalls Stevens, who left Butler in 2013 to become head coach of the NBA's Boston Celtics.

"I asked my guys if this was okay with them. To a man, they said, 'Hell, no! We're not here for entertainment purposes. We're nobody's underdog!'"

Stevens says his team went into the final with the expectation of winning it, and their staunch refusal to go along with the Hollywood script pleased him greatly.

"The way they all stood together and displayed their faith in themselves and in the program . . . I was very proud of my team that day."

Avery Jukes, a senior backup center on the 2010 team, recollects the lead-up to the final in much the same way. He says his team, while well aware of the *Hoosiers*/Cinderella hype, did their very best to ignore it.

"But, if Gordy's shot goes in," adds Jukes, "well, now *that* would have been something else."

Indeed. Glass slippers and golden carriages from Here to Hinkle.

As for the Dukies, they, too, were fully cognizant of the mythical milieu in which the game was played, but were much too caught up in the action to care.

Nevertheless, as the final 3.6 seconds ticked down, they could not help but experience the echoes of Bobby Plump's last shot.

"I'm a fate kind of guy," acknowledges former Duke player and 2010 assistant coach Chris Collins. "So I'm watching that shot hang in the air for two hours and thinking all the way to the hoop, 'This one's going in.'"

Fortunately for Duke, what's past is past, and whatever it is that the basketball gods call Fate is beyond human understanding.

The Butler Way

Many organizations, be they college basketball programs or corporate entities, have their "Ways." For example, there was Dean

Smith's much-admired "Carolina Way," which was essentially shorthand for players treating the university like a seat of learning instead of a pit-stop on the express lane from high school to the NBA.

Butler's basketball program had its own Way. However, there was, and is, a marked distinction between the "Butler Way" and the Ways of many other big-time college basketball programs. Butler actually walked this Way.

Jukes, who played at the University of Alabama before transferring to Butler, says the Butler Way was treated by everyone involved as a way of life. You either lived according to that credo, or you transferred out.

The Way, originated in the 1920s by legendary Butler coach Tony Hinkle (as in Hinkle Fieldhouse), was predicated on five locker room principles: passion, unity, servanthood, thankfulness, and humility. Brad Stevens added a sixth: accountability.

Six years after graduating, Jukes is able to rattle five of the six guiding principles off the top of his head (he forgot thankfulness).

"I guess you could say it was brainwashing," he says. "But the good kind."

Nevertheless, no amount of brainwashing, good or bad, can overcome the natural tendency of young people to resist authority. Research recently published in the *Proceedings of the National Academy of Sciences* suggests that educators who nurture their students' "benevolent defiance" find that this kind of defiance quickly transmutes into an even stronger desire to work together toward a shared purpose (as evidenced in the team's unanimous refusal to measure the height of a basket). Butler's 2010 Bulldogs were hardly the farm boy cast of Milan High or its filmic equivalent, Hickory High. They were an iconoclastic bunch, inclined to make their own kind of music.

Matt Howard, the wild-haired center, was the nearest thing to a hippie in the state of Indiana, with an almost feral approach to playing basketball and with more eccentricities than Howard Hughes. Gordon Hayward, a video game nut, reportedly chose

Butler over Purdue because Butler's 6:30 a.m. practices wouldn't interfere with his computer science classes. And Avery Jukes (a distinctive figure in name alone), while still in his junior year, created a non-profit foundation to help Ugandan students pay their secondary school tuitions. And, then, there was reserve guard Shawn Vanzant, who was ten days short of his second birthday when his mom passed away, followed by the death of his overworked father and the incarceration of his older brother. At sixteen, Vanzant was alone in the world, with nowhere to go but Cleveland to live with his grandmother.

In a scenario reminiscent of *The Blind Side* (indeed, there *are* other inspirational sports films besides *Hoosiers*), Vanzant was taken in by the Tampa, Florida, family of Lisa Litton, the designated den mother of his high school team. It was supposed to be for a couple of weeks, but it turned into a couple of years. Vanzant was used to taking care of himself, having grown up in an environment that didn't know from curfews and being accountable for taking out the family trash. The Litton Way eased his eventual transition into the Butler Way.

"It helps when you've got a few good values coming in," says Vanzant, who has been playing for a Canadian pro team and is still hoping for an NBA shot.

Stevens says the players' indoctrination into the specifics of the Butler Way began in the early recruitment stage.

"The first two slides of our PowerPoint presentation spelled out everything the university and the basketball program were about," explains Stevens. "Every kid who signed on knew from the beginning what was expected of him."

Matt Graves, an assistant Bulldogs coach in 2010 and currently head coach at South Alabama, says what truly brought this team together and kept it together was the competitive fire that burned in each and every player.

"We didn't go after highly-recruited guys," he says. "We were looking for smart kids who would run through walls ... the kind of kids who would create their own identity as a team."

They also went after players with chips on their shoulders, like Shawn Vanzant. For example, when a reporter at the Final Four casually suggested to Vanzant that mid-major schools like Butler were inherently disadvantaged relative to the power conference schools, Vanzant took it as a personal affront, and the discussion became heated.

No punches were thrown, according to Vanzant, "but we did go at it [verbally] for a while."

Practice scrimmages were where fists regularly flew, not surprising given the personalities involved.

And finally, there was the experience of the previous year's Bulldogs, which added even more fuel to the 2010 team's competitive flame. Terry Johnson, a member of the Butler staff for ten seasons before joining Ohio State, says the coaches set the 2008–09 bar much too low, telling the players before the season that they had a legitimate shot at the NCAAs. So when the team got to the tournament and were bounced out in the first round, the players' dissatisfaction quickly turned to anger and a commitment not to let that happen again.

"The next year, our guys were primed right from the start to go a lot deeper into the tournament," says Johnson.

As for all the other stuff—the individual quirks and whatnot—that was mere window dressing.

In Brad Stevens, Butler had the perfect coach to preside over a group of very pissed off freethinkers with attitude.

At age thirty-three, Stevens was the second-youngest Division I coach in the land, but the youngest-looking thirty-something since Dick Clark turned sixty. One observer at the 2010 final remarked that Stevens looked a lot closer to twenty-three but even that number was on the high side. Truth is, Stevens, at thirty-three, still closely resembled the boy who grew up in Zionsville, Indiana, exhibiting equal passion for the game of basketball and solving puzzles. While his basketball skills were modest (he did earn four varsity letters at DePauw University), his analytical skills were awesome and his intangible qualities formidable. Stevens is described by his old college coach, Bill Fenlon, as one of the most selfless, team-oriented players he ever coached. Hence, the Butler Way came naturally to Stevens.

Quite apart from that, Stevens's players were enamored of his coaching style, which relied heavily on getting to know them as players and people and adjusting his strategies to fit their skills and temperaments. They liked that Stevens was a whiz with the Xs and Os, relied heavily on statistical analysis, didn't get rattled when things were going poorly during games, and wasn't afraid of shaking things up in mid-game. They also liked that their coach was not above bumping backs with his guys in a winning locker room. He was a coach young enough to relate to his players on their terms but emotionally mature enough to command their respect. In other words, Coach K: The Next Generation.

"Brad had an uncanny ability to take what seemed like a negative and turn it into a positive for you as a ballplayer," says 2010 reserve guard Zach Hahn, who, like Jukes, managed on the fly to come up with five of the six Butler Way principles (forgetting only accountability). "And Brad was *always* calm, never yelled at anyone. If he raised his voice even a bit, it was just to emphasize a point. I never saw him waver in his demeanor, not ever."

The 2009–10 season was Stevens's third at Butler, where he had already amassed an impressive record of 56–10, with two trips to the NCAA tourney. In Division I basketball history, only North Carolina's Bill Guthridge won more games in his first two years as a head coach. But to most college basketball fans, who don't keep close tabs on the doings in the Horizon League, Stevens and his team remained unknown quantities.

Butler kicked off its schedule with a win over Davidson, then lost two of their next three games against ranked non-conference opponents. The team got a big win against 13th-ranked Ohio State before capping off the non-con part of the schedule on December 22 with a dismal 10-point loss to the University of Alabama-Birmingham. UAB closed out that game on a 10–2 run.

During any season, nearly every good team experiences at least one inflection point, an instance when the road bends or curves and the wheels feel like they're coming off. For Butler, the 2009–10 inflection point was the UAB game.

"I remember a deep sense of disappointment after that game," says Matt Graves. "There was a feeling among all the players and coaches that we weren't achieving at the level that was going to get us where we wanted to go. It was less about strategies and [personnel] moves than it was about recharging ourselves, all of us reflecting and refocusing and starting to pay much more attention to detail."

Terry Johnson attributes the problem to the fact that the players, as much as they all loved one another, had grown sick of each other.

"It was three days before Christmas, and everybody just wanted to go home already and get far away from basketball and teammates. There was a lot of bickering, really silly stuff, going on at that time. The kids just needed a break from it all."

A minor player-coach interaction during this period speaks volumes about the importance of the little things in redirecting a group toward its mission. According to several players, Stevens walked into the locker room one afternoon with a fist full of orange toboggan caps, each embroidered with the image of a duck, or a creature that looked like a duck. The players were dumbfounded.

"Coach Stevens handed each of us one of these winter hats, and pointed to the design," recalls Zach Hahn. "'As of today,' Brad told us, 'we are no longer the hunted. We are the hunter!'"

That was the mind-set that a few months later would be reflected in the team's revolt at the Final Four.

Standing at 8–4 at Christmastime, Butler embarked on a 20-game regular-season win streak, going undefeated in the Horizon League. The hunt was officially on.

The team's toughest conference test was a 64–62 overtime win against Detroit Mercy in a first-place showdown on the road. After shooting guard Shelvin Mack scored the go-ahead basket with under a minute left in OT, Detroit threw up its own desperation three-pointer. The glass slipper was on the other foot that day, and Butler narrowly escaped with its perfect conference record intact.

Stevens bristles at the suggestion that his team had a smoothly-paved road to the NCAAs, playing in a soft conference.

Aside from there being a few pretty good teams in the Horizon League, Stevens notes, they had all played against much the same Butler team the previous year, and they "knew our players and our tendencies well. It was hard to throw any new wrinkles at them."

In the NCAAs, Butler, seeded only fifth in the West bracket ("not a lot of respect there for the Horizon League," says Johnson), played its opening round game against 12th-seeded University of Texas El-Paso. Through the first half, it looked like a throwback to Alabama-Birmingham.

The Miners, NCAA champions from way back (see Chapter 8), over the first 20 minutes channeled the Spirit of '66, taking a six-point lead into the locker room. Over the next 20 minutes, Butler unleashed a flurry of long-range jumpers en route to a 77–59 rout.

Nevertheless, Stevens and his staff were less than enthralled by this performance.

And it got tougher, as it usually does, in the second round. With 25 seconds left against 13th-seeded Murray State, Butler went up 53–50 on a Ronald Nored layup and free throw. Murray State cut the lead to one and fouled Matt Howard on Butler's ensuing possession. Howard hit the first but missed the second free throw with just under five seconds remaining, giving Murray State its chance to wear the glass slipper. But Gordon Hayward deflected a pass, and the clock ran out before Murray State could recover the ball.

"We were very fortunate," says Graves. He was the assistant assigned to scout fourth-seeded Vanderbilt, Butler's anticipated second-round opponent, but when Murray State upset Vandy in the opening round, Butler had very limited data on their next foe. All they had, in fact, were a few snippets of film demonstrating how other teams effectively employed zone defenses against Murray State's continuity ball screens.

"That didn't help us at all," quips Johnson. "We didn't play zone. We were man-to-man all the way."

"As I recall," says Graves, "we struggled to defend their screens all game long. Murray State ran a patterned offense with very patient guards, and it threw us off."

Zach Hahn says Murray State's star player, freshman guard Isaiah Canaan, was the Bulldogs' chief tormenter.

"That guy might have been the best player we came up against in the whole tournament," says Hahn.

In the Sweet 16, against Syracuse, seeded No. 1 in the region and No. 4 nationally, the buzz on Butler started getting loud. The Bulldogs played a terrific first half, building a 10-point lead. But Syracuse roared back in the second half, taking a 54–50 lead on a fast-break dunk with 5:23 left. Stevens took a timeout, after which Butler held Syracuse scoreless over the next five minutes, and they led, 60–54, with under a minute left. They held on for a 63–59 victory to advance to the Elite 8 for the first time in school history.

The regional final vs. Kansas State followed a similar pattern, with Butler going up 7 at the half and withstanding a 13–2 Kansas State run late in the game to come out on top, 63–56. It was after this game that Butler revealed to the public Brad Stevens's secret flying back-bump, which it had adopted a few games earlier.

In the Final Four semifinal against Michigan State, Butler faced its toughest test to date. It was yet another lockdown defensive cliffhanger that came down to two big foul shots by Nored and a game-clinching rebound by Hayward, sealing a 52–50 win. Butler, interestingly enough, shot barely over 30 percent for the game and played much of the second half without Shelvin Mack and Howard—Mack was out with leg cramps and Howard suffered with dizziness after sustaining a mild concussion. Longtime MSU coach Tom Izzo, whose teams have earned a reputation for extreme physical—some would call it thuggish—play, praised Butler's fighting spirit and its physicality.

"They play like a Big Ten team," said Izzo.

"That was a street fight," recalls Graves. "That's how Michigan State plays, but we could be pretty good street fighters ourselves. Michigan State was also very good in transition, and that was the thing we worked on the most all week in practice. That night we played some solid transition defense."

For the first time since the adoption of the shot clock twenty-five years earlier, a team had held five consecutive NCAA tournament opponents to under 60 points.

It was a flattering statistic, says Coach Stevens, but he and his staff didn't believe that Butler had played to its potential in any of those first five tournament games.

They would have one last opportunity to do so. Next up for the Bulldogs on their Cinderella ride was Duke, another team with a distinctive Way about it.

The Krzyzewski Way

Mike Krzyzewski was not always "Coach K," a figure so beloved within the hallowed halls of Duke that he has to remain constantly vigilant in the event that someone might take his status as a living monument literally and begin pouring slabs of concrete over his body to get a head start on his statue.

Nevertheless, outside those halls, K's status is somewhat less exalted. A November 2011 piece in *The Atlantic*, headlined "Why Everybody Hates Coach K," offers a number of reasons why so many college basketball fans are disinclined to join the Cameron Crazies in celebration of the coach's manifold accomplishments. These include: the "smarmy, dirty-playing" style exhibited by many of his teams over the years (see Christian Laettner, Cherokee Parks, Grayson Allen, et al.); and the elitist, "country-club" vibe that emanates from the coach's condescending smirks and his nasal-toned voice.

Lastly, there is the coach's abject failure to use his mega-victory pulpit to chip away at the corruption at the center of the college basketball business. When pressed on this issue, the coach has invariably stood firmly as the quintessential Company Man.

But, hard as it may be to imagine now, Mike Krzyzewski was not always Coach K. In the beginning, he was just one more devoted student at the basketball academy of Robert Montgomery Knight, better known as Bobby, whose disposition was such that he is nicknamed "The General." The General, while head coach at Army, drilled into cadet Krzyzewski the need to establish within the confines of a basketball court an aura of stern discipline. The right way, the wrong way, and the Knight way, as it were.

Carol Krzyzewski, known as Mickie, alluded to her husband's then state of mind in a 2015 interview in the *Duke Chronicle*. Mickie noted that she has been a basketball fan since the couple's courting days in the 1960s, but her tastes at that time ran to the hey-look-me-over style of play epitomized by Louisiana State's ragin' Cajun, "Pistol" Pete Maravich.

"I used to tell Mike, 'Well, I like Maravich,'" noted Mickie, "and that would just drive him insane!"

Not insane enough, of course, to keep him from marrying her, siring three daughters and living in a home bedecked in pink and lace.

Nevertheless, while the coach has never lost his disdain for disorder on the court, his coaching style has reportedly evolved quite a bit since he arrived at Duke in 1980. His former players and assistants are his biggest fans and they applaud these changes.

Chris Collins, who played for Coach K for four years in the early-to-mid-1990s and coached under him for thirteen years before taking the head job at Northwestern in 2013, is one such acolyte.

"Coach has adapted beautifully to the changes in today's players and to the game itself," insists Collins, referring, among other things, to the advent of the one-and-done freshman superstar.

"For another thing, over the years he's finally learned how to delegate authority. He no longer attempts to micromanage everything that goes on in his program. During that [championship] season, he gave his three assistants a lot of added responsibilities. I started doing halftime press interviews. Assistants give [pregame] speeches now and take more responsibility for running practices.

"I think it's been a struggle for Mike, coming out of the Knight mold," acknowledges Collins. "But he's found the right balance. One thing I do know for sure: I wouldn't be head coach at Northwestern now if I hadn't had him for a mentor."

Steve "Wojo" Wojciechowski, a 2010 Duke assistant who graduated to head coach at Marquette, says Coach K has gradually come to recognize that he didn't need to alter his core values to coach twenty-first century student-athletes, he just had to change how he communicated those values.

"He's been willing to learn and grow as a teacher," says Wojo, "and as the generations have changed, so has he."

The 2009–10 Blue Devils in no way resembled those nasty, elitist Duke squads reviled by so many. They were a working-class team right from the get-go. Duke began the season ranked ninth and won thirteen of its first fourteen games, three against Top 20 teams. Subsequent losses to Georgia Tech and North Carolina State preceded a nasty beatdown by seventh-ranked Georgetown in late January. That loss was especially disheartening, as it seemed to signal to the players that 2010 might not be their year.

Chris Collins recalls starting guard Jon Scheyer coming into his office distraught and near tears, thinking his final season at Duke was about to spiral downhill. That loss to Georgetown became Duke's inflection point.

Coach K and his staff, after some difficult discussion, elected to shake things up by revamping the starting lineup and installing a new offense to go with it.

It was determined that the team needed more senior leadership and a more physical presence inside. The Plumlee brothers—Miles and Mason, a sophomore and freshman, respectively—were replaced as starters by a couple of seniors, center Brian Zoubek and forward Lance Thomas, a top-notch defender. The Zoubek move in some respects was a bold one, as the center had seen only limited service over his first three-and-a-half years on the team and lacked the speed and athleticism of most of his teammates. But he had always been willing to embrace the down and dirty aspects of playing the center position, and he responded to this promotion just as his coaches had hoped, emerging as a major rebounding and defensive force, averaging 10 boards a game over the rest of the season and dominating on the offensive glass throughout much of the NCAA tournament.

"We were prepared, if things didn't work out, to scrap the [new look] immediately," notes Wojo. "But when Brian went out in the next game against Maryland and scored 18 points with 16 rebounds [actually 16 points with 17 rebounds], we knew we were off to the races."

"Everybody wants to start, so obviously Mason and I weren't thrilled about the changes," acknowledges Miles Plumlee, currently a member of the NBA's Atlanta Hawks. "But the seniors deserved it. They'd been through a lot together, and we all rallied around them."

The personnel moves necessitated significant changes in Duke's basic offensive strategy. The team switched from running a spread pick and roll offense—which relied heavily on speed and quickness to break down a defense—to more of an "old-school style" offense, featuring increased ball movement and lots of off-the-ball screens and back screens.

"With [a less fleet of foot] Zoubek in there, we obviously couldn't keep running pick and rolls," says Miles, "but I believe the changes helped us become a grittier, grind-it-out kind of team. We had some excellent players, but no superstars here, and what we needed more than anything at that time was a strong collective will. The match of wills was ultimately what made the final against Butler such a great game."

Following the Georgetown loss, at 17–4, Duke got on another hot streak, winning twelve of its next thirteen, entering the NCAAs as the No. 3 team in the country and the top seed in the South region.

They glided through the first five tourney games on cruise control, winning four by double-digit margins and besting Baylor by seven.

Now an even grittier and considerably more confident band of brothers, they were hunters too. And fully loaded for Bulldog.

The Game

For Butler, the morning of the championship game played out like any other Monday morning in early spring. Eight Bulldogs went to their classes on campus. Funny thing is, more than seven years later, they tend to remember what happened in those classes more than they do what transpired that evening on the basketball court.

Zach Hahn explains this particular form of selective memory:

"We're taught as players to run a play and spring forward into the next one and the next one. Ultimately the whole game, and the whole season, runs together in one long cycle. Even today, I have a lot of trouble looking back on any game I ever took part in and recollecting individual moments."

Indeed, as regards the Duke-Butler final, apart from those last, thrilling 3.6 seconds, there were no recallable signature moments. It was your basic 40-minute defensive slog, with baskets harder to come by than Duke fans in Chapel Hill.

Chris Collins, for his part, mainly remembers the three buckets that Duke scored off of inbounds passes under the Butler basket in the first nine minutes of the second half.

"We had scripted all three of those underplays, and we executed them flawlessly," says Collins. "Any time you could get even one easy hoop in a game like this, it's big, because it was so hard to score in the half-court game or in transition. Those were six crucial points for us."

Terry Johnson says Brad Stevens so bemoaned those six points that the following season, with those three scripted plays in mind, he retooled Butler's under-defense strategy to ensure that no opponent would ever again score on the Bulldogs with such impunity.

The tone of the 2010 final was established right from the opening tip: solid rotating man-to-man defense, played to near-perfection by both sides, relatively unencumbered by the referees and very light on the chippy stuff.

Duke went up early, 6–1, and over the first seven minutes held Butler to just two field goals—a pair of three-pointers by Shelvin Mack. Duke's interior defense in the first half was particularly stellar, exemplified by a terrific Jon Scheyer block on a Willie Veasley breakaway dunk attempt. An 8–0 Duke run beginning at about the 12-minute mark stretched their lead to 26–20. That six-point lead would be the biggest by either team in the game.

After a much-needed Brad Stevens timeout with 5:08 left before halftime, Avery Jukes, subbing for Matt Howard, who was forced to the bench with two fouls, responded with the finest five minutes of basketball in his playing career—a 10-point explosion featuring two three-pointers and two layups.

"We all played our roles that season," says Jukes, basking in the moment, "but [explosive bursts of scoring] wasn't my role. I just got in a zone there for a while."

A 7–0 run put Butler back on top by one before the half ended with Duke up, 33–32.

The second half played out much as the first, back and forth, possession by possession, only without any big scoring bursts. The outburst by Jukes was a fluke, notes Brad Stevens, and it could hardly be expected to reoccur.

With only six minutes gone in the second half, Matt Howard picked up his fourth personal foul (Duke's big man, Zoubek, picked up his fourth shortly thereafter).

Butler then took its last lead of the game, 43–42, on a Ron Nored trifecta. It was answered by a Kyle Singler three-pointer that put Duke in the lead for good, at 45–43. A gimme layup by Brian Zoubek and a very questionable charging call on Gordon

Hayward helped Duke maintain its slim scoreboard advantage. More than that, Duke's continuously fierce interior defense and a second-half rebounding surge appeared to be wearing Butler down. The Bulldogs were still making big plays on the defensive end, but their shooting touch had completely vanished, and it was only at the foul line where they were managing to keep their title hopes alive.

With Matt Howard back on the floor, Butler trimmed the Duke lead to 56–55 with 5:02 remaining on two Hayward foul shots.

A Singler jumper and two Nolan Smith foul shots got the Duke lead back to five at 60–55 before a pair of Howard layups (Butler's first baskets in nearly eight minutes) once again whittled it back to one, at 60–59.

With under a minute to go and CBS pumping up the TV audience with the inspirational theme music from *Hoosiers*, the stage was set.

Kyle Singler missed an open 12-footer, and after a mad scramble underneath the basket, the ball kicked out of bounds off Brian Zoubek's leg with 33 seconds left.

Ball to Butler.

The Bulldogs worked for a good shot for the next 20 seconds before the ball was deflected out of bounds by Zoubek. Brad Stevens then took the first of his two remaining timeouts to set up the last shot. But trying to make the inbounds pass from the corner of the baseline, his sight lines impeded by Zoubek's impressive wingspan, Gordon Hayward couldn't make the pass and was forced to call Butler's final time-out with 13.6 seconds on the clock.

Matt Howard took over the inbounding duties and tossed the pass out to Hayward well beyond the top of the key. Hayward took off toward the left side of the basket but Singler cut him off and, glued to Hayward's left hip, forced his man toward the right baseline where Hayward jump-stopped and put up a slightly off-balance, fadeaway jumper over the outstretched arms of Zoubek. The shot bounced off the back of the rim and was rebounded by Duke's big man, who was immediately fouled with 3.6 seconds left.

In Italian, it's called La Forza Del Destino (*The Power of Fate*). *Here, Gordon Hayward sends up a last-second prayer to the Basketball Fates. This one went unanswered.*

Zoubek went to the line with the following directive from Coach K: hit the first shot and miss the second, the strategy being that with 3.6 seconds remaining, no timeouts, and the ball under their own basket, there would be no time for Butler to secure the rebound and get down the court for a decent shot. It was a sound strategy, to be sure, but one that came pretty darn close to backfiring. After making the first shot, Zoubek, as instructed, missed the second. Hayward rebounded, dribbled a few times just across the midcourt line, and let fly with 0.5 seconds on the clock...

And this, folks, is where we came in, at the end of a busted fairytale.

Brad Stevens, who hasn't watched the game in more than six years, remembers it as the best game his team played in the tournament.

Zach Hahn agrees, and, upon further reflection, does recall a relatively insignificant detail of that last play.

"Look again at the video of Gordy's shot," he insists. "There I am, down court, wide open, waiting for the pass."

We checked it out and, yes, there was Zach Hahn, standing out there all by himself. Had there been, say, another three or four seconds on the clock, Hayward would have had time to spot the wide-open Hahn and pass him the ball for a game-tying layup.

What might that have wrought?

Perhaps another popular sports bar in downtown Indianapolis, "Hahn's Last Shot." Has a nice ring to it, no?

Since then, various mathematicians and sports scientists with lots of free time on their hands have calculated the difference between a Hayward make and a miss. The numbers they've come up with range from three inches to just under one inch.

Matt Graves is familiar with this academic exercise and has a very definite opinion about it.

"One thing I'd like to do," half-jokes the former Butler assistant, "[is to] find the guys who calculate these numbers and punch them in the mouth."

Aftermath

Butler proved to be more than what is known in the music business as a "one-hit wonder." The Bulldogs made it all the way back to the NCAA final the following season without their best player, Gordon Hayward, who had left for the NBA after his sophomore year. On its second try, Butler again came up a little short, losing to perennial power Connecticut in another defensive duel, 53–41. Butler later left the Horizon League to move into the more prestigious Atlantic 10 conference, and after a brief stay, they jumped to a power conference, the Big East, where the Bulldogs currently compete twice a season against the likes of Georgetown, Villanova, and Marquette.

Brad Stevens's move to the NBA came as a surprise to some of his former players, given that he had passed on a number of multimillion-dollar offers to become head coach at power conference schools.

"I figured, if he turned down Oregon and ten million bucks, it meant he wanted to stay and build on his legacy at Butler," says Avery Jukes. "But you can't fault him for [moving up in] his career. So far, he's done a fantastic job in Boston, as everybody knew he would."

Moreover, one could argue persuasively that Stevens's legacy at Butler was already well-established. For example, Terry Johnson says in preparing his 2016–17 Bulldogs for the rigors of the new season, he dipped into the files for vintage tapes of Butler's 2009–10 practices, looking for ideas on how to instill in the new kids some of the competitive fires of old.

There is also a Stevens coaching tree slowly taking root across the land. It will never become the mighty oak that is the Coach K tree, but branches like Matt Graves, Terry Johnson, Zach Hahn, and Willie Veasley, now an assistant at North Dakota State, will eventually make their mark. If nothing else, members of the Stevens tree will bring to the college basketball world a much-needed measure of calm leadership.

As for the Duke basketball program, its glory days never pass by. Coach K's 2014–15 squad delivered him his fifth NCAA title, a total exceeding Adolph Rupp's four and putting K second only to John Wooden's 10 championships. As of this writing, Coach K's resume also lists 1,071 career wins (998 at Duke), putting him at the top of that all-time list.

Today, with its horde of Cameron Crazies and its strong rooting traditions, Duke basketball remains an immense source of pride and unity among the student body, faculty, and alumni.

As it happens, the 2010 championship came four years after a horrendous sexual abuse scandal that engulfed the university, the town of Durham, and the entire nation. Three white players on Duke's lacrosse team were accused by a black stripper of having raped her at a party at the home of two team captains. The headlines were lurid, invoking some of the most sickening aspects of America's racial and class divide. In some local quarters—including the District Attorney's office and segments of the Duke community—the three suspects were judged guilty by suspicion. Even after all the allegations had been proven false, all the charges dismissed with prejudice, and the rogue DA sentenced to prison, the lives and reputations of those players and their coach were irrevocably damaged. It could well be considered the worst period in Duke's storied history, and there are some who say the stench of the scandal still wafts over Duke's majestic gardens.

Just three months after Duke completed its 2010 championship run, the university finally got around to tearing down the house at 610 North Buchanan Boulevard where the rape reportedly occurred. It had been unoccupied since 2006, an empty reminder of a time that nearly everyone, especially the Duke administration, would dearly love to forget.

There is no evidence of any direct connection between Duke's title and the razing of the house. A university spokesman states that the presumption of such a connection is "absurd." Nevertheless, a symbolic connection can be drawn between the glory that is Duke basketball and the tarnish of the lacrosse scandal. Former students and Duke supporters believe that basketball helped, at least in some small way, to soothe the raw feelings and the frayed nerves of a profoundly wounded and divided community.

Wojo, who was coaching at Duke in 2006–07 and well aware of the firestorm burning all over the campus, responds to a question about the relationship of basketball to the scandal the way one would expect a dedicated coach to respond:

"Whatever there was going on outside our little world, our main concern was about basketball, putting out the best team we could."

On this point, the evidence is abundantly clear. Nine hundred and ninety-eight wins' worth.

Chapter 2

The Improbable Game: Michigan vs. Seton Hall, 1989

Call it the Improbable Game.

When the season began, Seton Hall was picked to finish near the bottom of its own conference while Michigan's coach when the season started would not be sitting on the bench when it ended.

The last play of the 1989 championship game was also highly improbable—and certainly one of the most controversial in the history of the NCAA tournament.

To say that Seton Hall University was a barely recognizable name in the college basketball world that year would be an understatement.

The Catholic school, located in the New York City suburb of South Orange, New Jersey, had fielded a team since the turn of the century, but had received only one previous NCAA tournament bid.

In the early '40s, guided by coach John "Honey" Russell and All-American guard and future pro star Bob Davies, Seton Hall won forty-one straight games and competed for the first time in the National Invitational Tournament (NIT).

Russell guided Seton Hall to the 1953 NIT championship by defeating archrival St. John's. A point-shaving scandal in 1961 brought the basketball program to a low point, but coach Bill Raftery, better known later as a TV commentator, returned the Pirates to the NIT in the mid '70s.

Although Seton Hall became a charter member of the Big East Conference in 1979, the basketball program languished, so in 1982 the university brought in a young local wunderkind with an impressive basketball pedigree named P. J. Carlesimo to turn the school's roundball fortunes around.

The Michigan Wolverines certainly had a higher profile than the Seton Hall Pirates, but the massive university in Ann Arbor was known as a football school first and foremost.

Under Bo Schembechler, then the winningest football coach in the country, Michigan went to seventeen bowl games in twenty-one years and regularly played in front of over 100,000 fans.

Although the Michigan basketball program played second fiddle to their pigskin counterparts, it was hardly second-rate.

The basketball team had won twelve Big Ten championships and had been invited to a dozen NCAA tournaments.

One of the country's best coaches, Johnny Orr, raised the program's stature during a highly successful twelve-year stint that ended in 1980.

Rebuilding in South Orange

Meanwhile, in South Orange in 1982, Peter John Carlesimo was looking at a long-term rebuilding project. The team had won only two Big East games the previous season, finishing next to last in the conference.

Carlesimo won a grand total of seven Big East games the next four seasons, finishing last each year.

But the good fathers at the university had patience, and Carlesimo was able to draw solace and sustenance during those bleak years from a highly sympathetic—and knowledgeable—source.

His father, Peter Carlesimo, was a Jersey guy, born in Newark, right next to Seton Hall.

He went to college at Fordham University in the Bronx where he played football alongside Vince Lombardi, then spent twenty-six years in Scranton, Pennsylvania, where P. J. was born and raised. After coaching the University of Scranton's football, basketball, and cross country teams, as well as being the school's athletic director, Carlesimo Sr. returned to his alma mater as Fordham's athletic director.

In 1978, Peter Carlesimo became the executive director of the National Invitation Tournament and revived the NIT's status—and coffers—by starting a preseason tournament in New York and moving early-round postseason NIT games to campus sites.

One of ten children, P. J. followed in his father's footsteps, attending Fordham, where he played under coach Digger Phelps and then became a coach himself. His high-energy passion, engaging personality, and success at Wagner College in Staten Island, New York, caught the attention of the media in Manhattan, and his father's high profile in the metropolitan area didn't hurt either.

Only thirty-three and single when Seton Hall named him head coach, P. J. faced a formidable challenge. The team was lousy. Media attention was perfunctory, at best. The basketball team played in a 3,200-seat gym on campus that rarely filled up. There were only two baskets in the training facility and no workout rooms to lift weights or train.

But Seton Hall was in the Big East, not just a rising power conference featuring star-studded teams like Syracuse, Georgetown, and St. John's, but a media darling that played its championship tournament in Madison Square Garden.

And Seton Hall was located just twelve miles from New York City and its fertile recruiting prospects.

Carlesimo crossed the Hudson River and went to work.

"There was nothing magical about the turnaround, it was all about recruiting," says Bruce Hamburger, who worked with Carlesimo as an assistant coach at Seton Hall for nine years. "P. J. is a very charismatic guy. He would walk into a room and take it over with his personality. And he has a great ability to put people at ease. I think P. J. appealed to recruits because he was honest, consistent, personable, and worked hard in recruiting kids that he wanted."

The breakthrough came in 1984 and literally occurred in Seton Hall's backyard.

Mark Bryant, who went on to a long career in the NBA, was from South Orange and went to the local high school, where he was coached by Hamburger.

"Mark Bryant really got the program set on the right course," Hamburger says. "He was a Top 50 national player, and his commitment to Seton Hall opened up a lot of people's eyes."

A year later, Carlesimo reeled in John Morton, a sharpshooting guard from the Bronx; Gerald Greene, a skilled point guard from Brooklyn; Daryll Walker, a sturdy power forward from Manhattan; and Ramon Ramos, a rock-solid center from Puerto Rico (where Carlesimo had been coaching in the summer).

The groundwork for a highly competitive team had been laid, but patience was required as the players adjusted to the Big East and to each other. Despite four consecutive losing seasons and protests from students and restless alumni, the school's faith in the bearded bachelor finally began to pay dividends in 1987 with the Pirates' first NIT invite in a decade.

Aiming High in Ann Arbor

The situation in Ann Arbor when Bill Frieder took over from Orr in 1980 couldn't have been more different.

Before leaving for Iowa State, Orr guided the Wolverines to ten consecutive winning seasons, two Big Ten championships, and four NCAA tournament appearances, including a title game in 1976 against Indiana, the last team to have an unbeaten season.

A Michigan graduate, Frieder was coaching high school teams in Flint to state championships, but desperately wanted to return to Ann Arbor. He hounded Orr for a job, at one point saying he would work for free.

The school brought Frieder on as an assistant in 1973 for $14,000, and he quickly developed a reputation as a top recruiter, helping the Wolverines land Rickey Green and Phil Hubbard, who were instrumental in the team's '76 title run.

He could coach, too. Michigan won the NIT in 1984 and the Big Ten regular season championship in 1985 and '86. Beginning in 1985 the Wolverines also never missed an NCAA tournament during Frieder's tenure.

The Wolverines got knocked out of the tournament in the second round three consecutive years, but in 1987–88 the team reached the Sweet 16, led by All-American guard Gary Grant and Big Ten scoring champion Glen Rice.

Grant graduated, but Rice, who would finish his career as a consensus All-American and the highest scorer in the history of the Big Ten conference, returned for his senior year, along with fellow senior and co-captain of the 1988–89 team, rugged big man Mark Hughes.

Rice and Hughes were joined by an impressive quartet of extremely talented and athletic juniors: Rumeal Robinson, who replaced Grant at point guard; Sean Higgins, a smooth shooting forward; and reliable rebounders and scorers Terry Mills and Loy Vaught.

"The expectations for that team were through the roof," says Mills. "You had four McDonald's high school All-Americans: myself, Glen, Sean, and Rumeal. We felt we had underachieved in '88, not winning the Big Ten championship and losing to North Carolina in the Sweet 16. So we were definitely hungry."

In New Jersey, the Seton Hall Pirates had a much lower profile but similar confidence.

They too were a veteran group who had been to the school's first NCAA tournament the previous season.

All-American Mark Bryant had graduated and went to the NBA, but Morton, Greene, Walker, and Ramos, who had played together for three years, were back. And they were joined by a high scoring 6-foot-7 forward from Australia named Andrew Gaze, who proved to be the missing piece to the Pirates' puzzle.

Gaze, a reliable three-point shooter who could also pass and get to the basket, was already considered to be one of Australia's best basketball players in 1988. He starred on the country's Olympic team that summer and was introduced to Carlesimo through his father, a coach who knew Carlesimo's father.

Despite the previous season's success and the return of a core group of talented seniors, Seton Hall was only picked to finish seventh in a brutally tough Big East conference stuffed with stars such as Derrick Coleman and Sherman Douglas at Syracuse and Alonzo Mourning and Charles Smith at Georgetown.

After his first few scrimmages with the Seton Hall players in South Orange, Gaze says he thought to himself, *My goodness, if this team is one of the worst teams in the conference, it must be one of the greatest conferences in the history of the world!*

Morton says the preseason slight didn't faze the players.

"We were veterans, and we felt very comfortable with our team," he recalls. "We had a taste of the NCAAs and wanted to get back. We never had to talk about it. We just got out on the court and enjoyed playing. When Andrew came it was like he had been here for four years. He just fit right in."

Bill and Bo

As Bill Frieder was preparing for what was shaping up to be a dream season in Ann Arbor, he was jolted by some unexpected and unwelcome news: Bo Schembechler had been named Michigan athletic director.

Schembechler was the ultimate straight arrow, an old-fashioned company man—a no-nonsense football coach who equated winning with discipline. Frieder was a free spirit, loosey-goosey basketball geek who didn't impose a dress code, was close to his players, and left the X's and O's to others.

If Schembechler was a Knute Rockne throwback, says Mark Hughes, Frieder was more like The Dude in *The Big Lebowski*.

"They were like oil and water," Hughes says. "Schembechler could be truly intimidating, and Frieder was a laid-back guy who showed up to practice in flip-flops. Frieder was not Bo's kind of coach, and we weren't Bo's kind of players."

As if Frieder's freewheeling ways didn't rub Schembechler the wrong way to begin with, an incident in the spring of 1988, when Michigan was preparing to play in the NCAA tournament, further and arguably fatally undermined the football coach's respect for his basketball counterpart.

Schembechler was the Michigan Man personified. He had been at the school for over twenty years, was the winningest coach in its history with a national championship under his belt, and was greeted at games by students chanting "Bo is God."

In March 1988 it was reported that Frieder was being considered for the head coaching position at the University of Texas. Then it came out that Frieder had approached Texas, not the other way around. The next shoe to drop was that Frieder had allegedly planted the Texas-is-interested-in-me story to give him more leverage when his contract came up for renewal at Michigan.

To put it mildly, this did not sit well with Bo Schembechler.

After Schembechler was installed as athletic director, he restricted non-players' access to the basketball team, cut charter flights, reduced the number of tickets Frieder was allowed to sell or give away, and publicly criticized Frieder's weak pre-Big Ten schedule. When the team traveled to Hawaii for the Maui Classic, Schembechler sent one of his aides to accompany them, ostensibly to help with "travel arrangements"—wink, wink.

"When Schembechler became the athletic director," Frieder said in an interview with CBS Sports years later, "he gave me no indication he would be behind basketball the way I needed him to be behind it."

Frieder may been chafing under the new regime, but the players were oblivious.

"The tension didn't filter down to us," says Terry Mills. "We just went out and played."

The Wolverines beat Vanderbilt, Memphis State, and Oklahoma to win the Maui Classic in December, then won eight more in a row, albeit playing a less than formidable schedule, including games with South Dakota State, Northern Michigan, and Youngstown State.

One opposing player that season called Michigan "a young pro team," an assessment that rang true: every Michigan starter and its sixth man were drafted by an NBA team; Rice had a 15-year pro career and was a three-time All-Star.

But an abundance of talent is rarely trouble-free.

Higgins, a highly-sought after high school star, wasn't thrilled about not starting and had a reputation as a hotshot playboy from LA who thought he was too cool for school. By the end of the year he had been suspended three games for breaking team rules.

The Wolverines were also accused of being too cocky, not taking opponents seriously, and not playing hard enough, especially on defense.

And the team's reputation for underachieving the previous season reemerged with an embarrassing loss to lowly Alaska-Anchorage. The Wolverines didn't exactly set the Big Ten on fire either, compiling a mediocre 7–5 conference record in their first twelve Big Ten games.

Frieder was hardly blameless. He already had a reputation for doing well in the regular season but failing to push his teams far enough in the NCAA tournament. He was considered a first-rate recruiter but a less than stellar bench coach. And constantly kidding around with the players had a downside, according to assistant coach Mike Boyd.

"There are times when a coach has to be a jerk on the floor," Boyd told John Beckett in *Mission Accomplished: Michigan's Basketball Miracle, 1989*. "Sometimes when you're a jerk on the floor but a friend off it, I don't know how much of what you say on the floor gets through."

Nonetheless, the Wolverines continued to have faith in themselves and Frieder.

"We always felt we were really good," Mills recalls. "With all the talent we had, it could be hard to feed egos. But we all came together, we were all close, we all pushed one another. We learned to go with the hot hand. If one guy got it going, we would cheer him on and not pout because we weren't scoring."

Over their last six conference games, Michigan only lost once. Ironically, it was that loss—and another Big Ten defeat earlier in the season—that proved to be just as meaningful as the wins.

The first time Michigan played Wisconsin, they lost because Robinson missed two free throws at the end of the game. Robinson hated to lose, and he vowed never to let it happen again. He began coming to practice early to shoot 100 extra free throws.

Michigan's final home game was against Illinois, who had beaten them earlier in the season. Riding a five-game win streak, the Wolverines were supposed to avenge the earlier loss on Senior Day and give Rice and Hughes a fitting send-off.

Instead, Illinois humiliated Michigan, 89–73.

"We played like crap on senior day in front of a national TV audience," Hughes recalls. "It was bad. They killed us on the offensive glass. That was a high flyin' Illinois team with lots of attitude. They were dancing and prancing all over the floor. It was hard to take."

Mills says the players were so stunned and embarrassed they sat frozen in the locker room and didn't leave until midnight. "You can't imagine how bad we felt. We said if we got another shot at them, there would be a different result."

Big East Battles

The team they would eventually meet in the championship game also began the season with an impressive tournament win, beating Utah, Kentucky, and Kansas in the Great Alaska Shootout.

The Pirates reeled off ten more consecutive wins, capped by an upset over fifth-ranked Big East rival Georgetown at the Meadowlands Arena, the first time Seton Hall sold the arena out and the largest crowd to ever see a college game in New Jersey.

Seton Hall's first loss was a shellacking, but losing to No. 2 Syracuse in front of 32,000 screaming fans at the Carrier Dome wasn't exactly shameful. The Pirates went on to lose only four more games in the regular season to finish second in the Big East behind Georgetown.

Having four seniors in the starting five plus the twenty-three-year old Gaze (who stayed at Seton Hall for all of six months) was key to Seton Hall's success. Gaze's experience, besides the

Olympics, included time with an Australian club team coached by his father, which later raised questions about his amateur status.

"We were a mature group," Gaze recalls. "We had good balance inside and out, we shared the ball, and P. J.'s system enabled us to exploit those skills."

Morton agreed.

"We were veterans," he says. "We definitely had a complete unit—we knew our roles and we knew what to do. No one had to hype anybody up. We just went about our business and enjoyed playing basketball."

As the team's confidence grew as the season progressed, Carlesimo kept things loose off the court but provided a steady hand on it.

"He kept everybody laughing," Morton says. "His mom and dad were always around, and we'd joke that if he got out of hand we'd call his mom and get him in trouble. But he showed us how to do things the right way, and I admire him to this day because he showed us how to become men."

Carlesimo "made it easy on players" and was "extremely generous with his time," Gaze says. But Carlesimo also had "a very authoritarian approach" to coaching, according to Gaze.

"He was very demonstrative about the way he wanted things done. There was no gray area. It was very defined and understood what your role was and what was expected of you."

Ranked 11th in the country at the end of the season, Seton Hall beat seventh-ranked Connecticut in the Big East quarterfinals but lost—for the third time—to third-ranked Syracuse.

Hamburger thinks the loss and the resulting extra rest it gave the players was a blessing in disguise. A three-seed in the NCAA tournament, the Pirates were about to spend three solid weeks on the road, traveling successively to the Rocky Mountains, the Southwest, and the Pacific Northwest.

Detour

The Michigan Wolverines' tournament route was less circuitous but far more turbulent.

On Selection Sunday, Michigan, also a three seed, learned they would be traveling to Atlanta to play Xavier in the first round. On Wednesday, they learned they had a new coach for Friday night's game.

Arizona State, meanwhile, had a coaching vacancy to fill for the coming season, and ASU athletic director Charles Harris was a former Michigan assistant AD (and a candidate for the Michigan top job) and a friend of Frieder.

The two men had been in touch informally, and towards the end of the regular season Harris contacted the Michigan athletic department for official permission to talk to Frieder. Permission was granted, but no one from Michigan reached out to Frieder—now in his 16th year with the basketball program—asking him to stay.

When Purdue coach Gene Keady turned the ASU job down, Harris made a formal offer to Frieder, but he needed an answer quickly.

As much as Frieder loved Michigan, it was clear Schembechler didn't love Frieder. Plus, Arizona State was offering a guaranteed multiyear contract with considerably more money. Frieder flew to Phoenix and accepted the offer on Tuesday afternoon.

By Tuesday night, rumors were flying. The Michigan players had a tape session to prepare for Xavier at 9 p.m. Tuesday night, but Frieder wasn't there. Schembechler received an anonymous call around 11 p.m. telling him that Frieder had taken the ASU job.

"I don't think that's accurate," Schembechler said, according to *Mission Accomplished*. "He hasn't said anything to me. Why, he's getting his team ready to play in the tournament."

In the middle of the night, Frieder called some of the players to tell them he would be going to Arizona State next season, explaining that he had to do it for his family. But he told them he would still coach the team through the NCAA tournament.

Early the next morning, Frieder called Jack Weidenbach, Michigan's associate AD, and Schembechler. He fully expected to coach the team in Atlanta.

"In his mind this was no big deal," says co-captain Mark Hughes. "After all, football coaches quit all the time and get to coach their teams in bowl games."

Bo Schembechler had other ideas.

The athletic director said later the decision to fire Frieder on the spot was a "five-second job." Frieder hadn't kept him informed about the new job, and he hadn't shown up for a practice before the start of the NCAA tournament. "It was the only choice," Schembechler explained, "and any man sitting in this chair would've made that choice."

At a press conference that afternoon, Schembechler famously declared: "I don't want someone from Arizona State coaching my team. A Michigan man will coach the Michigan basketball team."

That man would be assistant coach Steve Fisher.

The Michigan Man

If Fisher seemed like an unassuming, small town kind of everyman when he was thrust onto the national stage, it's because he was. He grew up in Herrin, Illinois, a farming and coal mining town, went to Illinois State, and settled in suburban Chicago, where he was a high school basketball coach for eleven years.

Fisher told John Beckett he would never have left if his friend Les Wothke hadn't offered him a job as his assistant at Western Michigan. In 1982, he accepted an offer from Frieder, and after seven years the two men (and their wives) had become close friends as well as colleagues, and they worked well as a team.

"Frieder was a manager more than a coach," Hughes says. "He did a great job of putting players in the right positions and was a good delegator."

He left the X's and O's to Fisher, who "had as much say-so at practice as Frieder did," according to Mills. Fisher also suggested strategies and lineup changes during games, recommended game plans, and broke down tape of opposing teams.

When Fisher stepped up to head coach, "it was completely seamless for us," says Hughes.

Fisher admitted later he was "scared to death" when he took over, but as former Xavier coach Pete Gillen once put it: "A nuclear power is still a nuclear power, no matter who the president is."

Fisher's strategy for the tournament was straightforward: break it into two-game chunks and worry about the next level when you get there.

Michigan did beat unranked Xavier and South Alabama in Atlanta, but Schembechler wasn't thrilled with the way the Wolverines won and the way they were playing, particularly Sean Higgins, who had let it be known he wasn't happy with his floor time and was thinking of transferring or turning pro.

"There was no sugarcoating with Bo," Mills says. "He got right to the point and laid it down."

"He told us we're a bunch of underachievers who need to start playing for the name in front of our jerseys instead of the names on our backs," Hughes recalls.

He called out every starter, told them what they needed to do, and then turned to Higgins.

"Do you want to leave here?" Schembechler asked. "Your goddamn transfer letter is on my desk . . . you either join this team or get out."

And if Higgins did go to Lexington, Kentucky, for the next round, Schembechler let him know he would be expected to dive for loose balls, hustle every minute he's on the court, and run to the coach when he was substituted out of the game.

"I'm sure no one had ever talked like that to Sean Higgins before," Hughes said later.

Higgins stayed with the team, whose next game was against fifth-ranked North Carolina—the team that knocked the Wolverines out of the tournament each of the past two years.

Glen Rice made sure that 1989 would be different, however. Michigan's all-time leading scorer poured in 34 points, going 13-for-19 from the field (8-for-12 from three-point territory) and leading Michigan to a hard-fought 92–87 win.

When a reporter complimented Fisher on coaching a good game, using smart substitutions and timeouts, Fisher replied, "All I did was go out there and say, 'Get the ball to Glen Rice.' Glen Rice would make any coach look good."

After Michigan's next win, a nearly 40-point blowout over Virginia, Steve Fisher was obscure no longer. The team's victories, combined with his ruddy cheeked, guy-in-the-next-cubicle persona was making him a national celebrity.

And the back story was irresistible: the quiet, loyal number-two man getting a one in a million shot to prove that he is every bit as good if not better than his boss—and pulling it off.

Indeed, it did not go unnoticed that in this tournament, instead of being the talented underachievers, the Michigan Wolverines were hustling, sharing the ball and focused—and were going to the Final Four.

Western Odyssey

The team they would meet in Seattle was Michigan's mirror image in reverse: while Seton Hall played hard every game and didn't have a reputation to live down, expectations that the Pirates, going to only the second NCAA tournament in the school's history, would advance very far were not, to say the least, very high.

But, improbably, advance they did—against some very good teams.

After easily dispatching Southwest Missouri State and Evansville in the first two rounds, Seton Hall traveled to Denver to confront the Big Boys, starting with eighth-ranked Indiana and Bobby Knight.

The other coaches in the regional semifinal? Only Lute Olson and Jerry Tarkanian.

"We never worried about the coaches we were facing," Morton told the *Newark Star-Ledger*, "just the players."

And lo and behold, behind a lockdown defense that held the Hoosiers to just three field goals over the final 15 minutes of the game, Seton Hall cruised to a surprisingly easy 78–65 victory, handing Indiana its worst NCAA tournament loss ever at the time.

Then the Pirates caught a break—kind of. They wouldn't have to play number one-ranked Arizona. But the team that pulled the upset was Tarkanian's Runnin' Rebels from UNLV.

When they played, however, the team that did the running was Seton Hall. Holding UNLV to an abysmal 30 percent shooting percentage, their lowest of the season, Seton Hall beat Nevada-Las Vegas soundly, 84–61, led by Gaze's 19 points, five rebounds, and three steals.

Carlesimo then made a decision which may have been as important as any he made on the sidelines the entire season.

Despite having been on the road for two weeks, instead of flying back to New Jersey for a few days and then traveling west again all the way across the country to Seattle for the Final Four the next weekend, Seton Hall went to Santa Monica, California.

"There was no Internet then, no cellphones, no way for our kids to know what was going on back home," says Hamburger, who had flown back to scout Duke in the Eastern semifinals at the Meadowlands. "I saw how people were going nuts in New Jersey. Meanwhile, our kids were living in a noise-free bubble with nothing to do but focus on the next game. I think not getting caught up in all the frenzy back home helped keep their heads on straight."

Morton and Gaze agreed.

"It definitely helped us," Morton says. "It was like a vacation."

"If we had gone back, we would have got caught up in the excitement," Gaze says. "In Santa Monica, we were isolated. No one knew who Seton Hall was."

The country was about to find out.

Final Four Face-Off

Michigan and Seton Hall both had formidable Final Four opponents: Duke for the Pirates, while the Wolverines faced, of all possible teams, their Big Ten rival Illinois, who had beaten them twice and embarrassed them in front of their own fans just a few weeks earlier.

Fabled Duke was led by All-American Danny Ferry, winner of the Naismith Award as the national player of the year in 1989, and sure enough, when the lights went on at the Seattle Kingdome before 39,000 fans and a national TV audience, the young men from South Orange got stage fright. They came out jittery and tentative, and the Blue Devils jumped to an early 26–8 lead.

"We were getting annihilated," Gaze recalls. "We had to regroup to get back in the game."

They did just that.

Carlesimo called a timeout with 11 minutes to go in the half and his team down by almost 20. "He just told everyone to settle down and play one possession at a time," reserve forward Anthony Avent told the *Newark Star-Ledger*. "There was no panic. He just told us to keep playing our game."

The Pirates regained their poise, as well as their shot and their stifling defense. They whittled the Duke lead to five by halftime, and in the locker room, guard Gerald Greene, the team's "hype man," according to Morton, rallied this teammates.

"He said this was it, this was when we had to prove ourselves," Morton says, "and everyone knew what they had to do."

Led by Greene, who finished the game with 17 points and eight assists, Seton Hall roared back, shut down Ferry and Quin Snyder, and romped to a 95–78 victory.

The second semifinal game was all Michigan could have asked for: a rematch with Illinois.

The Wolverines wanted revenge, and playing Illinois was "like a dream come true," says Mills. "Our attitude was 'Bring it on,' but we knew we had to avoid their runs. That was our whole game plan—try to avoid their runs. If you played run and gun with them, you lost."

And for good reason. Illinois was ranked third in the country and had an explosive offense featuring future pros Kendall Gill, Nick Anderson, and Kenny Battle. But funny things happen when a determined defensive player gets good position on even the best offensive player.

And the Wolverines had a secret defensive weapon, a 6-foot-7 swingman named Mike Griffin who came off the bench to clamp down on the opponent's best player. Griffin got overlooked playing behind five future NBA players, but he had the best plus-minus ratio on the Michigan team.

The game was a battle from start to finish, with thirty-three lead changes and seven ties, but the Wolverines prevailed at the end by two points as Griffin held Gill to 11 points while Rice poured in 28 for Michigan.

So two teams that both overcame "an unusual set of circumstances," as Gaze put it, were set to meet in an improbable championship game.

"We felt good about our chances," says Gaze, "but we knew Michigan had talent. And we knew they had Glen Rice."

"We didn't know a lot about Seton Hall," says Mills. "But we knew they had to be good to get past Duke."

Winner Take All

Michigan opened the game strong, never trailed in the first half, and led by five points when the half ended. Robinson hit 5 of 9 shots for 13 points, attacked the basket and dished out assists, and Griffin, who had carefully studied videotape of Andrew Gaze's shooting habits, harassed the Australian sharpshooter into missing all of his field goal attempts.

The Wolverines extended their lead to 12 in the second half but went cold at the same time that John Morton was catching fire. He made two baskets and four free throws in two minutes to cut Michigan's lead to 61–59 with six minutes to go.

Rice had been guarding Morton and wanted Hughes to switch out on him the next time Seton Hall came down court. But Ramon Ramos, the broad-shouldered Pirates center, "set one of his monster picks," Hughes recalls, "and I was slow getting there and Morton drained another three. Man, Glen was angry at me!"

Led by guard Rumeal Robinson (21), shown here getting by Seton Hall's Daryll Walker (24) and Andrew Gaze (10), Michigan never trailed in the first half of the 1989 championship game. The Hall caught up in the second half, but Robinson won the game for the Wolverines with clutch free throws with three seconds left.

Morton kept scoring, and Seton Hall was up by two points with 1:12 to go. But Rice hit a three and Higgins made two free throws, and Michigan went up 71–68. Seton Hall wouldn't go away. With 25 seconds left, Morton, on his way to a game-high 35 points, hit a clutch three-pointer to tie the game and send it into overtime.

The OT was the first in twenty-six years for the championship game. Fisher broke the tension in the Michigan huddle by telling the team a quirky story about a man from California who anonymously called him up the night before to tell him Michigan would beat Seton Hall in overtime if Mark Hughes stayed in the game.

The teams traded baskets in overtime, and with 48 seconds to go, Seton Hall had the ball, up 79–78. Fisher encouraged his team to hang tough on defense, but instructed them not to foul, a strategy that paid big dividends when Morton forced up a bad shot with time running out on the possession clock, and Michigan snared the rebound with 13 seconds remaining.

Rice passed the ball to Robinson, who dribbled downcourt. He said afterwards he wanted to shoot, but was guarded closely by Greene, who knew his moves well from playing with Robinson in summer leagues on the East Coast. Chest-to-chest with Greene, Robinson passed to Hughes, who was open in the corner, waiting to fulfill the mysterious California man's prophecy.

But a whistle blew, stopping play. Greene had been called for a blocking foul before the pass, putting Robinson on the foul line to shoot a one-and-one with three seconds to play.

It would be very hard to argue that referee John Clougherty hadn't blown the call, reacting instinctively to incidental contact and prematurely blowing the whistle.

He admitted as much later on, and even Robinson would later concede the call was highly dubious.

"It was no foul," says Morton, who was just a few feet away from the play. "It was just a brush-by."

But refs are human and calls are part of the game, and the fate of the Michigan Wolverines season was in the hands of a 64 percent free-throw shooter.

As it happened, that shooter was the most tough-minded player on the team, says Mills, and one who vowed to avenge his performance when he lost the game for his team at the line in Wisconsin.

"We were very confident," Mills says. "We didn't say a word to him. We were all positive. When Fisher was in the huddle, he just talked about how we would play defense after Rumeal makes those shots."

Robinson stepped up to the line and swished the first shot to tie the game. Seton Hall called timeout. It didn't matter. Robinson said later once he made the first one he knew he'd make the second one. He did, and Michigan was ahead by a point, 81–80, with three seconds left.

Seton Hall could only scramble for a last-second desperation shot by Daryll Walker which fell short, making Michigan national champions for the first, and to date, only time.

Ironically, one of the enduring memories of the 1989 championship game was the class shown by the losers after a very bad call had arguably cost them a national title.

Carlesimo and his players never complained or made excuses.

"It's my clearest memory of that game," says Hamburger. "I was a young guy, only twenty-seven, walking off the court after the biggest disappointment of my life, and when I walked into the locker room, there was P. J., exhibiting the kind of poise and class that has stuck with me ever since.

"He had the ability to talk to the team at their lowest point and get them to hear what he was saying. When players talk about games they played in decades ago, these are the kind of things they remember."

The improbable game had one more irony.

Bo Schembechler, the ultimate Michigan Man, left the university the next year to become president of the Detroit Tigers.

"If I had known Schembechler was leaving," Bill Frieder said later, "I'd still be at Michigan."

Chapter 3

A Perfect Game from an Imperfect Team: Villanova vs. Georgetown, 1985

Joe Trimble, a *New York Daily News* sportswriter assigned to write the story of Don Larsen's 1956 World Series perfect game, sat and stared at the blank page in his typewriter, unable to come up with words to describe the indescribable. His colleague, Dick Young, never one to shy away from flaunting his writing chops, reached across Trimble's desk and typed out seven little words. Those seven words are now enshrined in journalistic lore among the all-time greatest sports leads:

"The imperfect man pitched a perfect game."

One could say that the Villanova Wildcats team of 1984–85 was the closest thing to the Don Larsen of college basketball. A good, but flawed, group of players who, on the biggest stage of their lives—the NCAA tournament final against Georgetown University—flirted for 40 minutes with the art of perfection and won the title, 66–64.

Just how imperfect were the 1984–85 Wildcats?

Well, for one, their starting point guard and field general, Gary McLain, was addicted to cocaine, which is generally not conducive to athletic success. Although McLain claimed in a 1987 self-penned essay in *Sports Illustrated* not to have snorted coke on the day of the final, he did admit to getting high forty-eight hours earlier, just prior to Villanova's semifinal win over Memphis State. And, since cocaine is said by specialists in the field of drug addiction to remain in the bloodstreams of casual users for two to four days and even longer for frequent users like McLain, it is reasonable to assume that he was playing the final while at least partly under the influence. In which case, it was arguably the finest game ever played by a point guard in that condition. McLain maintained his poise against Georgetown's full-court pressure defense, turning the ball over only twice, establishing the deliberate tempo so crucial to keeping Villanova in the game, and, in the process, converting several key baskets and free throws. He was rewarded with praise and a trip with his teammates to the White House, where McLain met with President Reagan while "flying high" on coke. Apparently, Reagan didn't notice it, either.

Just Say No, indeed.

McLain hinted in his controversial and dispiriting memoir—a *Naked Lunch* for jocks—that his coach and teammates knew about, and enabled, his drug abuse. This has never been confirmed, although by some accounts, coach Rollie Massimino had at least an inkling that something was amiss with his point guard, who was hanging with some rather unsavory companions. But the coach, according to these accounts, felt he lacked any "solid evidence" upon which to take action. Nevertheless, even if this situation was known only to insiders, Villanova's other fallibilities were well out in the open. These included a baffling inconsistency, unusual for a squad with strong senior leadership, and a knack for saving some of their worst basketball for the worst possible times.

The 1984-'85 'Cats lost a total of 10 games, eight of them in the Big East conference, and five against their two biggest Big East rivals, St. John's and Georgetown. They played Georgetown tight in both their losses, but in the three games against the Redmen (now known as the Red Storm), Villanova was outclassed.

They closed out their regular season schedule with a nationally-televised 23-point blowout loss at Pittsburgh. At halftime, Massimino advised his starters that they had five minutes at the start of the second half to justify their remaining in the game. If they kept up their rotten play, admonished the coach, he would yank them all. Just two minutes into the second half, Massimino, still frustrated by a lack of effort and senior leadership, called a time-out. "You've got one more minute," he told his starters. A minute later, he called another timeout and pulled them all. The second-stringers played the final 17 minutes. It was not a pretty sight, and surely no way to impress the NCAA tournament selection committee in the lead-up to "Selection Sunday."

A win in the first round of the Big East tourney over that same Pittsburgh team secured Villanova an eighth seed in the NCAA's Southeast Region. Even here, the committee was being generous.

By contrast, Georgetown, the 1984 NCAA champs, had it all going on entering the NCAA tournament. Having just crushed their toughest rival, St. John's, in the Big East final, they came into the Big Dance ranked first in the nation with a sterling mark of 30–2 and a 12-game winning streak. Georgetown was led by senior center and team captain Patrick Ewing, later to become a member of the NBA's All-Time 50 Greatest Players club. Georgetown was a 9 1/2-point favorite to repeat, and after a relatively easy four-game sojourn through the East Regionals and another rollover win against St. John's again in the Final Four semi, consecutive Hoya titles were a foregone conclusion among followers of college hoops.

"I don't think there was a living ass in the country who didn't think we were a better team," summed up Georgetown coach John Thompson in a 2004 *Sports Illustrated* retrospective on the '85 final.

This was the era of full-blown "Hoya Paranoia," a term originally coined to refer to Georgetown's feelings of being slighted and mislabeled by the media, which, at least to some degree, led Coach Thompson to enforce very strict rules on media access to his players. But Hoya Paranoia later came to imply something broader in scope and more disturbing—a widely-held vision of Georgetown basketball as an "Evil Empire," populated by angry black thugs masquerading as ballplayers, intimidating their opposition into abject submission.

Michael Jackson, a member of the 1985 Hoya team, speaking in that 2004 *SI* piece, sloughed off the popular image. "We had fun [with Hoya Paranoia] that season," he said. "We just listened and laughed. The image sold papers and made people watch us on TV."

Thompson has been oft-quoted as saying that he never cared a damn whether his team was well-liked, only whether it was respected. If nothing else, the Hoyas had earned that.

In any event, a Georgetown victory was how this championship game was supposed to play out.

But the basketball gods were even more fickle than usual on an April Fool's night in Lexington, Kentucky. Villanova had been on a nice roll throughout the tournament, but the team that showed up for the final had fully unearthed its inner mojo, and, most important, was in no mood to back down in the face of a more talented and deeper opponent. They also came into the game inspired by thoughts of two legendary and beloved Villanova figures: the longtime former head coach Al Severance, who passed away of a heart attack on the morning of the final game; and Jake Nevin, their seventy-four-year-old trainer, stricken with Lou Gehrig's Disease, who watched the final from his courtside wheelchair, his beatific smile bestowing a kind of benediction upon the Wildcats.

In the final, Villanova shot an amazing 22 of 28 from the field—an unprecedented 78.6 shooting percentage—against a team that during the season had held opponents to a shooting average of 39 percent. And they shot a very creditable 22 of 27 (81 percent) from the foul line. Villanova's record field-goal shooting was a reflection not only of pinpoint accuracy, but of a game plan that slowed the pace considerably and maximized every possession, keeping the score in the 60s and sucking the air out of Georgetown's offensive juggernaut. Georgetown actually hit an impressive 55 percent of its shots that night.

The only blemish on Villanova's near-perfect offensive display was its 17 turnovers (versus only 11 for the Hoyas). But those 17 turnovers make Villanova's achievement all the more astounding. Take away those possessions from Villanova's fifty-eight trips down the court, and it's evident that on nearly every possession where Villanova didn't turn the ball over, it scored from the field or the foul line. 'Nova combined that offensive efficiency with superior ball control. With 5:56 remaining in the game, CBS TV posted a telling graphic showing Villanova possessing the ball nearly twice as long as Georgetown in the second half. Great shooting, great ball control, great defense—can't lose.

Looking back on this game thirty-two years later, from a purely technical standpoint, Villanova's effort clearly fell short of absolute perfection. But, then again, Don Larsen didn't throw a strike on every pitch.

Ricotta Rollie

Rollie Massimino, who passed away in 2017, was but one of two funhouse characters enlivening the Big East conference in 1984–85, the other being coach Lou Carnesecca of St. John's. Here were a couple of elfin children of working-class Italian-American immigrants, wily and excitable, rumpled (Rollie more so) and lovable (Louie more so). Both wore their coaching hearts on their sleeves and, in their own ways, were deeply challenged sartorially. Indeed, Rollie could have had a pretty fair second career typecast as a rotund Oscar Madison in summer-stock productions of *The Odd Couple*.

But when it comes to coaching comparisons, perhaps a more apt one is between Massimino and another second-generation, fast-talking Italian-American, Jimmy Valvano of North Carolina State.

While Valvano captivated his players with practices featuring only a net and scissors, Rollie went even further in implanting dreams of glory in his players' heads. Working with a communications student at Villanova, Massimino, armed with biographical material gathered on every recruit, created make-believe play-by-play radio broadcasts that put these recruits in starring roles in imaginary championship games.

According to *The Perfect Game* by Frank Fitzpatrick, the six-minute audiotape Rollie created to woo the highly sought-after Worcester, Massachusetts, swingman Dwayne McClain was prescient to the point of being downright eerie. The game chosen for

McClain was the 1985 final against, yes, Georgetown and Patrick Ewing (McClain had played against Ewing in high school, but had never beaten him). However, all that disappointment was erased in McClain's fantasy tape, in which Villanova triumphed in a down-to-the-wire game, with McClain, the leading scorer, having his hands on the ball as the final buzzer sounded.

And, as it happens, this is exactly how it went down in the real world nearly five years later. Eerie, to be sure.

With Massimino, as with Valvano, the notion of family figured prominently in the recruiting pitch. Rollie's players didn't call him "Daddy Mass" for nothing.

Of course, there were the team dinners at Chez Massimino, catered with loving care by Mary Ann, aka Mrs. Daddy Mass.

Harold Jensen, a sophomore guard whose 5-for-5 shooting and 14-point output in the final is now the stuff of legend, describes those Sunday get-togethers as adhering to the finest traditions of the idealized American household.

Jensen says Massimino also had an uncanny knack for intuiting the feelings of his players, just as Ward Cleaver, the apotheosis of the idealized American dad, had with his son, "The Beaver."

"My first year and a half at Villanova were disappointing," recalls Jensen, who admits to having had a very tender ego that was in need of regular massaging.

"Maybe it was a fear of failure, but I was putting way too much pressure on myself. Coach Mass picked up on it, and he was great in helping me get in touch with those feelings and [to overcome] them."

Rollie's assistants were likewise deemed integral parts of the Massimino family dynamic.

Steve Lappas, an assistant in '85 and later Villanova's head coach, licks his lips in memory of the sumptuous dinners at the Massimino residence.

"Rollie wanted all of us there with him, including our wives and kids. My kids really loved dinner at Rollie's, especially the pasta and cheese. To this day, they talk about one particular Italian cheese that Rollie used to serve up in a brick and grate. It was Ricotta

Salata, but to my kids, who are all grown-up now, it will always be 'Rollie Cheese.'"

And, finally, Rollie reportedly liked to keep his guys loose by scrimmaging his black players against his whites. "The brothers verses the Joeys," as it was known. It was yet one more way of fostering bonds among his team—bonds that remain strong to this day.

Naturally, there was a less tender side to Daddy Mass, a tough-love side, which evidenced itself on the practice court. Jensen says the coach relied heavily on suicide drills and what they call "the 17s"—sprinting back and forth across the width of the court seventeen times—to get his players in game shape. Jensen recalls the assistant coaches bringing out buckets to accommodate the queasy stomachs.

But Daddy Mass's coaching tenure in Philly will be remembered more for the cheese than the heaves.

Big John Thompson, upon whom we expound at some length in Chapter 5, operated more in a disciplinary vein, although, he, too, was inclined at times to let his erring players off the hook. Big John was his own daddy mass of contradictions.

Three years after the crushing loss to North Carolina, the big man's countenance and coaching style hadn't changed very much. He and his 6-foot-10 frame still prowled the sideline, wearing a towel around the neck and a look that said *Don't f--k with me.* His 1984–85 NCAA runners-up viewed him in much the same way as his did his 1982 runners-up, although by '85 Georgetown was no longer an up-and-comer, but a recognized national powerhouse. So Big John could dip into a deeper well of high school talent. To counter all the negative aspects of rising Hoya Paranoia—a Salt Lake City scribe called Thompson the "Idi Amin" of the Big East—Big John by 1985 had grown increasingly protective of his players, keeping them safe from an aggressive, and occasionally racist, media and constantly peppering them with lectures on competing and surviving as Black men in White America.

But, as much as Thompson had his players' backs, he could be curiously inconsistent in his dealings with them. This was evident in his approach to their academic pursuits. While nearly all his players eventually went on to graduate, some say Thompson was less than sincere in his demand that they avail themselves of a top-notch Georgetown education.

One of these players was Grady Mateen, a highly-recruited 6-foot-11 freshman center on the 1984–'85 team, who grew up idolizing Thompson back in Akron, Ohio. Mateen did not get off the bench in the final (Thompson wasn't big on playing freshmen in critical situations) and was unhappy with the overall playing time he received that season. But what bothered Mateen the most, he says, was an unfulfilled promise that Thompson made during his recruiting visit. Thompson, according to Mateen, "guaranteed" that there would be a "study table" available to those players who were as concerned with their academics as their athletics. Mateen says when he confronted Thompson about his broken promise, the coach brushed him off.

"He looked right at me and my family that day and he lied to us," says Mateen. "I was there to get an education, not just play basketball."

Mateen credits Thompson with being a terrific coach—smart, intense, and tough, yet fair, with all his players.

But the freshman couldn't get past this initial deception and transferred to Ohio State the following year.

"I'd lost respect for the coach," he says, "and I'd lost some of the thrill of playing basketball."

Craig Esherick, a Georgetown assistant in 1985 who succeeded Thompson as head coach upon his retirement in 1999, is loath to question Mateen's personal account, but notes that he never witnessed Thompson being anything other than sincere in wanting his players to obtain a proper college education. For Esherick, Big John remains a gold standard in college coaching.

"He taught me the coaching profession," says Esherick.

And, finally, there was this whole other John Thompson

persona, one not at all connected to a Hoya Paranoia narrative, which emerged for the first time in public during the 1984–85 season.

Many, in and out of basketball, who have had private interactions with Thompson over the years describe him as warm and friendly in conversation and not at all the fearsome, glowering figure he appeared to be. In particular, Thompson's fun side ("The guy could be hilarious," says one former player), tended to get short shrift. This side of his personality was finally displayed to the world via his relationship with Lou Carnesecca, who became famous (or infamous, if you were a fashionista) for the repulsively ugly sweater he wore during a lengthy St. John's winning streak. Louie called it his "lucky sweater," and it endeared this little man even more to the masses.

Before their teams' second meeting at Madison Square Garden on February 27, Thompson approached Louie to shake hands and suddenly whipped off his jacket to reveal a T-shirt replica of Louie's sweater that was every bit as repugnant as the original. The MSG audience went wild with laughter. This display of humor and good will, broadcast nationally, was a very good look for Big John.

Idi Amin to Clifford Huxtable in one small fashion statement.

The Road to Lexington

Georgetown began its regular season with 18 straight victories, buoyed by a relatively weak non-conference schedule. But they did secure a few big wins against highly ranked DePaul, Boston College, and Villanova (the latter two in overtime). Their first loss, a one-point defeat by No. 2-ranked St. John's at home, was followed by an equally tough two-point loss at Syracuse. The Hoyas rebounded strongly, going on to beat St. John's three times and gaining revenge against Syracuse back home.

Esherick insists the team faced no significant hurdles during the course of the season. At least none that required tinkering with personnel or with Georgetown's basic motion offense and full-court pressure defense. The players, according to Esherick, came into the season with eyes firmly focused on the Final Four and went into the NCAAs having already been tested by big-time Big East competition.

The very best the Big East had to offer that season were Carnesecca's Redmen, led by future NBA Hall of Famer Chris Mullin and forward Walter Berry. SJU won the regular season Big East title with a 15–1 conference record. But after that loss to St. John's in January, Georgetown made it abundantly clear that they had Louie's number.

"St. John's had great players and Louie was a great coach, but we had a lot of success playing a box-and-one [defense] on Mullin, which took away much of his effectiveness," explains Esherick.

The NCAA East Regionals were likewise a relative breeze for the Hoyas, featuring double-digit wins over Lehigh, Temple, and Loyola of Chicago.

In the regional final, however, they got a bit of a scare from Georgia Tech. Ewing was in foul trouble throughout and spent much of the game on the bench, and his backup, Ralph Dalton, committed four fouls of his own. Thompson was forced to set aside his distaste for using freshmen in key situations and inserted Grady Mateen into the game in the second half.

But, at crunch time, up by two with 14 seconds left, he had his senior, Dalton, out there on the floor. And Dalton responded with two crucial free throws to ice a six-point win.

The Final Four semifinal was Georgetown's fourth game against St. John's that season and its third straight rollover win. Chris Mullin, stymied yet again by that pesky box-and-one, scored a measly eight points in a 77–59 beatdown. After the game, Carnesecca listed Georgetown among the greatest college teams of all time, up there with the '76 Indiana Hoosiers and all those dominant UCLA teams in the '60s and '70s.

By this point, Louie was suffering from his own severe case of paranoia—Georgetown variety.

Villanova, as discussed, struggled most of the season to find its true character. Its three senior leaders—Ed Pinckney, McClain, and McLain—for whatever reasons, did not seem to be jelling in that role, and other major contributors, including Harold Pressley, were maddeningly inconsistent all season, says Steve Lappas.

The three seniors have never disputed that harsh assessment. "The chemistry—that senior year, it just wasn't happening," Ed Pinckney told *Sports Illustrated*. "I still don't know why."

The Wildcats won ten of their first eleven against mostly indifferent competition, although this early-season run did include a quality win against Syracuse. But the overall strength of the Big East conference weighed on them over the next two months, and Villanova compiled a mediocre 8–8 record during that span. While only a few of those losses were one-sided, the execrable loss to Pittsburgh tied a ribbon around a disappointing regular season. Again, as alluded to, it was St. John's that contributed the most to Villanova's misery.

"We couldn't match up with them," laments Jensen, who confirms that Villanova was desperately hoping that Georgetown would maintain its dominance against St. John's in the semifinal so the Wildcats wouldn't have to face the Redmen for a fourth time in the NCAA final. "Had we played St John's," he says, matter-of-factly, "we would not have been champions."

Once Villanova entered the NCAAs, however, it was a more motivated and confident squad. In the opener, 'Nova survived and advanced against a tough Dayton team, which, with under two minutes left and the game tied at 49, went into a four-corner-like stall to set up a last shot. That plan was thwarted by Harold Pressley's steal, and Villanova then went into its own version of a stall. However, Jensen, feeling his offensive oats at last, saw an opening and took off to the hoop for a winning layup with just over a minute remaining.

This was followed by tightly-played upsets of top-seed Michigan and fifth-seeded Maryland in the Sweet 16. Next up was second-seeded North Carolina in the regional final. Down five at halftime, Massimino delivered one of his most inspired pep talks—this one having to do with spaghetti and clam sauce—and Villanova went on to cruise, 56–44, into the Final Four.

The luck of the Final Four draw matched them against Memphis State, which had a beefy and talented front line of 6-foot-10 All-American Keith Lee, 7-foot William Bedford, and a 6-foot-7 forward with the delightful name of Baskerville Holmes—a moniker that, no doubt, has since been bestowed upon innumerable canines. Memphis State was another team with Georgetown on the brain, and, based on their statements to the media, the Tigers appeared to be looking past Villanova to a championship matchup with Georgetown.

Despite Lee and Bedford being in constant foul trouble—Lee fouled out midway through the second half—Memphis gave Villanova a tussle. But 'Nova finally put the Tigers away with several free throws in the final minute for a 52–45 victory.

Asked by a reporter after the Memphis State game what it would take for any team to beat Georgetown in the final, Gary McLain (who, you will remember, was high on cocaine that night) replied, "It will take a perfect game."

Clearly, narcotics had robbed McLain of neither his court skills nor his insight.

The Perfect Game

Rollie Massimino, never known as a before-game speechifier, gave an eloquent address at the pregame mass and meal at the Lexington Ramada. Not a rah-rah speech, but a contemplative one, invoking the memory of the departed Al Severance and encouraging all his players to go back to their rooms and visualize themselves beating Georgetown. The players were moved and, more important, according to Harold Jensen, they were calmed by Massimino's soothing words and relaxed temperament.

It was a calmness they would need to capture the correct rhythm and tempo, as important in basketball as in hitting a golf ball or playing a piano sonata.

In the NCAA grand finale, Villanova had both, in spades.

Shooting-wise, they were in rhythm all night, and tempo-wise, they were playing with just the right slow hand.

From the opening tip-off, CBS TV color analyst Billy Packer was talking up the necessity of Villanova keeping the score in the 50s or 60s in order to have any chance to win. A myth to this day is that Villanova did it with a slowdown, spread offense. In fact, with the exception of only four possessions, Villanova did not hold the ball on any trip downcourt for more than 45 seconds, which was the limit set the following season when the NCAA introduced the shot clock. Villanova was simply in no hurry to attack the basket. Massimino's instructions were to be patient, make the extra pass, and not try to force anything. But he also emphasized not being afraid to work the ball into Ed Pinckney going against Ewing in the paint, as Pinckney had had success against the Georgetown big man throughout his career. And that carried over to the final, where Pinckney wound up with 16 points and six rebounds versus Ewing's 14 and five, and he was named Most Outstanding Player of the Final Four.

On defense, as with all Massimino-coached teams, the '85 Wildcats were nearly impossible for an opponent to decipher on the fly. Indeed, Rollie has stated that, on occasion, all his defensive machinations confused even himself. Just listen to Massimino on YouTube, addressing his colleagues at one of his defensive coaching clinics, and you will come away thinking that consummate double-talkers such as Casey Stengel and Professor Irwin Corey had nothing on Villanova's head coach.

Generally speaking, Massimino's schemes are modeled on the art of deceit. Show an opponent all kinds of looks—a trapping zone that morphs into a 2-3 zone and finally into a straight man-to-man. Do this, goes the Massimino doctrine, and you can restrict the opponent's offensive flow and control the direction of the ball.

"We needed to take into account that Rollie constantly changes up his defenses over the course of a game," explains Esherick. "On one trip down the court, he'll throw in a match-up zone, and the next time down they're in a man-to-man or a 2–3 zone or whatever. You never know what he's going to do, and we had to adjust to that."

Esherick says Georgetown looked to counter Rollie's defensive legerdemain with increased ball movement.

"We didn't want every time we came down court to have to figure out what the defense was in order to run set plays. So, in that game, we focused instead on keeping the ball moving, trying to get everyone touches, and that strategy worked pretty well."

"In the end, all our multiple defenses (as many as thirty or more) were grounded in a basic principle," adds Villanova's Lappas. "The beauty of showing the opposition something and doing something else; keep the other guys thinking you're playing a zone when you're really playing man-to-man."

Villanova further changed up its usual coverage on Ewing, dropping a guard down low to double-team him from the blind side.

And, finally, one should not overlook the excellence of John Thompson's 94-foot pressure zone, which turned Villanova over 17 times, and made them earn most of those 22 baskets.

In short, if this were a chess match played between two defensive-minded coaches, you could quite accurately call the 1985 final a draw. It's sad in a way that the final score had to reflect otherwise.

The pregame introductions featured an act of racial hostility encapsulating the worst aspects of Hoya Paranoia—a banana tossed on the court in the direction of Pat Ewing. Ewing and his teammates apparently didn't see the piece of spoiled fruit before it was carted away. Michael Wilbon, the *Washington Post*'s Georgetown beat writer who did witness this travesty, didn't even bother to mention it in his next-day story. Such vile behavior toward Ewing was that common during his years at Georgetown.

Once it got down to basketball, it was like old home week for two veteran teams intimately familiar with one another. But this game would not be like any of those others.

There was a heightened intensity, right from the tip-off, as Georgetown immediately went into its 1-3-1 full-court trapping defense, in an effort to make Villanova play faster. And it worked. The early, rapid pace of the game was not to Villanova's advantage. Massimino had written "64" on the locker room blackboard as a defensive point goal, but Billy Packer noted at about the midpoint of the first half, with the Hoyas up, 20–14, that Villanova was looking at a game in the low 80s. In other words, they were looking at a loss.

"Villanova would be smart to pull it out some more," said Packer. Which they did over the next five or six minutes, working more deliberately, and successfully, to get the ball to Pinckney and McClain in advantageous positions in the paint. The play that tied the game at 20, a baseline spin-move to the hoop by Dwayne McClain followed by an arching shot just over Patrick Ewing's reach, underscored the fact that Villanova was in this game to the end. Running back up court after making the shot, McClain dramatized the point by spitting demonstrably on the hardwood.

"I was making a statement that we didn't come here to fear Georgetown," McClain told Frank Fitzpatrick.

It seemed that whenever Villanova attempted to switch up and speed the action, Georgetown's trapping zone took away the ball. But Georgetown was in an offensive funk that lasted more than six minutes. They came out of it briefly when Reggie Williams sliced through the lane to put back his own missed free throw to retake the lead at 22–20. And then, with just over three minutes left in the half, Georgetown exploded out of their scoring drought with three monster dunks from Patrick Ewing. It was by now evident to all those in TV land and in the arena that this affair was going to be nobody's rout.

Perhaps the signature moment of the 1985 final occurred with just under two minutes left in the half and Georgetown up, 28–27. In possession of the ball, Villanova wisely went into a four-corner stall (which would be the last one ever attempted before the initiation of the shot clock). Georgetown elected to stay back in its 1-3-1 zone and allow Villanova to milk the clock, a tactic that, in Billy Packer's view, played "right into Rollie Massimino's hands."

Harold Pressley put back a rebound with four seconds remaining to give Villanova a 29–28 halftime lead. On the final play of the half, after a David Wingate jumper misfired, Reggie Williams let loose a wild elbow to the neck and face of Villanova's Chuck Everson. Williams immediately ran off, leaving Everson and Massimino to raise hell with the refs for failing to call a flagrant foul on the play.

Steaming over the non-call, Massimino followed his troops into the locker room pumping his right fist. Perhaps he knew that in not blowing their whistles, the refs had done his team a favor, supplying a major shot of adrenaline.

Back in the locker room, "Rollie was very animated," says Harold Jensen. "He was telling us that no team was going to do that to us."

Only he was saying it loudly, repeatedly, and in much more colorful language.

Jensen notes after a few minutes, the coach calmed down, but the energy and passion he displayed in those moments set the tone for the second half.

Villanova came out even more patient on offense than they were in the first half, but they were equally determined to get the ball down low to Pinckney whenever possible. After a Ewing jumper put the Hoyas back on top by one, Villanova took back the lead on Jensen's third basket and went up by four on a three-point play by Pinckney, muscling up against Ewing and drawing the first foul on the star center. A jump shot by Gary McLain pushed Villanova's lead up to six, and Ewing committed two more fouls over the next two minutes, necessitating his short rest on the bench.

The next nine minutes could be described as slow (on offense) and furious (on defense), as the lead changed hands several times. Typical of the milieu in which the second half was played was McLain taking a charge under the basket from Horace Broadnax that nearly cemented his head to the floor. McLain came out of the game for all of six seconds. An Ed Pinckney jumper got Villanova's lead back to 53–48 with just under six minutes to go, at which point John Thompson called timeout amid the roars of a pro-Villanova crowd. The timeout was effective, with Georgetown proceeding to rattle off six straight points, aided by two Jensen turnovers (he had six in the game), to retake the lead with about 4:45 remaining. It would be the Hoyas' last lead.

After yet another Villanova turnover, Georgetown went into a stall, but a hard pass from Bill Martin rammed off the lower leg of Broadnax and into McClain's arms. It's a seminal play that keeps popping up in the minds of the Hoyas. "It cost us the game," Ewing has said. Martin has admitted to making a low pass, but suggesting that Broadnax could have caught it. For the record, this turnover's on Martin.

Villanova then held the ball for nearly a minute before finding Jensen open again for his fifth and final basket at the 2:35 mark, putting Villanova back on top, 55–54. Two foul shots from Pinckney made it a three-point lead. From here on, for Villanova it was all about poise and the ability to shoot fouls. Harold Jensen sank four free throws over the next minute and 43 seconds to pad the lead back to five, 61–56, with 52 seconds left. Villanova players began slapping fives—very prematurely, considering who the opponent was. And as if to emphasize that it's a 40-minute game, Ewing threw down a dunk on the next possession, and the Villanova lead was back to only three.

But with 41 agonizing seconds remaining, the Villanova senior leadership that had so often faltered during the regular season, asserted itself. Over the next 23 seconds, Dwayne McClain calmly sank four more free throws sandwiched around layups by Michael Jackson and David Wingate that kept the Hoya's diminishing hopes alive.

With 10 seconds left, Harold Pressley hit a final foul shot for a 66–62 lead. Jackson drove the length of the court for a layup with five seconds left. Back then, the clock didn't stop after made baskets, so this game was effectively over. That is, until David Wingate smartly punched the ball toward the stands, forcing the refs to stop the clock with two seconds left. Broadnax collided with McClain going for the inbounds pass, but the kid from Worcester had already

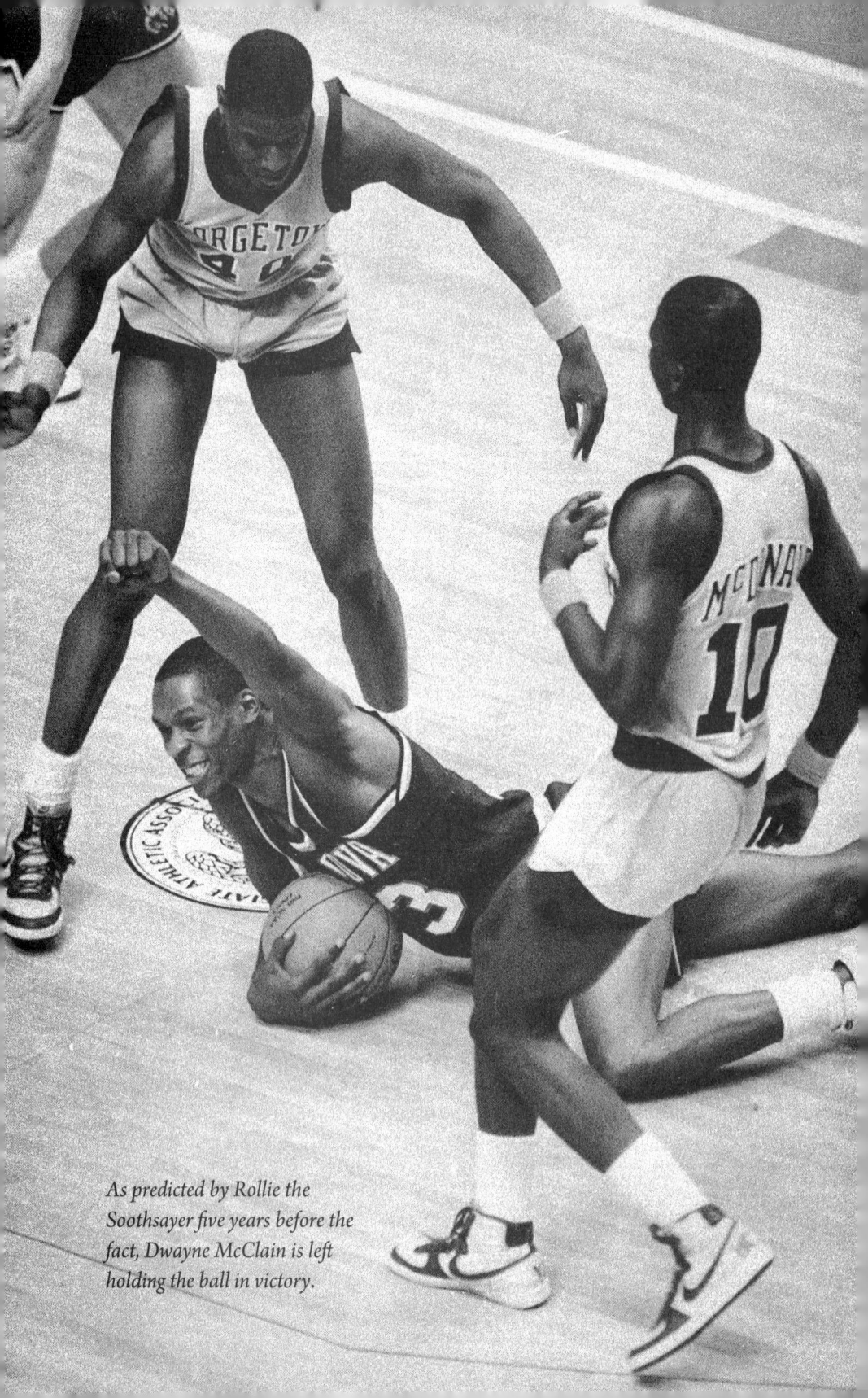

As predicted by Rollie the Soothsayer five years before the fact, Dwayne McClain is left holding the ball in victory.

heard the future five years ago on Rollie Massimino's fantasy radio show and knew precisely how this would all end.

Falling to the floor, McClain caught Jensen's inbounds pass and cradled it tightly, as the final buzzer intoned a perfect ending to an imperfect season.

Aftermath

For a team with the swagger and intensity of Georgetown, the mood in the postgame locker room seemed awfully strange, to say the least.

"No one looked down, no one was in tears," reports Grady Mateen. "There was a positive energy in the room. A distinct feeling among all the coaches and players that we had played a very good game, and it was just Villanova's night."

Craig Esherick concurs that there was little, if any, indication in the locker room that Georgetown had lost the game.

"I remember drawing strength from watching Patrick Ewing go out there with pride to accept his [runner-up] watch," notes the assistant coach.

Steve Lappas, however, isn't buying all this talk of serenity and acceptance.

"I know those Georgetown guys. They took it very hard that night and they still do."

Comments over the years, especially from Thompson and Ewing, tend to support Lappas on this point.

As for Rollie and his 'Cats, they naturally reveled in their accomplishment. At the hotel, they partied hardy into the next morning, followed by the White House visit and all the other championship perks that came with the university's first-ever national title.

And, then, two years later, out of nowhere, came Gary McLain's memoir in *Sports Illustrated*, for which he reported receiving a $35,000 freelance fee. It turned the joyful disposition of Rollie's close-knit basketball family decidedly sour.

"It hurt us all, but especially Rollie," says Steve Lappas. Not so much all the discussion of rampant drug use, but rather McLain's allegation that the coach was aware of McLain's problem and chose to ignore it, presumably to preserve the image of the basketball program.

According to Lappas, while McLain has since reconciled with Massimino and many of his teammates, the pain of having been thrown under the bus by a trusted family member lingers.

"It may have been forgiven," Lappas acknowledges. "But it is definitely not forgotten."

Lappas, Jensen, and other players remain insistent to this day that Massimino had zero knowledge of McLain's drug use and would most definitely have taken action if he had.

After the triumph of his life, Massimino turned down an offer to coach the New Jersey Nets of the NBA and remained at Villanova for another seven years, taking his team to the NCAAs four more times—including an Elite Eight appearance in '88—before resigning to become head coach at the University of Nevada, Las Vegas. UNLV was coming off probation and the forced resignation of its charismatic and freewheeling coach, Jerry Tarkanian, and it was hoped that Massimino would inject credibility and stability into that program. But things didn't work out that way, and Rollie was himself forced out after two years in a brouhaha over the amount of his salary.

The coach then moved on to Cleveland State for the next seven years, where the troubles got considerably worse—a losing record combined with more drug tales, allegations of academic improprieties, and players committing felony crimes.

Massimino's final stop on the coaching carousel was Northwood (later Keiser) University, a small college in West Palm Beach, Florida, where Daddy Mass quietly settled in and over a decade amassed an impressive won-loss resume.

It had not been his intention to finish his career in relative obscurity. Florida was originally his retirement destination, and

Massimino only agreed to take the Northwood/Keiser job as a favor to a friend.

But once back in the gym, this Italian leprechaun embraced it with the same passion—and the same pasta—of his glory years.

"Coaching keeps me young," he told a reporter several months before his death. "I'm a lifer."

Chapter 4

Hope Is a Thing with Leather (or Rubber): North Carolina State vs. Houston, 1983

The late Bill Guthridge, longtime assistant under Dean Smith and later head basketball coach at North Carolina, had a word he used to describe a certain kind of game: a victory so magically transcendent (or "transplendent," for fans of *Annie Hall*) that words fail and the only way to convey one's ineffable joy is via an individual or group hug. Guthridge called these games "huggables."

The 1982–83 season was, for the North Carolina State University Wolfpack and its irrepressible and charismatic coach, Jimmy Valvano, a season of huggables. So many hugs, in fact, that one would think that by the time NC State had scratched and clawed its way to yet another miracle victory in the NCAA final, there would be no energy left for hugs and no moisture left for tears.

But there were plenty of hugs to go around after that 54–52 last-second win over Houston in Albuquerque, New Mexico, on April 4. The irony was that State's coach and hugger-in-chief couldn't buy one.

The TV cameras captured the lasting image of Jimmy V in the immediate wake of the fulfillment of his lifelong dream, spinning, bobbing, and twisting his way through the hullabaloo on the court, searching in vain for someone—anyone—upon whom to administer an embrace. What wasn't widely known at the time was that V's mad dash was enabled by the IV fluids he received before the game to counter a nasty case of the flu. A flu that was bad enough to send him right back to bed after he had completed his postgame media interviews.

The flu bug notwithstanding, to this day that vision of Valvano, immersed in triumphant rapture and lacking only an outlet into which to plug it, ranks among the most memorable representations of the thrill of victory in the annals of American sport. Put it right up there with Yogi Berra leaping into the arms of Don Larsen and Joe Namath exiting Super Bowl III waving his index finger in the air.

One would think that Valvano's unforgettable victory dance would be his finest hour.

One would be wrong.

> *"Sincerity—if you can fake that, you've got it made."*
> George Burns

Valvano, the fast-talking middle child of Italian immigrants, wanted the NC State job desperately. But arriving in Raleigh in the spring of 1980 to take his place among the buttoned-down barons of the Atlantic Coast Conference, the dyed-in-the-wisecrack Corona, Queens, native was feeling out of place.

"I get to the airport," quipped Valvano years later in front of a live audience, "and a guy introduces himself, 'Hi, I'm Billy Ray Bob!' Okay, I say, where are the other two guys? Anyway, I did want to fit in so I said, 'It's very nice to meet you all. I'm Jimmy Tommy Tony.'"

You can imagine how this Noo Yawk shtick went over with many people on Tobacco Road. His fellow ACC coaches, including the venerable Dean Smith and Maryland's Lefty Driesell, found the league's new rock star more than a little obnoxious and in over his head in America's premier basketball conference. Indeed, before Valvano had coached his first game at NC State, he was already a local TV and radio celebrity. This, too, didn't sit particularly well with the ACC's august coaching fraternity.

"Never, and I mean never, have I met someone who took over every single room he ever walked into like Jim Valvano, " noted Dean Smith's wife, Linnea, as quoted in John Feinstein's book,

The Legends Club. Mrs. Smith added that Valvano "didn't just own the room, he *became* the room." Mickie Krzyzewski, spouse of Duke coach Mike Krzyzewski (aka Coach K), who had arrived on Tobacco Road about the same time as Valvano, had an even more visceral reaction to the news of Valvano's hiring. "Oh, shit," the normally demure Mrs. K is said to have exclaimed.

Meanwhile, Valvano's players, recruited by former NC State coach Norm Sloan, who had just left them to return to his former job at the University of Florida, didn't quite know what to make of the new guy. Was he conning them with a basketball-minded rendition of "76 Trombones"? Or was Valvano what he was telling them he was—a sincere and dedicated basketball coach with a dream of winning the NCAA championship who was going to make his personal dream come true for all of them?

Two of Sloan's most prized recruits, Dereck Whittenburg and Sidney Lowe, out of DeMatha High School in Washington, DC, had been hoping their DeMatha coach, the highly-respected Morgan Wootten, would accept an offer to coach at NC State and reunite with two of his favorite players. If there was ever a personality antithetical to that of Valvano's, it was Morgan Wootten's.

"We were excited," says Whittenburg. "We told Coach Wootten, 'Please come on down, we need 'ya here.'" But Wootten, after careful consideration, turned the job down.

Waiting in the wings was Valvano, who, according to Whittenburg, started in on his players from day one, constantly talking up his crystal-blue-persuasion vision of NCAA glory. In limning a portrait of that vision, Valvano went so far as to run occasional practices without a basketball. The props for the day included just a net and a pair of scissors with which to cut it down. Still, the more the man talked, insists Whittenburg, "the more we listened. We began to see what he saw and dream what he dreamed."

Ray Martin, one of Valvano's assistant coaches, says the team was lucky to have had a strong leadership triumvirate composed of Whittenburg, Lowe, and forward Thurl Bailey.

"Those three guys knew that V was the real deal, and they bought into his vision pretty quickly," says Martin, "and the other guys followed."

While it may have taken a bit of time for the vision thing to completely sink in, one thing his players sensed about their new coach right from the very outset was that he was, at heart, a kid like them—rambunctious and unpredictable—and that heretofore they would do well to expect the unexpected.

Max Perry, a former player and a graduate assistant coach on the 1982–83 team, tells a story about Valvano, shortly after being hired, pulling his Mazda 300ZX into the parking lot of the converted hotel where most of the NC State players lived. At the time, they were playing touch football on an adjacent grass field. Risking injury to their knees and ankles would have been enough in itself to raise a new coach's hackles. But apart from that, the players were playing this game under the influence of a hearty keg of beer. The players readied themselves for a royal comeuppance. Instead, what they got was a compatriot.

"Coach walks right past the keg and cries out for somebody to give him a beer," recalls Perry. "Then, he turns to us and says, 'Okay, I'm the quarterback. Whose team am I on?'"

"That was the V I remember," adds Ernie Myers, a freshman guard on the '83 championship team. "I was in a nightclub one night after a game against Virginia, dancing and drinking, and I bump into some guy on the dance floor . . . it was Valvano. 'Hey, Ernie, how're you doing?' he says. V was cool like that. He treated you like a man, and he expected you to act like one. He didn't worry if you weren't in bed every night at ten. Be ready to play. That's what he told us."

As regards North Carolina State's administration, they may have had a few qualms of their own about Valvano's ability to fit neatly into the staid ACC mold, and they were no doubt aware of a mild taint that he carried from his tenure at Iona College in New Rochelle, New York. Valvano had been questioned by the FBI over allegations of point-shaving and gambling at Iona during the

1979–80 season, but had ultimately been cleared of any wrongdoing. There were also rumors of unseemly goings-on involving Jeff Ruland, Valvano's star center at Iona (ten years later, Ruland would reveal that Valvano had slipped him cash under the table). But these types of concerns were far outweighed by Valvano's success in transitioning Iona's sleepy little basketball program into a major Division I contender in just two years. And, besides, it wasn't like NC State was a stranger to the stain of NCAA sanctions. Sloan's 1972–73 team went 27-0 but was banned from the NCAA tournament due to irregularities concerning the recruitment of David "Skywalker" Thompson.

Since winning the 1974 title on Thompson's wings, however, State had not come close to kissing the sky, making only a couple of appearances in the NIT and one second-round exit from the NCAAs. It was fervently hoped by the NC State powers that be that Valvano would apply the full force of his giant personality and nonstop internal engine to get the Wolfpack back into the upper echelon of the ACC. That was the name of the game then, as it is now and will no doubt forever be.

But it wasn't just Valvano's impressive won-loss record, his quotidian energy level, or his amazing powers of persuasion that had NC State's administration and players eating out of his hand.

"What was most remarkable about the man was that when he looked you in the eye, when he *listened* to you, it made you feel like you were the only person in the world," recalls Michael Klahr, a former sports information director at Metro State College in Denver, who invited Valvano to speak at the school in 1984 to generate enthusiasm for bringing back a basketball program that had been shut down after losing 77 straight games. This speaking engagement was like mother's milk to Valvano, who loved nothing more than whipping up an audience to accomplish the near-impossible.

"Now, did the man really care about Metro State? Was his interest in everything I said to him that day genuine? I can't say for certain, but it sure seemed to be," continues Klahr, now a Denver sports radio talk show host. "However you may have felt about the guy, there was no denying he had this incredible gift, and it served him well."

Dereck Whittenburg, for his part, is quite certain that Valvano's sincerity was no charade.

"He wanted to know us . . . this man cared about us."

Adds his teammate and high school chum, Sidney Lowe, "V told me he loved me, and I believed it . . . we all believed it."

It is the unshakeable belief of his players, more so than the genuineness of Valvano's sincerity, wherein lies the story of the 1982–83 North Carolina State Wolfpack.

Dreamin' Is Free

Valvano took to the ACC like a thick slice of mozzarella.

Ray Martin recalls a coaches' meeting in 1980, before the start of his first season, after Valvano had just returned from one of his first recruiting trips.

"He sits down in his red swivel chair, his back to us, and suddenly spins around to face us with this big smile," says Martin, "'Hey, fellas,' he says. 'We're in the BIG TIME NOW!' Coach was just loving the whole thing."

The Wolfpack were, indeed, embarking on the big time, but Valvano's first year in the ACC was a success primarily from a learning perspective.

"We were young, our key guys were just sophomores, and the ACC, as always, was loaded with talent," says Martin.

The 1980–81 team finished a mediocre 14–13 (4–10 in the conference), and that was enough to generate the first hate letters, including one in which the author, upset about the team's two losses to North Carolina, stated his intention to come to Raleigh and shoot Valvano's dog. According to Joe Menzer's book, *Four Corners*, the writer provided his name and business address, to which Valvano responded with a letter of his own suggesting that this rabid NC State fan consider rooting for another team. Valvano added in a postscript that he hated to spoil the man's day, but the Valvano family didn't have a dog.

Whatever the mood of the NC State fan base at season's end, there remained a shared belief among the team that the V train was on track.

Forward Lorenzo Charles, center Cozell McQueen, and sharp-shooting guard Terry Gannon all came onboard the following year, and the train traveled as far as the NCAAs, where it was derailed by underdog Tennessee-Chattanooga in the first round. Not a resounding success by any means, but enough to quiet the potential canine assassins.

Valvano, however, never let up on the gas, never allowed his players to get down on themselves and cease dreaming their championship dreams. To a man, those players and assistant coaches revered him as a "players' coach." To wit, Valvano's practices, while well-organized and duly strenuous, were relatively enjoyable affairs, emphasizing scrimmaging over endless ball drills and suicide sprints. His former players say those scrimmages were where they learned to deal with the intense late-game pressure situations that would characterize the '83 season.

Max Perry, who knew Valvano as both a player and participant in his backstage strategy sessions, says V preferred to run just a few basic offenses and mix-and-match "a thousand junk defenses."

"In just about every game I was a part of, after a few minutes he'd take the whole [defensive] game plan he'd just presented to us and scrap it," says Perry. "He was all about going with the flow of the game, putting people in the best positions to be successful."

His reputation as a consummate players' coach further stemmed from his dealings with his players off the court. Valvano's open-door policy was open to the point where the door was a needless appendage. One didn't need an appointment to see the coach; indeed, half the time he'd simply grab a player out of the hallway and drag him into the office for a lengthy chat on subjects near and far.

"V was an English major back in college at Rutgers and a

voracious reader of everything," explains Perry. "He loved to stop in the middle of the day to talk about the Italian Renaissance, economic theory, the existence of God, or whatever topic he was reading about at the time. The idea that he didn't care about [our intellectual development] is simply not true."

Ernie Myers concurs. "V told us all the time that in the scheme of life, there are much bigger things than basketball. If you, as a player, chose not to use college as a place to expand your mind, then that was on you, not him."

Although Valvano's reputation for not caring a whole lot about his players' academic achievements is not without validity—only about 11 percent of them graduated during V's tenure at NC State—the charge does not apply to the '83 players, nearly all of whom received their bachelor's degrees.

Valvano further gained the respect of his players by not playing favorites and being willing to reach all the way to the end of the bench for guys who would lay it on the line for dear old NC State.

"He would always tell us, 'I don't pick the guys who play, you guys do,'" recalls Myers. "He was open to playing anyone who could help us win games."

The Wolfpack entered the 1982–'83 season ranked 16th in the country, as befitting their experienced roster and 22 wins the previous year. And they backed up that ranking with seven Ws in their first eight games, including impressive wins over 20th-ranked West Virginia and Michigan State, sandwiched around a close loss to No. 14 Louisville. But after a second loss against 15th-ranked Missouri, the wheels came off the V Express when senior captain and shooting guard Whittenburg went down with a broken foot in a losing effort against No. 2 Virginia.

The loss of Whittenburg was doubly dispiriting, as the ACC had adopted the three-point shot that season, and long-range shooting happened to be Whittenburg's forte. Although his replacement, Myers, did an admirable job filling in by averaging about 17 points a game during Whittenburg's absence, NC State, for the most part, was up the creek without their leader and three-point specialist.

During this stretch, the Wolfpack got shellacked by North Carolina and Wake Forest and lost closer games to Notre Dame, Maryland, and Memphis State. Everything they had worked for and dreamed of was seemingly coming apart.

After the January 29 loss at Maryland, which dropped their record to an unenviable 9–7, Valvano rallied the troops once again with his inimitable mixture of burning intensity and a loosey-goosey personal style ("the perfect pregame locker room balance," according to Ray Martin). NC State responded with seven wins in its next eight games, including one over No. 3 North Carolina. Whittenburg, although not entirely healed up, was given the medical okay to return to the court on February 27 at Virginia. NC State lost that game by 11—a disappointment, but hardly a surprise. But when State tanked again in the following game against unranked Maryland, it bothered the captain to no end. Taking a page from Valvano's motivational playbook, Whittenburg ushered the coach and his assistants out of the locker room and addressed his teammates in the strongest terms he knew. In the moving 2013 ESPN documentary film, *Survive and Advance*, which chronicles the 1982–'83 season, Whittenburg recalled that players-only meeting.

"I told them either you're gonna play hard or put up your dukes and you and I are gonna go at it." Valvano, listening through closed doors to Whittenburg's impassioned speech, was smiling a deep smile of satisfaction.

Whether it was Whittenburg's invitation to fisticuffs or the hundreds of motivational speeches already laid upon them by their coach, the entire team once more responded to the call to action. They put a 41-point pasting on Wake Forest in their final regular season conference game, and, at 17–10, went into the ACC tournament understanding that they needed to win it to get back to the NCAAs. They drew a much more resilient version of the Wake Forest team in the first round, squeaking by, 71–70, on a steal by Sidney Lowe and a free throw by Lorenzo Charles in the final three seconds.

In round two, they upset Michael Jordan and North Carolina in another nail-biter. Carolina's Sam Perkins narrowly missed a jumper at the end of regulation that would have won it for the Tar Heels. ("That ball bounced around the rim," remembers Thurl Bailey in the ESPN documentary. "It was a quarter of an inch from sending us all home.") In OT, Carolina went up by six, and Valvano had his guys start fouling in hopes that the opposition would miss those pressure free throws. Brad Daugherty, Jim Braddock, and Curtis Hunter all missed the front end of one-and-ones, and Whittenburg hit several big shots. NC State emerged with a 91–84 win and a major confidence boost.

"Who's Michael Jordan?" asked Whittenburg at game's end, lifting his coach with a great, big bear hug.

In the ACC final against "Superman" Ralph Sampson and Virginia, which had beaten NC State twice already that season, Valvano scrapped his defensive game plan and came out in a "triangle and two" junk defense, with two guys shadowing Superman and the triangle covering the rest. The contest was yet another thriller, coming down to a steal by Terry Gannon, stripping the ball away from Sampson with 35 seconds remaining, and two Whittenburg free throws with six seconds on the clock. Final score: 81–78, NC State. The Wolfpack had finally slain the mighty Sampson and were now back in the NCAAs. This time they were just getting warmed up.

However, in their NCAA opener against Pepperdine, Valvano's crew found themselves in the unusual (and uncomfortable) position of being the favorite. It wasn't a particularly good look for them, and they underperformed throughout most of the game. With Pepperdine up four, 59–55, with 29 seconds remaining in overtime and Dane Suttle, one of Pepperdine's best foul shooters at the line ready to salt the game away, V's dream was hanging by a closely manicured fingernail. Pepperdine players were high-fiving each other and talking trash. Even NC State's biggest daydream believers had pretty well stopped believing. Another one-and-done NCAA tournament looked imminent.

"We were dead," Whittenburg says.

Not so fast, Dereck.

Suttle missed the front-end of the one-and-one, and Thurl Bailey responded with a dunk with 23 seconds left to close the gap to two. Three seconds later, State put Suttle right back on the foul line, and he missed again. On the other end, Whittenburg was fouled on a drive to the basket with nine seconds left. He missed the first free throw, but Cozell McQueen rebounded and put it back in the hoop with three seconds on the clock.

The game went into a second OT where NC State finally prevailed, 69–67. They had survived and were advancing once again, but this time with an even deeper awareness of how thin the line is between dream and nightmare.

In the second round against UNLV, it was (cliché be damned) déjà vu all over again. NC State was down 12 with 11 1/2 minutes left in the game, and Sidney Green, UNLV's star forward, who had been dismissive of Thurl Bailey's skills in pregame interviews, was having his way with the Wolfpack all game long. And then, once again out of nowhere, Bailey & Co. awoke from their lethargy and embarked on another big run. Poetic justice reigned supreme when Bailey's rebound basket in the closing seconds was the difference in NC State's 71–70 victory. Green got the treatment in his postgame press conference, when Whittenburg inquired, "How good is Thurl Bailey now, Sid?"

A 19-point battering of Utah in the Sweet 16—a welcome change of pace for the "Cardiac Pack"—was followed by yet another game against arch-nemesis Virginia in the regional final. Beating the Cavaliers once in a season was a prodigious feat. But twice? This was pushing the pacemaker a bit far. So this time, Valvano upped the ante as the game wound down, calling out to his players to intentionally foul Virginia's Othell Wilson with the game tied and about a minute left.

"This was taking the coaches' handbook and throwing it completely out the window," says Whittenburg. "Who intentionally fouls a guy like Othell Wilson in a *tie* game? This was just plain crazy!"

Wilson missed one of two, and at the other end, Lorenzo Charles, a relatively poor foul shooter, was hacked under the basket.

What occurred in the huddle before Charles's free throws was right out of the movie *Hoosiers*. Like Gene Hackman in that film, Valvano instructed his team on what to do not *if*, but *when*, Charles sank his two foul shots.

Charles, as envisioned by his coach, made both free throws with 23 seconds left. And when two Virginia shots on their final possession went astray, State had a 63–62 win and a ticket to dance at the Final Four.

By this time, the letters—nice letters, for a change—were arriving in huge mail sacks from folks across the country. The wife of a coma victim wrote in that watching the team come back time and time again from near-certain defeat had given her a reason to believe her husband might eventually emerge from his coma. Even Coach K, heretofore not a fan of Jimmy V's, was "flabbergasted" by NC State's run to the Final Four and deeply impressed with the quality of Coach V's in-game strategizing. Coaches K and V thus began a close friendship that lasted until V's death in 1993.

V, himself, was hanging ten on a wave of victory, reveling in the letters, the pep rallies, and the media attention. He had, by this point, honed his comedy act to the level of a Rodney Dangerfield.

Asked about administering a heightened degree of discipline to his players on the eve of the Final Four, Valvano told reporters he had gone so far as to institute a bed check for the first time in his coaching career.

"I want to assure you all," he said, "that all the beds were there."

NC State disposed of a weaker Georgia team, 67–60, in the Final Four semifinal and awaited the last call to destiny.

Phi Slama Jamma

The University of Houston Cougars more or less flew into the Final Four. It would be hard to name any team in NCAA tournament history that possessed as much raw athleticism, speed, and swagger as did the 1982–83 Cougars. In a January 3 *Houston Post* article, sportswriter Thomas Bonk coined the term *"Phi Slama Jamma"* (PSJ), to refer to their run-and-gun, playground-style offense, and the name stuck.

The PSJ fraternity brothers, most of whom were given nicknames reflecting their on-court personas and skill sets (i.e., center Akeem "The Dream" Olajuwon, Clyde "The Glide" Drexler, Larry "Mr. Mean" Micheaux, and Michael "Silent Assassin" Young), embraced their growing reputation, as did their veteran coach, Guy Lewis.

Lewis told the media he not only condoned his players foregoing short jump shots for "high-percentage" dunks, and fast-breaking in lieu of running set plays—he insisted upon it. The players, naturally, loved playing in this high-speed, freewheeling style. And why not? It perfectly suited their skills and it yielded tremendous results.

After losing to Syracuse and Virginia in mid-December, the Cougars ran off 26 straight wins before entering the NCAA final at 31–2.

"Nothing unusual about that," says Micheaux, who currently runs kids' basketball camps and has long eschewed the "Mr. Mean" label.

"It just took us a little while to establish our own chemistry ... isn't that what the first few games are for?"

Among those 26 wins leading up to the NCAA final were fewer than a handful of close ones—a couple of one-pointers over Pepperdine (remember them?) and Louisiana-Lafayette and two three-point victories over Texas Christian, one in mid-January on the road and one in the Southwest Conference tourney final. Otherwise, for PSJ, it was mostly a season of slamming, jamming laughers.

This wild and crazy style of play reflected much less well on the late Guy Lewis than it did on his players, however. Despite five Final Four appearances and 592 lifetime victories over his long career, Lewis continues to garner little respect, as compared to other coaching giants of his era, such as John Wooden and Dean Smith, who ran more methodical offenses emphasizing fundamental basketball skills over sheer athleticism. Any half-decent coach, say Lewis's detractors, could have won with players of PSJ's caliber.

To many of Lewis's former players, their occasionally imperious old coach is deserving of greater admiration.

"Coach Lewis won with all kinds of teams," argues Reid Gettys, a key backup guard on the '83 team. "Before Phi Slama Jamma, he won with teams that featured only slow, plodding white guys, and then he won with more athletic teams with the likes of Elvin Hayes and Otis Birdsong." Gettys also credits Lewis with bringing college basketball to prime time, instigating the memorable, nationally-televised 1968 regular-season matchup with Wooden's championship UCLA squad. Not to make too fine a point of it, but Lewis bested Wooden that night.

Moreover, much of what Lewis accomplished as a coach, adds Gettys, occurred on the practice court, out of sight of the fans.

"When Clyde Drexler arrived in Houston," observes Gettys, "he was a 6-foot-7 forward who couldn't dribble or shoot. Guy Lewis developed him into a future Hall of Fame NBA guard. And Coach Lewis worked almost every day with Akeem (later Hakeem) Olajuwon in practice, helping him master his footwork and rebounding fundamentals."

Finally, Gettys, Micheaux, and other former Lewis players applaud the coach's willingness to adapt and change. Indeed, in this and several other respects, Lewis and Valvano were kindred coaching spirits. Each focused on running scrimmages in practice, to get their teams game-ready. And they were equally fearless about switching tempos, making unorthodox substitutions, and otherwise taking big strategic gambles at crunch time in big games.

Houston, after dispatching Texas Christian in the SWC final, kicked off the NCAAs with double-digit wins vs. Maryland and Villanova and a seven-point triumph over Memphis. But PSJ was most impressive in a semifinal dismantling of Louisville. A mere three years earlier, the NCAA-champion Cardinals had earned the nickname "The Doctors of Dunk."

Those doctors were no longer practicing by 1983, but their legend lived on. This game represented a superb opportunity for the PSJ fraternity brothers to distinguish themselves in the manly art of slama-jamma. In that breathtaking, high-speed 94–81 demolition of Louisville, Houston notched a remarkable fourteen thunder-dunks, eight in a row during one second-half stretch.

It was now time for Houston to take its Phi Slama Jamma show to the Big Show.

The Game

Before we begin the discussion of the 1983 NCAA Final, let's dispel a few lingering myths.

Myth 1: That Jim Valvano had actually planned "to hold the ball until Tuesday" against the awesome PSJ. That was another pre-game joke he told the media. Valvano planned all along for his team to come out on the attack.

Myth 2: That Houston was flummoxed by NC State's up-tempo offense and its odd-looking match-up zone that featured four players arrayed along the baseline to shut down Olajuwon and another chasing Michael Young, Houston's best shooter, all over the court. "The Hollywood line is that Valvano snookered us," laments Gettys. "It's nonsense. Guy Lewis had us ready for whatever Valvano was going to throw at us."

Myth 3: That Houston's hotshots had little regard for Valvano's dream believers. "This was a team that, with Dereck Whittenburg in the lineup, went 17–3," says Gettys. "Believe me; we knew they were really good."

Houston's major problem, insists Gettys, was not overconfidence, nor confusion, nor poor coaching.

"It was a case of our being out of sync most of the night . . . we just couldn't put anything together. It was, without question, the worst game we played all season."

The game kicked off with State, as expected, coming right at the Cougars. An opening Thurl Bailey dunk began a six-point run. Houston then reeled off a seven-point run of its own, and the teams settled into a semi-sloppy seesaw contest over the first 12 minutes. On the plus side for Houston, Alvin Franklin, their poised freshman point guard, was doing a superb job shutting down Whittenburg, and Olajuwon seemed to be playing at a different altitude than everyone else, well above the basket. On the downside, Drexler picked up three personal fouls in the first eight minutes, and by about the midway point in the half, the Houston players were starting to feel the effects of playing the game at 5,100 feet above sea level. So, too, were the Wolfpack, but the thin mountain air seemed to have a more pronounced effect on the high-flyin' Cougars.

With about seven minutes left in the first half, NC State, playing with a small lineup and recognizing the impact of the high elevation on their opponent, went into a spread offense to get Houston to chase them around. Gradually, the Wolfpack stretched the lead, led by Bailey, who had 15 first-half points. The Wolfpack went up as much as 10 late in the half. Worst of all for Houston, Clyde Drexler, who had begged Lewis to let him stay in the game with three fouls, was whistled for his fourth—an offensive foul—at about the 17-minute mark. On the play, Terry Gannon appeared to grab Drexler's legs as Gannon was falling to the ground. Drexler has never let go of the firm belief that the call should have gone the other way (indeed, eight years later, at the 1991 NBA All-Star Game, Drexler sought out Gannon, then working as a TV reporter, and addressed this matter with him in very colorful language).

The first half ended with NC State leading, 33–25. Guy Lewis, having seen his explosive PSJers crash to earth, spoke calmly, but bluntly, to his players in a despondent locker room.

"We just played the worst half of basketball we have ever played," the coach stated. Message: it can't get any worse, so relax, get out there, and start slamming and jamming.

The Cougars responded affirmatively to that suggestion.

With Clyde Drexler riding the bench, Houston went on a ferocious 17–2 tear, beginning with a couple of Benny Anders baskets (they called him "Instant Offense"), a few bad NC State turnovers, and a few more big-time Olajuwon blocks. By the 12-minute mark in the second half, Olajuwon had racked up 18 points, 17 rebounds, and seven blocked shots. Unfortunately for Houston, he had also racked up a severe case of altitude-induced fatigue. With Houston now up, 42–35, and its star center in need of oxygen therapy, Lewis elected to slow things down with Drexler back in the game, to protect the lead while Olajuwon was being treated on the sidelines.

Lewis's decision was not perceived as a mistake in the moment. Quite the contrary. "It's a smart move with Olajuwon on oxygen," noted TV commentator Billy Packer.

But the stalling tactic backfired, as the momentum quickly shifted NC State's way. Two big Whittenburg buckets followed by a steal and basket by Sidney Lowe, and the Houston lead was whittled to two, at 44–42. With Olajuwon back in the game, but still playing slowdown to lessen the effects of the altitude, Houston, on baskets by Franklin, Olajuwon, and Young, managed to get the lead back up to six, at 50–44, with just under four minutes remaining.

But Sidney Lowe, heating up, hit two more jumpers and Whittenburg buried another two, and with 1:54 on the clock, it was all even at 52.

And then it was time for Valvano to trot out his risky fouling strategy. On what would be Houston's last possession, he instructed his players to back off and allow Alvin Franklin to bring the ball up court. Once there, they were told to foul the freshman guard as soon as he got the ball back in his hands. At 1:05, Whittenburg fouled Franklin, as directed. The freshman, no doubt intimidated by the pressure of the moment, missed the front end of the one-and-one. Valvano called a timeout with 44 seconds left to set up the last shot.

The plan was simple. Work the ball around the perimeter before getting it into the hands of the point guard, Sidney Lowe, with about 10 seconds left. Lowe would then have time to penetrate to the basket and dish to an open Whittenburg or Terry Gannon, State's best outside shooters. In the event of a miss, there would still be a couple of seconds left for an offensive rebound and put-back.

But Guy Lewis, strictly a man-to-man man, tripped them up, sending his team out on the floor in a 2–3 zone trap defense. Having no more timeouts, the Wolfpack had to improvise on the fly. They passed the ball carefully around the perimeter, until it wound up in Lowe's hands with 10 seconds left. He passed it to an open Bailey in the left corner, but Houston immediately collapsed on him, and Bailey, in desperation, at the seven-second mark threw a very poor and misguided overhand pass to Whittenburg, who was positioned about 35 feet from the basket. The pass was nearly intercepted by the fleet Benny Anders, but Whittenburg was able to corral the tipped ball and heaved it in the direction of the basket with three seconds left.

One scenario has it that Olajuwon, reacting to Anders's move and thinking that Anders had stolen the ball, took a step away from the basket, giving Lorenzo Charles an opening to go up and grab it. Another take on the final three seconds has Olajuwon electing not to go up for the ball for fear of a goaltending call.

Either way, Charles, realizing the ball would fall short of the basket, leaped up, grabbed it, and dunked it through the hoop as the buzzer sounded.

Strangely enough, Charles's basket was the only one scored by a North Carolina State frontcourt player in the entire second half.

But, to paraphrase Valvano, it didn't matter a damn who scored which basket. All that mattered was who was standing on that basket at game's end to cut down the net.

Practice makes perfect. Jimmy Valvano puts all those net-cutting exercises to good use after his signature triumph.

"A knife through my back," is how Larry Micheaux recalls the final three seconds. "That's what I remember feeling for a long time."

Nevertheless, the events that followed the 1983 final would one day provide a new lens through which Micheaux and every participant in that game would view that moment in time.

Now What?

The NC State basketball program, in the wake of 1983, would never be the same—not for its administration, coaches, or players. And, most of all, not for its head coach, still just thirty-seven years old, whose initial thought, after taking scissors to net, was "What do I do now?"

V was now a true, board-certified rock star, and for a restless intellect and spirit like his—not to mention his supersized ego—the wealth of new opportunities and career options that came his way in the months and years following the '83 season would be just too tempting to resist.

"V was your classic Renaissance man," notes Ray Martin, who went on to coach under Valvano at NC State for another five years. "While he loved basketball, there were so many more things that he wanted to accomplish in his life. There just wasn't enough time in the day."

Valvano leaped right into media-land, hosting his own (lame) TV show called *Sports Bloopers* and guest-hosting regularly on Bob Costas's national radio broadcast. He also did a daily five-minute radio spot every morning on a local Raleigh station, as well as some color game commentary for NBC. And, with all that, he somehow found the time to recruit prospects and fly all over the country on speaking engagements, for which he was now getting paid handsomely.

Moreover, Valvano took on the added job of Athletic Director at NC State. The expanded duties and the increasing pressures to which he would be subjected from alumni and boosters, coupled with all his outside pursuits, were regarded by his family and friends as too much, even for a man with Valvano's voracious drive and ambition.

Nevertheless, Valvano proved himself to be a highly competent AD, at least in one respect.

"He made sure to take care of everybody in the sports department," says Martin. "All the coaches, especially, loved the guy because he always had their backs."

Nor did Valvano forsake his players, but while his door continued to remain wide open to them, says Max Perry, all too often "there was no one behind the door."

Those players who arrived after '83, continues Perry, "never knew V the way we did."

And, even more disconcerting, on those rare occasions when Valvano was in his office, ready and willing to bestow words of wisdom upon the younger generation, the recruits in the post-championship years were less interested in soaking up his wisdom than they were in playing basketball while maintaining their meager grade point averages via sham courses.

Dereck Whittenburg, who stayed on as a graduate assistant after that championship season and continues to work in a community relations capacity at NC State, places the blame for the decline of player academic performance squarely on the players themselves.

Valvano, says Whittenburg, longed to be coaching the kind of players he coached in his first three years at NC State.

"Trust me, the only reason he stayed here was because he was given the AD job... what V really wanted was the UCLA [coaching] job. With him, it was 'OK, I can do this. Now let's see what else I can do.'"

Valvano's teams did benefit somewhat from the glow of 1983. It enhanced Valvano's already-demonstrated ability to charm recruits and their families. While the '84 team failed to qualify for the NCAAs, Valvano's teams reached the big dance in each of the next five seasons, getting as far as the Elite Eight in 1985 and 1986 and the Sweet 16 in 1989.

But, ultimately, as his friends and family had long feared, Valvano's reach far exceeded his grasp, and he lost control of what was going on all around him. For example, it is one thing to admit scholarship athletes with questionable academic credentials—in fact, it's business as usual in most major college programs—but another thing entirely to accept "student-athletes" such as Chris Washburn, a profoundly troubled youngster with a combined score of 470 on his Scholastic Aptitude Tests (one receives 400 points for signing one's name correctly). To be sure, NC State was not the only school to go after Washburn, and Valvano, once Washburn was enrolled there, did try to help the kid navigate this unfamiliar terrain.

As could be expected, the experiment failed. Washburn played just over one full season at NC State, where he stole some stereo equipment and was sentenced to five years' probation. He later encountered problems with drug abuse in the NBA and lived on the street for a while, before finally turning his life around.

Similarly, when Charles Shackleford, a center from the mid '80's, explained to reporters that he could shoot with both hands because he was "amphibious," it didn't help the basketball program's academic image.

All these negatives and a great deal more came to a head with the publication of *Personal Fouls: The Broken Promises and Shattered Dreams of Big Money Basketball at Jim Valvano's North Carolina State*. The book, by Peter Golenbock, alleged a slew of major abuses on Valvano's watch, including the existence of secret stashes of cash reminiscent of Watergate and the fixing of player grades. The charges that were actually substantiated were relatively minor infractions, such as the selling of game tickets and shoes by players. Valvano was cleared of wrongdoing after lengthy investigations by the NCAA and the state-appointed Poole Commission, but he was cited for violating "the spirit of the law" through a marked failure of oversight.

Valvano, under pressure from the faculty and a new university chancellor, was forced to step down as AD in October 1989. Six months later, he negotiated a financial settlement with NC State and resigned as head basketball coach to go into broadcasting full-time.

In June of 1992, he received a diagnosis of terminal bone cancer. And this is where all of Valvano's empathic gifts came to fruition.

In the final ten months of his life, Valvano demonstrated to the world not only how to die with grace, courage, and a fully intact sense of humor, but how to live a meaningful life. Receiving an "ESPY" award from ESPN in March 1993, Valvano, with malignant tumors all over his body, delivered a televised address that will be replayed again and again as long as there are human beings on the planet. He spoke eloquently about his loving family and his will to go on fighting the disease. He told marvelously funny stories and reiterated to a worldwide audience the same advice he had given to Ray Martin any number of times. A "good day," Valvano insisted, is one in which you spend at least some time doing three basic things: laughing, crying, and thinking. Such a day, concluded Jimmy V, makes for a fine entry in anyone's book of days.

Jim Valvano died eight weeks later, at age forty-seven. As per his dying wish, the "V Foundation" was established in his name to raise funds for research on a cancer cure. To date, the foundation has distributed more than $170 million in grants.

Larry Micheaux says after watching Valvano's ESPY speech he stopped thinking about the 1983 final as a knife in his back.

"I think now that it was God's gift to Jimmy V, knowing his time on earth would be short," says Micheaux. "And it was a gift he deserved."

If you haven't already watched the ESPY speech, do so with someone to hug.

Chapter 5

Dean, Redeemed:
North Carolina vs. Georgetown, 1982

There's an old story about the legendary North Carolina basketball coach Dean Smith that traces to his days as a fledgling assistant at the University of Kansas in the early 1950s. The story was related by a reliable Kansas source on the Yucatan Peninsula, where an asteroid wiped out the dinosaurs 65 million years ago, paving the way for the invention of basketball.

As we heard it down Mexico way, there was concern at the time that Kansas's football team was getting better grades than the basketball team. Smith, a former benchwarming math major, was part of a group of basketball players who broke into the administration building in search of the answers to an upcoming class quiz. They reportedly ended up getting locked in the office where they had to spend the night huddled furtively behind some cabinets, before they were able to somehow sneak away unnoticed in the morning. A gun and a dead horse were all that kept this vignette from becoming an inspiration for a riotous scene in *Animal House*.

Delivering a John Belushi impression is not how one would picture Dean Smith, at any age.

"That sure doesn't sound like the man I knew," says a longtime Kansas newspaperman who was acquainted with Smith for over thirty years. Indeed, the Dean Smith known to most of us was a decorous uncle, a kindly mentor, a man whose acts of moral courage and generosity bespoke an extraordinary human spirit. And a man, who, for a wide variety of reasons, would never have been caught dead in such a compromising position, attempting to sneak an advanced look at some test questions.

Still, we're talking about a twenty-two-year-old kid, probably more than a little insecure, and perhaps still a little intimidated as the only math scholar and Kierkegaard reader in an arena of big-time jockdom. In any case, all this little tale suggests is that once upon a time, Dean Smith was a boy. A boy with a sly penchant for intrigue; a bit of a schemer.

It is a penchant that the future Hall of Fame coach would maintain throughout his career that helped bring him so much success.

Like so many great coaches in college basketball history, from John Wooden and Adolph Rupp, to Larry Brown and John Calipari, Smith was a grandmaster at tweaking the rules and regulations, artfully manipulating refs and in-game situations, and otherwise jockeying to give his teams every edge in a dog-eat-dog competitive environment. Smith knew how far to push the envelope and when it was time to get back to the fundamentals of basketball. And Smith practiced this art form in a more discreet and stylish way than most of his peers. Not baiting refs, a la John Wooden, but rather planting a subtle thought in a ref's head that might cause a call to go Carolina's way down the stretch of a close game. "It was just Dean being Dean," in the words of close friend and adversary John Thompson of Georgetown. A man adept at covering every angle, whether in the final seconds of a tight basketball game or hitting an approach shot into the 18th green.

But as much as this might disappoint denizens of Duke and other Atlantic Coast Conference members and others who saw arrogance and hypocrisy rather than deep humility and sincerity in Smith's reserved demeanor, there is no credible evidence to indicate that the man was anything other than what he appeared to most of the world to be: honorable, morally upright, compassionate, and thoroughly committed to the well-being, and the future success, of all his student-athletes (a whopping 96 percent of whom obtained their college degrees). Coach Smith was very much a man of his time; a time well before the current Age of Authenticity, where the highest value is attached to allowing one's true self to be seen by others. Dean Smith was not about exploring his inner self and making it known to everyone. He worked strictly from the outside-in, practicing diligently to become the man he was until those positive behaviors became second nature.

As an intensely private man, he kept hidden not only his emotions, but his vices, which included a nasty nicotine habit. Matt Doherty, a 6-foot-8 starting forward on the '82 championship team, treasures a photo on his office wall, which pictures Coach Smith, a cigarette dangling from his lips, standing among a group of men. For Doherty, the rare glimpse of his old coach enjoying his little vice is a reminder of the basic humanity of the man who influenced Doherty's life in so many meaningful ways.

As far as Smith's ability to coach the game of basketball, let's just say he was more than worthy of the sobriquet, *hoop genius*.

Smith, who passed away in February 2015, was, like Wooden, a "systems coach," who possessed the flexibility of mind to adapt his system to exploit any offense or defense and any perceived personnel mismatch. Smith's contributions to the game of basketball are on par with those of the Wizard of Westwood. The one for which the Dean is probably best known, and most despised, is the "four corners," which was actually two distinct offenses—one aimed at spreading out a defense before attacking the basket, and the other designed to kill time and run out the clock. Smith also pioneered the "run and jump," a simple but highly effective double-teaming defensive maneuver now used around the world at all levels of play; and the use of multiple screens to beat a zone defense. Smith further applied his math student's acumen in the service of "possession-based analytics," now a standard instrument in every basketball coach's toolkit. Prior to 1959, when Smith first introduced this concept at UNC, the only statistics being used by coaches to guide their strategic decisions were raw metrics, like overall field goal and foul shooting percentages. Smith went so far as assigning team managers to track such detailed stats as points scored and allowed per possession or per 100 possessions.

"Teams, especially in college, play at different rates," Daryl Morey, general manager of the NBA's Houston Rockets and a strong proponent of advanced statistics, explained to the *New York Times* in 2015. "So if you're trying to judge how good a defense you were, you couldn't just look at [raw numbers of points]. You had to look at [total] points and divide that by chances."

By the fall of 1981, Dean Smith had been head coach of the North Carolina Tar Heels for twenty years, having taken over from Frank McGuire in 1961. McGuire, himself a legendary New York figure who possessed oodles of charm, charisma, and a touch of the blarney, had won a national title in 1957 and was credited with popularizing the "underground railroad," a pipeline that transported great New York City playground players—whites only—south to "Tobacco Road." But McGuire ran afoul of the school administration over major NCAA violations and rumors of point shaving and was given his walking papers. His third-year assistant, Dean Smith, was hired in his place. Smith had none of McGuire's charm nor his gift of gab. He was still just a quiet, unassuming math whiz, a relative pip-squeak. It did not help at all that in the wake of the scandal, UNC deemphasized basketball, cutting the 1961–62 schedule to only 16 games and reducing scholarships, thus further limiting Smith's already meager recruiting power.

The worst of it came in Smith's fourth season, 1964–65, when the team arrived home from a brutal loss at Wake Forest and found an effigy of their coach hanging outside the gym. Even without the history of hatred defined by the image of the dangling man, seeing their respected coach strung up like that was too much for his team to bear. Billy Cunningham, one of those players and a future NBA Hall of Famer, ripped down the effigy and kicked it aside. The coach himself fell into despair. A 1982 story by Frank Deford in *Sports Illustrated* addressed the depths of that despair and how Smith managed to overcome it and embark upon a legendary career trajectory. The answer came in a book given to Smith by his sister, called *The Power of Helplessness*, which, according to Deford, helped Smith understand how little control we as human beings have over events and how we can turn our inadequacies into faith, and thus redeem ourselves.

A few days after hanging in effigy, as the story goes, Coach Smith delivered a fiery pep talk—something he never did—before a key game against Duke. Carolina went on to win that game, and Smith ultimately kept the job that he so desired and had seemed to be on the verge of losing.

Fast forward seventeen years to the 1981–82 season, by which time Smith had notched 436 wins, six Final Four appearances, and an NIT title—but no NCAA championship to show for all that. His archrivals and naysayers, as might be expected, took a Schadenfreude-like pleasure in disparaging Smith's failure to "win the big one." This, of course, was a load of horse-hockey. Smith, suffice it to say, maintained a stiff upper lip, insisting for years that it was no big deal, and that getting to six Final Fours was, at least in Smith's mind, a far greater accomplishment than winning a single title. Whether this air of nonchalance reflected his true feelings is an open question. In keeping with Smith's usual close-to-the-vest approach to his emotions, he did not share any feelings of disappointment with his players. But the slur nevertheless grated on them. In the weeks leading up to the '82 NCAA championship, point guard Jimmy Black hosted a team meeting to rally the players around the ultimate goal of finally getting their esteemed coach the Big Win. Black noted at the time that he was simply sick and tired of hearing his coach unfairly denigrated as a loser.

"We players cared a lot about getting him the title, but I don't think coach did," argues Doherty. "He was a teacher, a servant-leader, not like most people in a sport where end results are all that matters. For one thing, Coach Smith was a man of faith and he trusted [in God's will]. What he said right after the final game about not being a better coach than he was two hours before ... that statement, I believe, showed his real feelings about the whole thing."

Nevertheless, the '82 NCAA Final—a heart-pounding 63–62 victory over Georgetown University, on March 29 in the Louisiana

Superdome—would forever alter the perception of Dean Smith as a champion choke artist. And that's not all. That game, which featured sixteen lead changes, not only took an asterisk off one Carolina legend; it kicked off another. Because the relatively unknown freshman who drained the left-baseline, go-ahead jumper with 17 seconds left to give Dean Smith his first NCAA title was none other than Michael Jordan (or, just Michael, as in Magic, Kobe, or Beyonce). Toss in a superlative Carolina cast of characters, including future NBA greats James Worthy and Sam Perkins; an estimable opponent in the Hoyas of Georgetown, with their own freshman sensation, Patrick Ewing; their own larger-than-life-size coach, John Thompson; and their fiendishly competitive drive, and you've got a hell of a ballgame. A college All-Star game, as it were, only with all the participants playing at full capacity, their place in history on the line.

A Coach in Full

"The true measure of a man," it is written, "is how he treats someone who can do him absolutely no good."

This immortal quotation is often attributed to Samuel Johnson. Others, of a less literary bent, credit it to Ann Landers. But it appears that neither of these luminaries said or wrote any such thing. No doubt, wherever they are, they wish they had. Nevertheless, to quote Bill Murray in *Meatballs*, it just doesn't matter. For our purposes here, we'll attribute this bit of acquired wisdom to anyone of a less than exalted position who was fortunate enough to come into contact with Dean Smith.

Indeed, the sentiment could well have come from a little-known small college assistant basketball coach named Doc Kennedy, who posted a touching posthumous tribute to Dean Smith on the *Tar Heel Blog*. Kennedy, a UNC alumnus, never met the Dean. He wrote him a letter around 1994 telling him how much Smith's book, *Multiple Offense and Defense*, had meant to him, and asking the coach to sign his personal copy. Smith sent back the book with an inscription offering best wishes on Kennedy's recent promotion from high school to college coach and noted that he would now be following Kennedy's progress at his new position at tiny St. Augustine's College.

"The thing is," wrote Kennedy, "I hadn't told him what college I was going to coach." Smith had cared enough to look it up and compose a personal note of good wishes.

A few years later, the head coach of St. Augustine's passed away. Soon a letter arrived from Dean Smith, offering Kennedy his condolences and encouraging the young assistant coach to remain strong for his players.

"People will often forget what you did or even said," concluded Kennedy of Smith, paraphrasing a famous line by the poet Maya Angelou. "But they will never forget how you made them feel. I was no one of any importance, and twice, the greatest basketball coach of all time took the time to make me feel like I was the most important person he knew."

This view is shared by dozens, if not hundreds, of men who played for Dean Smith during his 36 years as head coach at UNC. It is hard to imagine, after listening to their heartfelt testimonials, that any human being could be so thoughtful, considerate and utterly selfless.

"Coach was an example to all of us of how to conduct ourselves as human beings," says Eric Montross, a star center on Smith's 1993 championship team. As a professional UNC basketball broadcaster, Montross has grown accustomed to weighing his words carefully. But the words can be hard to find in describing a relationship that was seemingly so one-sided. Montross sees it as analogous to that of a father and son.

"Coach Smith would always tell us our only gift to him was how we represented the program and went on to live our lives. He expected us to pass all [his teachings] on to our own children and other young people we came into contact with. I cannot imagine him ever expecting, or agreeing, to take anything more than that from any of us."

Such a relationship can perhaps most easily be understood by an adult son who has just dined at a restaurant with his old man and attempted to pick up the check.

The meal reference here is especially apt. Coach Smith's final bit of largesse toward his former players came in his Last Will and Testament, in which he left each of his 180 lettermen $200 in cash with instructions to dine out on it. It was an inheritance, if you will, like a father would bequeath equally to all his offspring. In this case the gifts were made with deep respect and appreciation toward each beneficiary. It left some players wondering once again how best to pay the coach's blessing forward.

"On one hand, it was truly a wonderful gesture," acknowledges Montross. "But it seemed wrong, somehow, to go out and spend the money."

Montross believes that Smith, being a deeply religious man, meant his final gift as a benediction, right out of Corinthians 11:24.

"I think coach was making a specific reference to the Biblical passage [about] 'bread being broken'... he wanted all of us to share a meal with our loved ones."

Matt Doherty's half-joking thought, upon receiving his $200, was to make a reservation for three in a fine restaurant. "Two seats for me and my wife, and one for the coach."

Big John

John Thompson and Dean Smith became friends back in the early 1970s when Thompson was still coaching high school and Smith was recruiting one of his players. Subsequently, Thompson's son attended Smith's summer basketball camp and Smith named Thompson as one of his assistants on the 1976 US Olympic team. The affection between the two men was deep.

Like Smith, Thompson was a powerful force in the lives of his players, only a much brasher and more opinionated one. Thompson, too, was a father figure to many (especially those players without their own fathers) and was fiercely protective of all his "children." He was acutely aware of the need to shield his African-American kids from the racism they commonly faced on the road, and he placed very strict limitations on his players' availability to the media.

Thompson, as did Smith, did not demand his players' love in return, only a commitment to their teammates, their university, and to the process. If you played for either coach, you did what you were told to do, because that was part of the process.

But there were significant differences in their approaches to the job. For one, Thompson, at 6-foot-10, wearing a scowl of disapproval and the ever-present towel around his neck, cast a much more imposing figure than did his diminutive counterpart. Thompson's coaching style was right out of the playground; not in the sense of undisciplined freelancing, but rather the firm conviction to never give an inch to an opponent, in practice or in games. In attempting to get his "us against the world" message across, Thompson's speech tended heavily towards the profane. Coach Smith, on the other hand, rarely, if ever, screamed or cursed in the presence of his players. Smith also preferred to get his players in and out of the gym with reasonable wear and tear, whereas Thompson was partial to long, grueling practices that, to at least some of his players, bordered on the abusive.

Fred Brown, a member of the '82 team, is one of the very few who has been outspoken on the subject.

Speaking about his former coach to a *Washington Post* reporter in 2007, after Thompson had been honored at a gala commemorating the 100th anniversary of Georgetown men's basketball, Brown did not mince his words in accusing Thompson of using his pulpit like a schoolyard bully.

"To get up at a function twenty-five years later and say, 'I know I abused you all, but I loved you.' . . . Come on. 'I abused you?' We know you abused us, and a lot of people have a lot of feelings about that."

In the same article, Thompson stated that he still loves Brown but can't understand what drives his former player to say such things.

"It's something he has to deal with and not me," concluded Thompson.

Those close to both Thompson and Brown have a number of theories as to the true source of Brown's feelings of alienation. In the end, it just goes to show how fine the love/hate line can be.

Yet another striking difference between Thompson and Smith lied in their recruiting strategies; specifically, in the kinds of players they recruited. Thompson, whose program was well on its way to national prominence in 1981 but had yet to achieve the recruiting traction or cache of North Carolina, was more inclined to go off the grid in search of guys who, according to his former assistant coach, Bill Stein, "would fit into John's system." That meant hungry, scrappy kids, often from mean urban streets, grateful for the opportunity and willing to claw their way to a loose ball. Dean Smith, on the other hand, had easy access to McDonald's All-Americans (there were six of them on the '82 squad) and didn't need to go far afield to find the best high school talent.

Ed Spriggs, recruited by Thompson and Stein in 1978, exemplifies Georgetown's recruiting ethos. Spriggs, at age twenty-two, was no high school hotshot when he came to Thompson's attention—he was already a full-grown man, holding down a full-time job in the US Post Office. Spriggs was big, strong, and athletic and liked to mix it up underneath the basket. He was also mature enough to appreciate the opportunity being presented by an athletic scholarship to one of America's finest universities.

But, oddly enough, Spriggs didn't immediately leap at the offer. He had other career priorities.

"I initially turned it down," explains Spriggs. "I was a driver, and the post office was getting ready to transfer me to tractor-trailers. I was really excited about driving those rigs. But it turned out that at 6-foot-9, I was too big to fit into the cab. So my goals changed."

At Georgetown, Spriggs got his chance to drive the big rig—The Georgetown University Transit System "GUTS Bus."

"Ed drove it in the summertime for all the kids on campus," says Gene Smith, a sophomore forward on the '82 team. "I worked on campus every summer, too, just to stay close to the program and keep in shape."

It was the lunch-bucket guys, comprising most of the '82 Georgetown roster, who set the tone and kept everybody in line, notes Smith. None of them was more effective at drawing those lines than Big Ed Spriggs.

"Freddy Brown was highly recruited [out of the Bronx] and when he first arrived at school, he got on Spriggs's bus," relates Smith. "Freddy at this point had no idea who the driver was. So he says something disparaging to Ed, something like, 'Yeah, boy, just drive the bus.' Ed puts the bus in park and walks over, all 6-foot-9 of him, and gets right up in Freddy's face. 'You see a boy?' says Ed. Spriggs didn't care who you were, you just had to show respect. He was teaching Freddy a lesson."

Spriggs, a co-captain of the '82 team and still a lunch-bucket guy, is a Georgetown perennial. He is currently assistant director of the university's Yates Field House.

John Thompson, now a grey eminence in Georgetown basketball, has softened a bit over the years. But not to the point where he can let old losses go. Big John, as he will be forever known around campus, declined to speak about the 1982 final. Ask me about Georgetown's 1984 championship season, he said. I'll talk your ears off.

That was Big John being Big John.

Walkin' to New Orleans (with Talky Tina)

North Carolina at the start of the 1981–82 season was an extremely confident team, as they had every reason to be. They had four returning starters—two sophomores, one junior, and one senior—a freshman named "Mike" Jordan, and a pretty solid bench. One of their starters, James Worthy, bore the nickname "Big Game James" (more on that later).

Off the court, they were reportedly a close-knit bunch. Senior point guard Jimmy Black, in an autobiography published in 2006, says the team bonded around typically adolescent pursuits, including *Twilight Zone* reruns (the "Talky Tina" episode being one of their favorites) and a constant musical soundtrack programmed by freshman Lynwood Robinson, who carried around a radio/tape player the size of a small refrigerator. It played a steady musical diet of R&B—Earth, Wind & Fire and Stevie Wonder, with a dollop of Rolling Stones to please Matt Doherty.

The Heels were ranked No. 1 entering the year, and except for a brief period after a loss to Wake Forest in midseason where they fell all the way to No. 2 (Sam Perkins was ill and did not play in that game), Carolina held the top spot in the polls from November right through March. Carolina lost only one other game that season on its way to a 32–2 record. Virginia, led by the freakishly talented 7-foot-4 center, Ralph Sampson, vanquished the Heels by 16 in early February. But Carolina got payback in the ACC tourney final, a game that would have an impact on college basketball well beyond 1982. With Carolina up 44–43 with 7:34 left, the Heels went into their classic four-corner stall, in an effort to draw Sampson away from the basket. Virginia coach Terry Holland refused to bite, and for the next seven minutes or so, the crowd chanted "BOR-ING," as Carolina played catch around the perimeter. Finally, with 28 seconds to go, Virginia had committed enough fouls to send Doherty to the free-throw line. Doherty hit one of two, and after a Virginia turnover, he hit two more to ice the win.

To be sure, other low-scoring games figured into the inauguration of the shot clock in 1985–86, including a 1973 game between Temple and Tennessee which ended 11–6, and a 1979 Carolina-Duke matchup that saw the Tar Heels hold the ball for 11 minutes. The halftime score of that game was 7–0, Duke.

But, according to Jimmy Black, the '82 Heels cared not a whit about boring the daylights out of the fans. Their only concern, says Black, was getting the coach his first title.

Nevertheless, that dream nearly died in the first round in the NCAA regionals against James Madison. Shooting poorly from the foul line against a much less talented, but very well-coached team, Carolina barely slipped away with a 52–50 win. It was the kind of win, wrote Black, that every championship team needs to remind itself that a championship is built one win at a time. Carolina played much better in the next two regional wins over Alabama and Villanova.

When the Heels arrived in New Orleans, assistant coach Roy Williams, possessed of a superstitious nature, picked up a piece of local juju that spitting into the Mississippi River brings good luck. Williams, on his normal morning jog, stopped by Old Man River and let loose a loogie into its rolling waters. Williams passed along this tip to other Carolina rooters, and thus did the mighty river run with saliva on Final Four weekend. All that salivary input certainly didn't hurt, as Carolina shot 59 percent from the field in the semifinal—Perkins was 9-for-11—and defeated an excellent Houston team led by Akeem Olajuwon and Clyde Drexler, 68–63.

Georgetown's road to the Big Easy was drier and bumpier than Carolina's. The Hoyas opened in the Great Alaska Shootout, getting beaten by Southwestern Louisiana and Ohio State, before running off 13 straight wins against mostly inferior competition. The highlight of this run came against No. 20 St. John's at Madison Square Garden in New York. The Hoyas jumped out to a 41–9 lead on the way to a 30-point rout.

"We were feeling pretty cocky during our warmup," says Stein. "I remember when we busted out of the locker room to take the Garden floor, I turned to Big John and said, 'I've been here ten years. Now let's just go and kick some ass.' Big John didn't say anything, just turned to me with a smile."

But, in January, the Hoyas experienced a tough stretch, losing to Big East rivals Syracuse, Connecticut, and Providence in the course of six days. Their open shots had stopped falling, and Hoya nerves were fraying.

Before practice on the day before the next game versus Villanova, Thompson set up a TV in a conference area and plugged in a VCR tape. The players were expecting to see Villanova in action. Instead, it was a tape of the Madison Square Garden massacre, in five-part harmony.

"This is how I know you all know how to play," Thompson told his team. Later, down on the court, continuing the theme of positive reinforcement, he had each of his players say something uplifting and original. Then it was time for Stein to present his customary review of the upcoming opponent.

"Screw that," said Big John. "Let's play the game."

Georgetown took apart Villanova and went on another lengthy run, soundly beating Seton Hall, Syracuse, and St. John's, before upsetting No. 4 Missouri at home. They continued in this vein in the Big East tourney, with three double-digit wins, and went into the West Regionals feeling pretty near invincible.

The University of Southern California, one of the other teams in that regional, had assistant coach Rudy Washington scouting Georgetown. Washington phoned St. John's assistant Ron Rutledge, who had already had his fill of Georgetown, to get the full skinny on the Hoyas.

"Let me put it this way," Rutledge ruefully advised Washington. "When Georgetown substitutes, they get better."

The Hoyas knocked off Wyoming, Fresno State, and Oregon to enter the Final Four for the first time since 1943.

In the semifinal against highly-touted Louisville, the seniors stepped up. Eric "Sleepy" Floyd, the consensus All-American guard, and forward Eric Smith, who was named Georgetown's season MVP, did most of the scoring in a tough, defense-dominated win, 50–46.

"People don't talk much about that semi," says Eric Smith, "but it might have been an even better game than the final, and Louisville an even better team than Carolina."

Nevertheless, the stage was now set, with two supremely gifted teams in high stride, cheered on by 61,612 fans, at the time the largest paid crowd in NCAA history. This time, all that spangled was, indeed, gold.

Blues in the Night

In the final, both teams were clearly tight from the tip-off. "There's a lot of nervous energy out there," remarked CBS TV's color analyst Billy Packer.

Nevertheless, Georgetown emerged with all systems go on defense, tossing in a fluid mix of a 2-1-2 match-up zone, a full-court zone press, and a dash of man-to-man, extending their half-court pressure 30 feet from the basket. In the first seven or eight minutes, they turned Carolina over four times, to Dean Smith's consternation. Center Patrick Ewing, Georgetown's first national blue-chip recruit, appeared to be coming out of his skin with anticipation during the player introductions. Thompson wanted his big man to waste no time demonstrating his dominance, and Ewing complied—in the extreme. He committed goaltending violations on Carolina's first four baskets (five, total, in the first half). At least a couple of those shots would, arguably, have missed the basket.

"The strategy didn't intimidate us at all," professes Matt Doherty. "All it did was hand us easy baskets when we needed them early in the game." Bill Stein insists Thompson had no qualms about Ewing's hyper aggressive defense, but the fact that Ewing stopped trying to block every shot by about midpoint in the first half suggests that cooler heads eventually prevailed.

The first-half Carolina offense, such as it was, consisted primarily of the 6-foot-9 James Worthy, who got gotten into the flow of things right from the outset. Over the first 20 minutes, Worthy soared, scored, and otherwise staked a strong claim inside the paint, Ewing's towering presence be damned. Worthy scored 16 of Carolina's first 22 points, all of them around the basket.

"They called him Big Game James for a reason," raves Doherty. "James was the kind of player who would have 10 points and eight rebounds against Furman, and against Duke, he'd have 29 points and 14 boards ... the better the opponent, the bigger he played."

Worthy was never bigger than this night, finishing with 28 points and five monster dunks.

On the Georgetown side, after the initial nerves had calmed, its motion offense started clicking, led by the quickness and pinpoint shooting of Sleepy Floyd, who ended the half with 10 points.

The first half also offered a hint of Michael Jordan's multitudinous gifts, including a sequence in the final minutes where Michael snatched an offensive rebound over a defender and, switching seamlessly to his left hand in midair, banked the ball cleanly in the hole.

The half ended 32–31, Georgetown. So far, said the TV commentators, it was everything they expected.

The second half saw the pace of the game accelerate and the banging under the boards generate lots of heat and high-volume grunting.

Ewing, for his part, was all over the place, giving Carolina all sorts of problems—at one end, intimidating Jimmy Black into missing a fast-break layup, at the other end muscling his way to a basket after tipping the ball several times. Ewing scored nine points in the opening six minutes of the half. Jordan also stepped up his offense, scoring six points in the first few minutes, as the lead kept changing hands.

At 47–43 Georgetown, with about 12 minutes to go and Carolina's starters looking a little tired, their hands on their hips, the momentum seemed to be turning the Hoyas' way. Then, a couple of sequences flipped the narrative back into seesaw mode. After stealing the ball in the frontcourt and potentially taking it all the way to the basket for a six-point lead, Sleepy Floyd botched an easy layup and Sam Perkins hit a baseline jumper on the other end to cut the lead to two. And, on an ensuing Georgetown possession, with the Hoyas up, 49–45, Carolina's Buzz Peterson swiped the ball and pitched it to Worthy, who took off in full stride and slammed down a vicious dunk upon the unfortunate forehead of Sleepy Floyd. If all this wasn't painful enough for Floyd, he also got slapped with a foul on Worthy, who completed the three-point play, reducing the Hoya lead back to one. Over the remaining 11:41, neither team led by more than three points.

From there, the tension seemed to grow, as both teams had their composures severely tested. Every possession was fraught with drama, and the pushing and shoving got chippier. With about nine minutes left, Georgetown, in the space of just 20 seconds, committed three silly touch fouls far from the basket, putting Carolina in the one-and-one and ensuring that free throws would be a key determinant of the final outcome. Ewing and Worthy finally concluded their dunkathon.

With 5:11 left and Carolina in possession and leading, 59–58, Smith called up the four corners—not just to kill time, but to give his tired starters a breather and probe the defense in search of a potential backdoor layup. When Michael Jordan glimpsed that chance, he flashed to the hoop from the left side, throwing in a magnificent 12-foot runner with his left hand to increase the Carolina lead to three with a little less than three and a half minutes left. Ewing's jumper at the 2:30 mark cut the lead to one again, and Carolina went into another semi-stall, with Georgetown again going all out trying for a steal. With 1:16 left, Eric Smith thought he had one, poking the ball away from Matt Doherty and taking off down the court for an uncontested layup. The ref, however, saw it otherwise and sent Doherty to the line for a one-and-one.

"No way was that a foul," insists Smith, still smarting about the call. "Go back and look at the film. It was a clean steal. Just a terrible call at a bad time in the game."

In any case, Doherty missed the front end of the one-and-one, and Sleepy Floyd followed with a slick spin move and a gorgeous little head fake in the lane that sent James Worthy flying off into space, before tossing in a short jumper to put the Hoyas up, 62–61, with 53 seconds on the clock.

Dean Smith, with all his timeouts still in the bag, finally called one at 32 seconds to set up a play. He called for a "two-zone offense," the first option being a lob pass underneath to Worthy, and, barring that, getting it to Jordan for an open jumper. Georgetown, which, as expected, came out in a 1-3-1 zone, took away the lob pass, but Jimmy Black managed to swing the ball crosscourt to Jordan, who hesitated not an instant before releasing the ball at the 17 second mark.

Nothing but net.

Thompson did not use his last timeout to set up the final shot, so as not to give Smith a chance to position his defense. Freddy Brown brought the ball upcourt and stopped his dribble just outside the key. According to Bill Stein, what happened next was in no small measure a matter of color. Georgetown, which had worn white uniforms in each of its previous NCAA games, was decked out in blue for the final, with Carolina all dressed in white. On that play, Sleepy Floyd cut to the basket, leaving James Worthy hanging out there on the right perimeter, far from the hoop and out of position. Turning toward Worthy in that sudden flash of an instant, perhaps expecting a white-clad teammate to be there, Brown passed the ball to the wrong guy.

Worthy, just as surprised as everyone else to receive the errant pass, dribbled quickly downcourt before getting fouled with two seconds left. He missed both free throws, but Georgetown's desperation heave fell well short, and Dean Smith was off the hook. Not that he cared, but the coach was observed in the moments after the victory sporting what appeared to be a smile and a glint of a tear.

Brown, downcast to the point of desolation, was consoled by Thompson, who draped his big left arm on Brown's shoulder. It was a sight with which the Georgetown players were unfamiliar.

"Big John was no hugger," says Gene Smith, "but in that one moment, he was there for Freddy in the way you'd want your coach to be. That image of the two of them together is something I'll never forget."

Aftermath

Freddy Brown got his redemption in 1984, when as a senior, his Georgetown team beat Houston to claim its first-ever NCAA title.

Above all, Jimmy Black wanted to win the 1982 championship for his beloved coach, Dean Smith. But Jimmy clearly appears to be enjoying it, too.

Nine years later, in another championship final, Michigan's Chris Webber called timeout with his team out of timeouts and trailing by two points. This bizarre mental error resulted in a technical foul against Michigan and helped hand Dean Smith his second NCAA title as the coach of North Carolina.

Watching history grimly repeat itself on TV, Brown dialed up Bill Stein at home.

"Can you believe that?" asked Brown, with a mix of empathy and amazement at the mysterious ways of the basketball gods.

Later, Brown penned a letter of condolence to Webber. Once again, says Stein, the 1982 team was a source of pride to its coaches and its university.

As for Dean Smith, he coached at North Carolina through 1997, growing his win total to 879, making him at the time the winningest coach in college basketball history. After retirement, Coach Smith became a highly vocal and effective advocate for the repeal of North Carolina's death penalty law and for other progressive social causes. But, sadly, by the mid-2000s, Alzheimer's dementia set in, and over the final years of his life, Smith not only lost his singular cognitive abilities and his steel-trap memory, but became completely isolated from all the people who adored him and wanted nothing more than to shower the old coach with love and affection.

But, whether in dotage or fully intact, that was a shower Dean Smith could never take.

Chapter 6

Too Much, the Magic/Bird Show: Michigan State vs. Indiana State, 1979

Opening nights on The Great White Way are a great big deal, whether it's Marlon Brando opening in *A Streetcar Named Desire* or the one and only performance of *Moose Murders*, a comedic drama from the 1980s that is widely considered the worst play ever performed on any stage, anywhere.

It doesn't matter. It's opening night. Put on your best duds, hop in the limo, and grab a piece of theatre history.

And so it was that theatre history was made on April 11, 2012, when a new drama called *Magic/Bird* opened at the Longacre Theatre. The play itself was less than memorable, falling into that immense creative divide between Marlon and Moose. *Magic/Bird* opened to tepid reviews and closed after only thirty-seven performances. But the opening night audience got its money's worth, when the true stars of the show emerged after the curtain came down. What ensued between Magic Johnson, Larry Bird, and their rapt audience was, indeed, Broadway drama of the highest order.

"I've never seen anything like it in the theatre," says Fran Kirmser, a Broadway veteran who produced the play with her partner, Tony Ponturo. "This wasn't just basketball fans, there were jaded theatre people in the audience who barely knew before the play who these two men were. They all leaped out of their seats as one and cheered. I had goosebumps. I can't imagine that anyone didn't."

Magic, by far the more loquacious of the two legends, began to tell the story of his first encounter with Bird, which occurred at an all-star amateur tournament in 1978 in which they were teammates facing off against an international team from Russia. The city boy and country boy were duly impressed by each other's amazing basketball skills, but did not immediately hit it off socially, given their hyper-competitive natures and their widely different backgrounds. Magic got only part of the way through the story and started breaking down in tears. Then Bird stepped in, put his arm around Magic, and picked up the tale. And then Larry Bird—yes, Laconic Larry, himself—began choking up, too. It was, to be sure, the only time that the word "choke" would apply to either of these two men and the first time that anyone could remember Bird weeping in public (unless you count the bitter tears he shed sitting on the bench, his head completely wrapped in a towel, after a loss in the 1979 NCAA championship game).

"What we all saw on that stage," continues Kirmser, "was love, a deep and lasting friendship between two men. My biggest fear in producing this play was that it would come off as some kind of fable . . . but I knew at that moment that the connection that Larry and Magic had between them was real, and it was very special."

Ponturo, who sat behind Bird and his wife at the opening, reports that he and Kirmser went to visit Magic back in December 2010 to convince him to sign off on the project. "If I'm comfortable with this, then Larry will be, too," Magic confidently told Ponturo. "That's what these guys had become by that point," explains the producer, "two minds acting as one."

Magic shortly thereafter came to New York to see *Lombardi*, an earlier Ponturo/Kirmser production about the life of football coach Vince Lombardi. Magic was concerned that a play about he and Bird could end up turning their private lives into a joke, but seeing how *Lombardi* treated its legendary subject with dignity, Magic was sold on the idea. He ended up having most of the input into the creation of the characters, although Bird did weigh in with some thoughts, as well.

When the curtain fell on opening night, notes Ponturo, both

men, although highly accustomed to entertaining large crowds, were overcome by the moment.

"You have to understand," says Ponturo, "they were seeing actors living out their lives on a live stage. That's something neither of them had ever experienced. That's why I believe they became so emotional taking their curtain call."

Ponturo looks back on *Magic/Bird* with a combination of pride and regret; pride in bringing their story to Broadway and regret that the play was not more successful and that the writer and producers did not do more to flesh out the human drama in the two men's lives.

"First, I think we should have allowed more of Larry's sly sense of humor to come out, and there were major dramatic elements that we didn't take advantage of." Those sensitive elements, says the producer, included the suicide of Bird's father and the obvious questions surrounding Magic's contraction of the HIV virus.

"In the process of trying to show respect for these two fantastic men, we may have forfeited drama which ended up hurting us with the critics."

Not coincidentally, the action of the play kicked off with a recreation of the first-ever competitive battle between the players, which occurred in that NCAA final between Bird's Indiana State Sycamores and Magic's Michigan State Spartans on March 26, 1979, in Salt Lake City. The action in that game, like that of the play, was less than compelling, as Bird had an uncharacteristically poor outing, shooting only 7-for-21, and Michigan State, behind a terrific match-up zone defense that stifled the Birdman and the stellar play of Magic and teammate Greg Kelser, won going away, 75–61. But, as the 2012 opening night on Broadway illustrates, it isn't only the live performance that creates the drama. What made the 1979 final worthy of inclusion among the most iconic NCAA championships is what it augured for the college game, the National Basketball Association, and for the world at large. Sometimes, one has to look beyond the live action to the moment of commencement of a journey, the impact of which would prove to be transformational.

The Bird-Magic final was just such a transformative moment, in more ways than one.

What's in a Game?

"The college game was already on the launching pad, and then Bird and Magic came along and pushed the button," is how the late coach and commentator Al McGuire summed up the '79 final in Seth Davis's book, *When March Went Mad: The Game That Transformed Basketball*. Davis posits that the '79 televised final, regardless of what transpired that night on the court, was the game that ushered in March Madness as we now know it. The evidence strongly supports his thesis. About 18 million households housing 40 million sets of eyeballs—translating to a 24.1 Nielsen rating—tuned in that night. That broadcast rating still stands as a record (although the impact of cable TV, live Internet video feeds, and social media interactions greatly skews the numbers).

Millions of members of the viewing class of '79 tuned in simply to get a look at the mysterious "Hick from French Lick," who hadn't mouthed a single word to the print media in months and whose team had appeared on national TV just three times that season, despite having gone undefeated to that point. Many of those newly-minted fans were surprised to discover that the Birdman was a white man. Naturally, the racial angle made the first matchup of the two best players in the college game all the more fascinating to viewers. A press agent could not have drawn up a better scenario upon which to construct a foundation of hype.

Jud Heathcote, who was in only his third year as head coach of Michigan State, remembered well his first, rather unpleasant, taste of March Madness. According to Heathcote, who passed away in August 2017 at age ninety, the members of the press in the days leading up, and immediately after the game, were utterly "relentless" in pursuing the story of "the Magic man and the Bird man," as if the NCAA final were a game of one-on-one.

"I had to take two players out before the game to meet the media," recalled the former coach, who at the time of this interview was preparing to host his final reunion of his 1979 champions. "So I decided to take along Magic, who was great in these situations, and Greg Kelser, an academic All-American who was also very articulate. Kelser comes back at the end of his media session and tells me all he got asked in the interviews was who did he think was better, Bird or Magic? And Magic says all they wanted from him was to say something negative about Bird, and that was, of course, the last thing Magic would ever do." Heathcote noted that he and his players treated the press onslaught as an opportunity to hone their skills in the game of cat and mouse. "It was a kind of con job we did on the media. We gave them nothing juicy."

Later, after the postgame press conference, just one lone freelance reporter was left in the Michigan State locker room, trolling for scraps of gossip. "He was going around the room, asking [Terry] Donnelly and [Mike] Brkovich and other guys about how Larry Bird had let down his team," said Heathcote. "I was eavesdropping on the conversation. I walked over to the guy and told him if he didn't stop trying to get my players to badmouth Larry Bird, I was going to pick him up and toss his little ass out of the building."

Besides heralding the age of the overbearing media, many other things about the college game would never be the same after the debut Magic/Bird show. The NCAA tournament, financially and metaphorically speaking, was on the cusp of moving from a mid-cap stock to the Fortune 500. The forty-team NCAA tournament expanded to forty-eight teams the next year and to sixty-four teams five years later. TV rights fees of $5.2 million in 1979 nearly doubled the next year, then quintupled in the next two years, and doubled again to just under $100 million by 1985. In the spring of 2016, the NCAA negotiated an extension of its TV deal worth $8.8 billion over eight years. As a member of Congress once observed, a billion here, a billion there, and pretty soon you're talking real money.

In basketball terms, the 1979 final also helped advance the notion that smaller schools from mid-major conferences, such as Indiana State out of the Missouri Valley, could compete with the big boys and in the process do wonders for the TV ratings. After all, nobody loves an underdog the way Americans do. The triumph of the small fry over the big guy has since become a staple in the March Madness narrative (see Butler, George Mason, Middle Tennessee, et al.).

"Here comes Indiana State and this big blond guy and four chemistry majors," broadcaster Dick Enberg remarked to Seth Davis. "The argument was, they played in a minor league. Are they really that good? And they're matched up against a Big Ten power. Dramatically speaking, it was truth strangling fiction."

Last, and definitely least, as regards the 1979 final's cultural contribution to the Madness of March, there was "Disco Bird," an execrable song parody produced at Terre Haute radio station WPFR that celebrated the exploits of Larry Bird. Of all the awful disco parodies of that period—"Disco Duck," anyone?—it would be hard to identify any that is less listenable than this Bird-brained confection.

Two Men, One Destiny

There are events in life that come under the heading of Historical Inevitabilities. Obvious examples include the Civil War, the Cold War, and the stain on Monica Lewinsky's dress. The first battle between Bird and Magic can also be seen as predestined, as has just about everything that has happened to the two men since.

As Bird and Magic have journeyed from their respective humble roots in rural Indiana and Detroit to an NCAA final, a combined eight NBA championships, an opening night on Broadway, and the executive suites of corporate America, they've carried with them this aura of inevitability. And, at bottom, it is not hard to see why, for the differences between the two men—in background, personality, and style—are skin-deep. Their commonalities, on the other hand, cut right to the bone. Each is a natural, inspirational leader; each lives and breathes competition; and each was possessed of all the essentials for basketball stardom, the most critical being a preternatural ability to make everybody around them better players.

Coach Heathcote asserted that anyone with eyes and some basketball knowledge could pretty much predict what the future had in store for Magic and Bird—entering the NBA together and proceeding to remake it in their own image.

"Writers would ask me about them back then, and I would say they'll be going to the NBA and they're going to make history," said the coach. "Speaking just about basketball skills, to me it mainly came down to two things. Each had great court vision and great hands, and those are qualities you can't teach. I've never seen two guys so built for success on the court."

"I knew the first time I saw Earvin and Bird together that they would be joined at the hip for all time," seconds Mike Brkovich, a member of the '79 Spartans, who fondly recalls the day Magic had him over to the family home to watch a ballgame with the folks. Brkovich's thoughts, as a player in the championship game, are of a piece with the theory that the game's long-term impact dwarfs the event itself. "Not a day goes by where I don't feel lucky to have been a small part of this story," he says. "In fact, that final probably means more to me now than it did when I was playing in it."

In their 2009 autobiography, *When the Game Was Ours*, written with journalist Jackie MacMullan, Magic and Bird acknowledge knowing each other even before they were formally introduced. Bird says in the book's introduction that the spirit of Magic Johnson began pushing him, goading him, dominating his thoughts from the time he first heard tell of this Motown phenom. Ditto Magic's initial ideations concerning Bird. Well before their initial encounter in a gym in Lexington, Kentucky, the two had been poring over each other's box scores in the newspapers, comparing their stat lines. Mutual respect, from the very beginning, was mixed with jealousy and a competitive flame that burned like Ali-Frazier. For a long time, given the fierceness of their rivalry, it was extremely hard for these two guys to like, let alone love, one another. The friendship, it is safe to say, took a long time evolving to the point where Magic and Bird were finishing each other's stories and sharing unscripted tears of joy under the bright lights of Broadway.

"We were trying to beat each other year after year," wrote Bird in reference to their NBA years, with Magic winning five titles in LA, and Larry winning three in Boston. "People kept comparing us. I wanted what he had, so I didn't want to get to know him, because I knew I'd probably like him, and then I'd lose my edge." Magic, on the other hand, was better equipped emotionally to couch his envious feelings in a laugh or a joke.

In short, what you had here was an odd couple on the outside and kindred spirits on the inside. Destined, as Larry Bird has often said, to be forever connected, whether they liked it or not. Bird long resisted the connection, until resistance became futile. As he and Magic grew into men, they grew to love each other and accept the inevitability of their common destiny.

Magic/Bird—the slash is almost superfluous.

The Road to Salt Lake

Both teams entered the 1979 NCAA tournament on a roll, Indiana State with a perfect 29–0 record, and Michigan State at 21–6, but winners of 10 of their last 11.

MSU, ranked seventh at the start of the season, jumped to No. 1 after a 17-point drubbing of Indiana in late December brought their record to 7–1. The fast start obscured some pesky personality issues. They included player resentment over Heathcote's frequent tirades and a feeling among some players that their cantankerous coach was tamping down an offense with the potential to be a lot more explosive. In addition, senior Greg Kelser, the team's all-time leading scorer, was chafing just a bit about having his leadership role usurped by the younger Magic Johnson. This was hardly a fault of Magic, who couldn't very well put a lid on his own superior skills and infectious personality, which captivated all his teammates, including Kelser. Moreover, according to his coach, Magic was virtually without conceit when it came to his individual accomplishments.

"He never looked at his game stats," said Heathcote. "The only thing Earvin cared about was the score. He loved publicity, for sure, and he loved playing to the crowd, but he was never a showboat. He was probably the least arrogant guy I ever coached."

Guard Terry Donnelly cites two other irritants: the pressure that comes with high expectations, as the previous season Michigan State was achingly close to going to the Final Four, losing a tight game to eventual champion Kentucky in the regional final; and, having been together for five or six months since embarking on a preseason South American tour, the players were itching to get a break from one another.

"We'd been together a long time," says Donnelly, "and after a while, all that togetherness gets to be too much."

As happens often in the course of a sporting season, relatively minor distractions like these hardly matter at all until the losing sets in. MSU lasted at No. 1 for only two weeks, dropping back to No. 6 after consecutive road losses to Illinois and Purdue. And in late January, MSU hit a rougher patch, losing to archrival Michigan by one in Ann Arbor and getting trounced 83–65 by lowly Northwestern (which finished the season 2–16 in the Big Ten). This was more than a loss; it was awfully close to a humiliation. Magic, for whatever reason, was not playing with his normal swagger, and, perhaps following his lead, all his teammates appeared to be enervated on the court. Heathcote and his coaching staff were appalled by the seeming lack of effort.

Indeed, if there was any point in the 1978–79 season where things could have permanently unraveled, it was at this crucial juncture. Fortunately for Michigan State, they had a reserve point guard named Mike Longaker, whose on-court contributions may have been miniscule but who possessed an extraordinarily keen mind and whose opinions carried considerable weight among his peers and coaches.

After listening to his teammates gripe about their over-restrictive, blustering coach at a team meeting, Longaker had heard enough. He got up to speak his mind.

"Look," he told the team, "the answers to all our problems are right here in this room. The coaches are here to coach, and we're here to play. If we're gonna wait around for the coaches to change their personalities, then we're finished. What happens from this point on in the season is completely up to us and no one else."

The players got the message, as did the crusty coach, who henceforth started toning down the volume of his tirades and letting up a little on the brakes. "I give coach some credit," says Longaker, "for being malleable in his thinking and not trying to keep micro-managing everything on the court."

Not at all surprisingly, backup guard Mike Longaker is known today as Dr. Michael Longaker, an internationally-renowned stem cell researcher at Stanford University.

Nevertheless, Heathcote insisted the turnaround would not have been complete had he not initiated a key personnel shift, replacing 6-foot-7 power forward Ron Charles with guard Mike Brkovich in the starting lineup. Heathcote explained that the move was aimed at "taking back our fast break."

As much as everyone got a big kick out of watching the world's first great 6-foot-9 point guard sweep the defensive board and take the ball end-to-end for a finishing layup, this was not a basis upon which to construct a viable championship offense.

"Teams were ganging up on Magic," noted the coach. "We needed someone who could take the outlet pass [off the rebound] and get it to Earvin in the front court so he could do what he does best."

To be fair, this move was not met with universal acclaim. Charles, who carried not one, but two nicknames—"Bobo" to his teammates, for his appeal to the ladies, and "No Sweat" to his coaches, for his relaxed approach to practice—knew this would end up reducing his playing time, which it did. But Charles came to accept the inevitable without lingering resentment, and peace descended over East Lansing.

From its lowest point, Michigan State, sitting at No. 14 in the country and 5–4 in the conference, embarked on a 10-game tear, beginning with a huge overtime win over No. 7 Ohio State on February 1. Within a month, their ranking had climbed back to No. 4, and MSU was rolling into the NCAAs with its mojo back intact. That confident air stood up in breezy wins over Lamar in the second round, and LSU and Notre Dame in the regionals in Indianapolis.

The semifinal in Salt Lake City, against Ivy League Pennsylvania, was one of those games that steps out of a player's sweetest fantasy. The final score, 101–67, doesn't tell the full story of that shellacking. At halftime, MSU was up, 50–17, having shot 63 percent to the Quakers' 17. Magic racked up 29 points, 10 rebounds, and 10 assists, the easiest triple-double of his playing career to date. There was, to be sure, no brotherly love for the kids from Philly. Late in the game, Mike Longaker failed to close out a Penn shooter and got a tongue-lashing from Heathcote.

"Coach wanted to win the second half," Longaker explains. "How much we were ahead on the scoreboard was not the issue. He just didn't want to see any slacking off."

The Sycamores of Indiana State, by contrast, came into the season, despite the presence of Larry Bird, unranked and unsung. The previous season, Bird & Co. were knocked out in the second round of the NIT, and four of that year's starters had since departed, leaving behind only Bird and the "four chemistry majors." Bill Hodges, the first-year head coach at ISU, recalls attending *Playboy* magazine's preseason shindig in Lake Geneva and hearing his team described as "Larry Bird and four weak sisters." Bird, now a fifth-year senior by virtue of having left Indiana U. and transferring to ISU, had been drafted by the Boston Celtics in 1978. There had been some question entering the new season whether he would jump ship to the NBA, but he elected to stay on for his final year of eligibility and became the first in his family to get a college degree.

On top of all this uncertainty and trepidation among the inhabitants of Terre Haute, the coaching situation was in considerable flux. ISU's previous head coach, Bob King, who had originally been hired as athletic director in 1974 but returned to coaching upon the arrival of Bird in 1975—thoughts of future glory in his head—suffered a heart attack four months before the start of the new season. That was followed by a brain aneurysm three months later. His assistant, Hodges, took over the top job on an interim basis just a few weeks before the first game. During the season, the interim tag came off, and Hodges assumed the position on a permanent basis (he coached but three more years at ISU, compiling a record over that time of 34–47, before being fired).

Slowly but surely from day one, ISU began inching its way into the national consciousness. They opened their Division I season on the road at Purdue, which ISU had beaten handily the previous season. Coach Hodges put his best man on Purdue's best man, center Joe Barry Carroll ("there's not a better defensive player in the country than Larry Bird," he explained), and the result was another convincing 10-point win. "Mackey Arena can be the loudest place you can imagine," says Bob Heaton, a senior forward who roomed with Larry Bird in 1978–79. "But at the end of that game, with everybody marching out, the place was absolutely dead."

On a more profound level, the end of the Purdue game marked a watershed moment in the Sycamores' season—a moment when the team's ability to pull together counted more than its talent. Two days after the game, the brother of forward Alex Gilbert was shot dead through a door in East St. Louis, Illinois.

"My brother was the reason I was here at Indiana State," says Gilbert. "I fell into a deep depression. The only reason I managed to get through the rest of that season without losing my mind was the [support] of my guys, especially Brad Miley and Carl Nicks . . . that friendship and camaraderie is what I will always remember about the whole season."

Two weeks and a half-dozen Ws later, including a two-point win over Illinois State and a four-point triumph at Evansville, ISU crept into the Associated Press poll at No. 20, and from there, they just kept climbing the charts.

On February 1, ISU journeyed to Las Cruces, New Mexico, to take on New Mexico State for the second time that season, having narrowly won by four in Terre Haute two weeks earlier. It appeared to all but a few at the Pan America Center that ISU's 18–0 record was about to fall to 18–1. ISU was down 83–81 with the clock winding down when Brad Miley rebounded a missed free throw by New Mexico State's Greg Webb and passed it to Heaton, who heaved in a prayer shot to send the game into overtime, where ISU ultimately prevailed, 91–89.

Congratulated thirty-seven years later on the 50-foot miracle shot, Heaton didn't miss a beat. "Fifty-two feet," he says. "The shot was fifty-two feet."

It was after this that the folks back home began to address Heaton as the "Miracle Man," and Heaton says he and his teammates began getting their first whiff of hoops immortality.

Throughout the season, according to members of the ISU team, there was little, if any, intra-squad friction. Bird would occasionally get down on guys for lack of effort or execution in practice, but winning every game put a damper on Bird's tendency to trample over teammate sensitivities. For example, during the 1975–76 season, as a non-playing transfer student at ISU, Bird was asked by his coaches to tone down his level of play in practice because he was decimating the collective psyche of the varsity. "To hell with them," Bird is said to have replied. "If they can't win, then they deserve to lose."

In regard to Bird's acknowledged obsession with the burgeoning legend of Magic, Heaton, his roommate, says while Bird might have been secretly scrolling through the Michigan State box scores, he cannot remember the two of them ever discussing Magic Johnson.

"Larry," says Heaton, with more than a touch of understatement, "was not one to talk about his feelings. Back then, he really was the hick from French Lick."

The two young men, both from tiny Indiana farming communities, shared hoop dreams and the occasional beer, but that was about as far as it went. "Larry had a few friends here, and I had some fraternity friends I hung around with," explains Heaton. "We got along well all season, but I can't say we were close."

Ed McKee, ISU's former sports information director, treaded lightly with Bird's media phobia throughout the season.

"He was very self-conscious about doing interviews. He used a lot of double negatives, and he felt out of place among groups of eloquent writers," says McKee, giving one major reason Bird did not do a single print interview leading up to the NCAAs. "And Bird had a previous bad experience with a magazine reporter who he had trusted to honor his wish not to go delving into family issues. So the guy goes back and writes a long article about Larry's father's suicide and all that very private stuff. I think that was really the last straw for Larry as far as talking to the press."

With or without that publicity, the team rolled on toward its destiny. They had but one more close call in their final 10 regular season games—a one-point win at Southern Illinois in mid-February. It was one of several games that season where the opposition managed to keep Bird in check, requiring a teammate to step up. In this case, it was guard Steve Reed, who hit two crucial foul shots in the last 14 seconds.

But it was Dick Versace, the too-clever coach of Bradley University, who provided a rough template for defending Larry Bird. On February 10, employing a double-team on Bird that became known as a "Bird's Nest" or "Birdcage" defense, the Bradley Braves shut the big man down completely, holding him to just two shots, four points, and seven rebounds. It was the only time in Bird's college career that he was held below double figures in scoring. Unfortunately for Bradley, ISU had four other guys on the court, and Bradley lacked the talent to keep those four from taking over. Carl Nicks poured in 31 points and Reed added 19, and Indiana State won easily, 91–72. Nevertheless, Bird's image of infallibility had taken a hit, and the competition had surely taken notice.

After dispatching their regular-season nemesis, New Mexico State, in the Missouri Valley Conference final, Indiana State went into the NCAA sub-regional in Lawrence, Kansas, where they won comfortably over Virginia Tech before moving to the regional in Cincinnati and doing the same to Oklahoma. In those games, Bird was slowed ever so slightly by a thumb injury sustained in the New Mexico State game.

Things got a lot tougher from there. A two-point win over Arkansas in the regional final again required the last-second heroics of miracle man Bob Heaton, who tossed in a short, off-balance jumper with two seconds on the clock to win it, 73–71. And, again, it was Mr. Miracle who made the game-winning shot in the semi against the Blue Demons of DePaul; a layup with under a minute left on a pass from Nicks, punching the Sycamores' ticket into the final. But Bird was the real story of the DePaul game, hitting 11 of his 12 shots in the first half and 16 of 19 overall.

Watching Bird fly over, under, and through DePaul in the first half were a few players from Michigan State. They were impressed, to say the very least.

"That was my first live look at Bird," notes Mike Brkovich. "I'd seen him on TV a few times, but that didn't capture just how fantastic this guy was. If any of my teammates had any doubts about Bird before that game, I have to tell you that watching him against DePaul eliminated those doubts completely. I remember the Michigan State fans at that game chanting 'We Want Bird.' Well, we got him."

Terry Donnelly was equally blown away by the high-flying Bird but relieved that the Spartans had avoided DePaul in the final.

"They had an incredible team with the likes of Mark Aguirre, Clyde Bradshaw, and Gary Garland. Indiana State didn't have that kind of talent, apart from Bird."

In any case, now faced with the challenge of containing the Birdman, Michigan State got right to work, trying to figure the best way to keep him in check without giving away the store to his teammates. Heathcote chose not to go all-out with a Dick Versace-like Birdcage. But he knew Bird was too heavy a load to lay on one defender. Michigan State ultimately elected to employ a "man and a half" match-up zone, ensuring that Bird would get double coverage whenever he put the ball on the floor and would get bumped every time he ventured into the lane. Equally important, the defense was geared to choking off Bird's passing lanes. At practice the day before the big game, Michigan State spent the whole time focused on implementing their Bird containment strategy. A few players took their shot at impersonating Bird, but none of them was close to being up to that monumental task.

Then Magic stepped into the breach. "You want the real Larry? Just watch me," he said.

Magic then proceeded to shred the mock match-up zone, tossing in all kinds of wild shots from all over the floor. The players found Magic's act amusing, but the coach emphatically did not.

"I got really pissed off," acknowledged Heathcote. "I was yelling at the guys, 'If we can't stop Bird in a [simulation], how the hell are we going to defense him in a game?'"

That night, by chance, both teams happened to take field trips to the same movie. When the theatre lights came on after the show and the teams noticed each other's presence, the Spartans began hurling some classic playground trash talk at the country boys from ISU. Carl Nicks, ISU's star guard who hailed from the mean streets of Southside Chicago, was well accustomed to such talk, and worse. But Nicks was uncomfortable with the reaction of some of his teammates, who appeared to him to be a little intimidated.

"It was another day at the playground for me, but except for myself and Alex Gilbert, we weren't a streetwise group," says Nicks. Nevertheless, Nicks was less bothered by the trash talk than by the Spartans' size and leaping advantage and the specter of facing a 6-foot-9 point guard the likes of whom had never been seen on any basketball court in the world.

Those concerns were, indeed, well-founded.

The Game

Sometimes, as they say in sports, it just ain't your night.

Brad Miley recalls getting that sick feeling walking into the ISU training room before the final game and bumping into Larry Bird, who was standing near Carl Nicks. "Larry turned to both of us and said, 'I hope you guys got it 'cause I don't feel it tonight.'"

It was not the kind of news that Miley wanted to hear on the eve of the biggest night of his life, but it would prove to be prophetic. Bird had sensed that this night was going be less about him than how well his fellow teammates would take on the weight of history.

Michigan State, although somewhat more confident heading in, had a few flies in its ointment, as well. Center Jay Vincent had a bad foot that would limit his effectiveness, and there were doubts about the availability of Terry Donnelly, who chipped his tailbone in the semifinal and had been battling a high fever for the past 48 hours.

The game began with Magic Johnson picking up a traveling call on the first possession, before giving America a taste of his genius, gobbling up a defensive rebound and setting off along the left side of the court, finishing with a magnificent driving layup and a three-point flourish.

"They had me guarding Magic early in the game," says Miley. "I remember he throws up that shot and it bangs off the back of the rim, bounces around, and goes through the basket, and I'm shaking my head and asking myself what that was that I just saw with my own eyes."

ISU's players, not only less athletic and undersized relative to MSU, were also more tired, adds Miley, having just slogged through a much tougher semifinal.

Meanwhile, Larry Bird, from the very outset, was feeling the pressure of the match-up zone, getting knocked around and closeted by Greg Kelser, Ron Charles, and Terry Donnelly whenever he crossed the lane or got his hands on the ball on the wings. Open looks at the basket were few and far between, and out of frustration, Bird was forcing passes he would not normally make. On defense, the Birdman was having a devil of a time dealing one-on-one with Greg Kelser's explosive first step to the basket. Kelser burned him

Bird helps Magic off the floor in the 1979 final. The mutual respect was already in full force. The love would come much later.

several times on drives to the hoop in the first half. But his defensive struggles paled in comparison to his inability to get into any kind of offensive rhythm.

"They're packing the zone, making it tough on Bird to do anything down low," noted NBC color analyst Al McGuire. Later, he pointed out that Bird "was getting buried in that zone."

Bill Hodges was not at all surprised by MSU's innovative defensive scheme. "Teams had been throwing up all kinds of junk defenses at Larry all year," he says. "That was nothing new. Like always, it was up to the other four guys out there to make things happen, and that night they just didn't."

On the defensive side, in addition to Kelser's quickness, ISU was nearly transfixed by the hydra-like talents of the Magic Man. It was like a Hollywood wag once said of Ginger Rogers—that she did everything Fred Astaire did, only backwards and in high heels. Magic did everything that Bob Cousy did, only he did it in the body of a power forward.

Attempts by the ISU players to get into Magic's head failed miserably.

"I'm out there doing everything I can to get under his skin," laments swingman Leroy Staley, who guarded Magic for much of the game. "I'm gritting my teeth, making ugly faces at him, and he's just smiling back at me. He was having fun out there making us miserable."

At the six-minute mark, MSU went up, 16–8. The next six or seven minutes featured an extraordinary leap by Bird to intercept an alley-oop pass, and a couple of baskets by Carl Nicks, who was trying his best to penetrate that thick 2–3 zone and take some pressure off Bird.

"I saw what was happening with Larry," says Nicks, "and that made me press too much and took me out of my game." While the same could be said for the rest of Bird's teammates in the first 20 minutes, Nicks, as the Scottie Pippen to Bird's Michael Jordan, takes the lion's share of the blame for not picking up the slack. "I was the guy who really needed to step up, and I didn't." His first-half travails concluded with Greg Kelser making a remarkable defensive play under the Sycamores basket, blocking and snatching the ball away from Nicks, who was going up for a put-back in the final minute.

MSU maintained a steady five to 12-point lead throughout the half, which ended with the Spartans up, 37–28.

Nevertheless, given how thoroughly Michigan State had negated Bird's offensive brilliance and had used their size and leaping ability to dominate under both baskets, nine points were hardly a safe cushion, especially with the two MSU stars, Magic and Kelser, each saddled with three first-half fouls.

The opening minutes of the second half belonged to MSU. Terry Donnelly, who rarely shot the ball and averaged only six points a game during the season, made the Sycamores pay dearly for constantly leaving him wide open on the wings, draining four jumpers in the first five minutes. Donnelly's offensive production in the final—15 points on 5-for-5 field goal shooting and 5-for-6 from the foul line—surprised everyone but himself.

"Coach took me aside at halftime and told me I could expect to get a lot of open shots as they had no choice but to double up on Magic to stop his penetration," explains Donnelly. "I had the green light to go ahead and shoot. I hadn't done much of that in college, but I was a good shooter back in high school... I was ready."

Bird, meanwhile, continued to comprise the middle of a defensive sandwich, barely managing to even touch the ball. MSU's lead quickly rose to 16, at 48–32. To everyone in the arena and millions watching at home, this much-heralded matchup had all the makings of a blowout. That is, until Kelser picked up an offensive foul, his fourth, plowing into Bird just outside the lane. With Kelser, the senior, now forced out of the game for a substantial period of time, the 1979 NCAA Final suddenly got interesting.

Carl Nicks, snapping out of his first-half funk, started penetrating and shooting like he was back in the Chicago playgrounds, and ISU initiated a full-court trap, causing several turnovers and rattling even the Magic Man.

"I feel the momentum turning," said Al McGuire.

Over an approximately five-minute span, ISU whittled 10 points off MSU's lead, getting within six at 52–46. "Michigan State," exclaimed Al McGuire, "has lost its composure."

Heathcote, witnessing things spinning rapidly out of control, had little choice but to get Greg Kelser back in the game with just under nine minutes left. The six-point deficit would be as close as ISU would get the rest of the way.

Magic and Kelser, together again on the floor, immediately settled their team down, spreading the offense and further tiring out the Sycamores, already exhausted from their comeback effort. Coach Hodges says he toyed with calling a timeout with about eight and a half minutes left, to allow his players to catch their collective breath and talk about how to defense the spread offense. To this day, Hodges regrets not calling a TO until just over five minutes remained and MSU had once again established control at 61–50, following a hellacious Magic dunk and a questionable two-shot foul call on Bob Heaton for undercutting Magic in the air.

Nevertheless, ISU was not quite dead yet.

Mike Brkovich, a superb foul shooter, missed a couple down the stretch and Donnelly tossed away a pass around midcourt, and ISU managed to slice the lead back to seven with several excellent chances to make it even closer. But Bird, still under intense zone pressure, misfired on several more shots, Steve Reed continued to miss open mid-range jumpers, and Bob Heaton, polishing off a dreadful 4-for-14 shooting performance, tossed up one last air ball. ISU's miserable night at the foul line (10-for-22 overall) continued right up to the closing horn.

It just wasn't their night.

While the Spartans celebrated with soda showers and Donnelly recounted the pleasures of being left alone to shoot uncontested jumpers ("I think it was more relief than joy"), the Sycamores reflected quietly in their locker room. Larry Bird declined to speak with the media. Through his tears, he dictated some comments to Ed McKee, who scribbled them down and cobbled together a statement for the press. The statement praised Michigan State's zone and lamented all the missed free throws and the opportunity gone by.

Carl Nicks, a junior, would be coming back in Terre Haute next season, but not without a deep reservoir of resentment.

"I was angry at myself and my teammates for not sensing the urgency of the moment. I was angry at the refs (Al McGuire had termed the refereeing "consistently incompetent"), and I was mad at Magic for being so damn good and ruining our perfect season.

"But I got over it," concludes Nicks, who currently works for the Indiana Pacers as the team's manager of player relations. "Considering where I'd come from, I'm grateful just to have been in that situation."

For Alex Gilbert, the season-ending loss only deepened feelings that had lingered since the death of his brother. Gilbert says his struggle with depression went on for many years, until he finally emerged on the other side.

"I was a footnote to the standard-bearers of the history of basketball," Gilbert says now. "And that is more than enough for me."

Magic played coy in a postgame interview about his future plans, but he wasn't fooling anyone. He and Bird had both played their final college games and would soon be leaving for the coasts. But they would always filter back to Middle America. Magic, to the one place where he could be Earvin Johnson. And, Bird, well, once a hick . . .

Aftermath

The mid-to-late 1970s were a low point in the history of the National Basketball Association.

Their new TV deal with CBS (which replaced ABC) did not work out at all. CBS did an extremely poor job of promoting the league, putting many games, including playoff games, on tape delay, meaning they could not be viewed until nearly midnight. ABC also put its college football and the *Wide World of Sports* programming up against the NBA, and the floundering league got toasted in that head-to-head competition. On top of that, player cocaine use and on-court fighting severely tarnished the league's image. The nadir came in 1977 during a game between the Los Angeles Lakers and Houston Rockets when a ruckus broke out and the Lakers' Kermit Washington decked the Rockets' Rudy Tomjanovich with a punch that nearly killed him. Attendance and TV ratings were in dive mode.

The 1979 arrivals of Larry Bird and Magic Johnson, along with a new cable entity called ESPN, brought the moribund NBA back to life. In effect, pro-style March Madness continued for a full decade. Every championship contested during that time featured either Magic's Lakers or Bird's Celtics, with those two teams copping eight of the ten titles. Magic and Bird won a combined six MVP awards during the 1980s, made funny TV commercials together, and cemented their "warrior" friendship. Bird also developed a well-earned reputation throughout the league as one its most wickedly caustic trash-talkers. One famous story has Bird turning to the Utah Jazz head coach Frank Layden in the middle of unleashing an offensive deluge on the Jazz, and asking, "Hey, Frank, haven't you got anyone on the bench who can guard me?" Layden looks up and down his bench, and, deeply chagrined, turns back to Bird. "No," he replies.

By decade's end, the NBA had new lucrative four-year TV deals with NBC and Turner, and it was on the crest of another marketing wave engendered by Michael Jordan and his Chicago Bulls. And Magic and Bird took a friendship that had been forged on the court to a much higher level, beyond competition, when Magic was diagnosed with HIV in 1991 and announced it at a major media event. Bird reached out to him in a way that no one else in Magic's circle could have done.

Appearing together on the *Late Show with David Letterman* on the day of the *Magic/Bird* Broadway opening in 2012, the two reflected on this difficult period in their lives. Bird said it was the first time he could ever remember not wanting to play basketball, and he equated his profound grief over Magic's illness with that of losing his father as a very young man.

"I had a pit in my stomach for days after," Bird told Letterman, who appeared as awed in the presence of these two men as the audience at the Longacre. "Even after I talked to Magic... because, in my mind, in nine or ten years he's gonna be gone."

"Forget the sports, forget the championships, forget the MVP," chipped in Magic. "He came to my side and supported me, and I'll never forget that."

Neither man choked up in front of Letterman. On the outside, at least.

Chapter 7

The Wiz Waves Goodbye: UCLA vs. Kentucky, 1975

Cy Young, 511 lifetime pitching wins. Cal Ripken Jr., 2,632 consecutive games played. Wilt Chamberlain, who averaged more than 50 points and 25 rebounds per game over an entire season. All sporting accomplishments that will never—can never—be equaled in this modern age.

Add to these illustrious names that of John Robert Wooden (born October 14, 1910, died June 4, 2010), who coached the UCLA Bruins basketball team to 10 national championships in a 12-year span, beginning with the 1963–64 season. This remarkable streak concluded with Wooden's final NCAA championship in his final game on March 31, 1975, in San Diego, California, a closely-fought 92–85 victory over the University of Kentucky. Given how the men's college game has evolved over the past forty-odd years, from actual student-athletes remaining in school the full four years to soak up all the hoops know-how they would need to succeed in the NBA, to the ubiquity of today's "one-and-done" freshmen sensations, the notion of another Division I basketball program ever matching Wooden's astounding twelve-year run is inconceivable.

Was the success of the "Wizard of Westwood" (Wooden hated that nickname as much as Wilt Chamberlain hated being called the "Stilt") a true measure of his coaching ability? Short answer: yes, and then some.

True, he did have the likes of Lew Alcindor (later Kareem Abdul-Jabbar) and Bill Walton as the bulwarks of his championship squads of the '60s and '70s. But Wooden coached-up those superstars like no one else could, or at least no one who coached in his era.

It is probably something of an exaggeration to state that Wooden invented offensive basketball as we know it, but not that big an exaggeration. The major strategic innovations that he pioneered in his early days of college coaching in the 1940s and '50s—notably the high-post and the high-low post offenses—were groundbreaking developments as critical to the creation of the modern game of basketball as the replacement of wooden baskets with iron rims and net cords. Out of Wooden's basic offensive sets, a team could run a great many plays, each offering a bevy of options, or "reads." In Wooden's offensive "system," every pass, every cut to the basket, every elbow to the chin, had its purpose.

Without getting too technical—many volumes of arcane literature exist on this subject—consider the fundamental UCLA high-post 2–3 offense, designed to combat a man-to-man defense. It generally begins with a pass from the 1-guard to the 2-guard and the center flashing from the low to high post, the goal here being to pull defenders as far from the hoop as possible. The 2-guard then has the option of making an entry pass into the high post or passing to the 3-forward on the ball-side wing. Should the pass go to the high post, both forwards back-cut to the hoop in hopes of an easy layup, while the guards cut to the middle and then to the wings. If the layup opportunity has failed to materialize, the center can pass to the 2-guard on the ball-side wing. The 2 then has the option of passing to the 3-forward posting up down low, at which point the center cuts into the lane for a pass from the 3 and a layup. If that pass is not there, the center sets a down-screen for the 4-forward, who can cut around the screen to receive the pass from 3 in the lane. If all these options are bottled up, the pass from the 3 goes out to the ball-side wing for an open jumper.

Got all that?

This is but a snippet from page one of the Wooden offensive playbook. It may seem quite complicated, but, in fact, the great beauty of the high-post offense lies in its simplicity. All these options flow smoothly out of the basic offensive set. Once you've run through them often enough in practice, all these maneuvers occur as naturally as honey from a bee. It is the height of basketball elegance, the champagne of offensive systems.

Just a few of the many advantages accruing from the UCLA high-post offense include ensuring that all five players are actively involved in the offense; that the players are spaced on the floor in proper balance at all times; and that when a shot goes up, a rebounding "triangle" is formed on the strong side of the basket, enhancing the prospect of an offensive rebound and a put-back.

Still, while the classic high-post offense was central to Wooden's overall system philosophy, he was flexible enough to tweak it or shelve it entirely, depending upon the particular skills of his personnel. Indeed, when Wooden had Alcindor playing center for him in the late '60s and winning three straight NCAA titles, Wooden scrapped the high post in a favor of a low-post offense that would take full advantage of the big man's awesome scoring and rebounding talents around the basket. And, when Wooden brought in center Bill Walton and forward Keith (later Jamaal) Wilkes to win another couple of championships in the early '70s, the team mostly operated a high-low post-style offense to get the most of their natural skill sets, which included outside scoring, passing, and rebounding.

Wooden remains best known as an offensive innovator, and for good reason. But not all his innovations were on the offensive side. To take one example, the full-court zone press, back in Wooden's day, had been employed exclusively in desperate catch-up situations at the end of games. Wooden was one of the first, if not the first, coaches to roll out the press at other points in the game, as a means of confusing and disorienting the opposition.

The 1974–75 team, Wooden's final championship group, did not possess the top-flight, NBA-quality talent of the Alcindor and Walton gangs, and thus was the perfect team to execute a high-post offense designed to blend together and maximize the unique abilities of everyone on the court. According to the members of that team, Wooden taught his pupils well.

"When you talk about John Wooden," sums up Ralph Drollinger, who stepped into the big shoes previously worn by Walton, "it ought to be as a professor, not a basketball coach. You might have a professor in class for a couple of hours a week for one semester. I had John Wooden for a professor every day for three years. To play for him, you didn't have to be a great student of the game. He taught fundamental basketball, not a lot of details. You just had to pay attention."

Coming from Drollinger, in particular, such praise is noteworthy, as the junior center from nearby Grossmont High School didn't much like playing basketball. Drollinger says he was drawn to UCLA more by Wooden's manner of teaching and his innate powers of persuasion, which to Drollinger recalled the iconic educators of ancient Greece. "With Wooden, it was about more than Socrates' *logos* (logic), the subject matter itself. It was the *ethos* (ethics) and *pathos* (emotions), those unspoken means of persuasion, which you picked up just being around the man."

Drollinger recalls an incident in the gym one afternoon when the players commandeered a court that had been set aside strictly for intramural use. "We had no business taking away the students' court," says Drollinger. "Coach walks into the gym and calls the whole team over. He says nothing, just gives us a look, and the look says it all . . . 'You guys screwed up. Now set it right.' Most of the time, that's how he was. He could deliver a powerful message simply with his presence."

Although the aphorism, "failing to practice is practicing to fail," is standard practice among all successful coaches, to Wooden it was gospel. He wasn't much of an in-game strategist. He rarely, if ever, called timeouts to diagram plays, believing that this would be an admission of a lack of pregame preparation. And he cared little about scouting opposing teams for weaknesses. Wooden's coaching was done almost exclusively on the practice court, where his sole focus was on growing the potential of the players he had. And he had a way of running his practice sessions that was unlike that of any of his peers.

Think of John Wooden's version of basketball education as a civilian West Point, with the juniors and seniors the upperclassmen and the freshmen and sophomores the plebes.

"It was run like a well-oiled machine," says Pete Trgovich, a starting guard on the 1975 championship team and a keeper of the Wooden flame. "Our practices were completely mapped and printed out in advance. He'd divide us into drill stations. Every drill had a time attached to it, usually five to ten minutes, sometimes a little longer. Very specific, finesse drills, like, say, running a 3-man strong-side drill to defend a screen coming down. You'd work it for the allotted time and move on the next station. The guys who'd been in the program for years knew all the drills, knew where to go, and the younger guys would just follow them from station to station. These things became habits . . . passed down from one [player] generation to another."

Wooden's attention to organizational detail was total and immersive. As stated in many Wooden biographies, it went so far as teaching his players how to tie their sneakers to avoid blisters and bunions and bringing in a tailor to have every player's uniform custom-fitted at the beginning of the season. "He believed the right fit would build our confidence," says Drollinger, who was nicknamed "Luggage" for all the traveling calls he got that season.

His focus on the minutest of details even encompassed his abhorrence for emotional outbursts by his players. Wooden believed such outbursts sapped their collective energy and diverted their thoughts away from the task at hand.

"I sat on the bench my entire freshmen year, and the guys figured we could get over on coach by moving our legs right to left, and then left to right, when something good happened on the court," recalls Richard Washington, a forward and the Most Outstanding Player in the 1975 NCAA Final Four. "But Wooden figured out what we were doing and put a stop to it fast."

Wooden's insistence on maintaining stricter discipline stemmed, at least in some measure, from the wayward Walton years of the early '70s, when he felt that his players were too involved in anti-war campus activities and other non-basketball pursuits. The coach believed that he could mold the 1975 group to fit his ideal of what a basketball team ought to be. Hence, flip-flops, long hair, and blue jeans, the attire favored by the Walton crew, were jettisoned, and the team began eating meals together once again.

This near obsessive-compulsiveness about the small stuff, combined with a quiet, but white-hot competitive fire, led Wooden to seize on every advantage—no matter how seemingly insignificant—to get a jump on the opposition. Some would say an unfair jump.

Seth Davis, an ESPN analyst, in his 2014 biography, *Wooden: A Coach's Life*, writes that the coach ordered the nets at Pauley Pavilion woven extra tightly so that after every basket, the ball would take an added second or two to hit the floor, thus giving his team extra time to set up its full-court press.

Wooden, naturally, was also a stickler about conditioning, but not in the manner of many other coaches. Washington says Wooden had an uncanny knack for building players' stamina without having to resort to suicide drills or other brutal endurance tests. "Every drill we ran was with the ball, and they always centered on finesse rather than punishment or strength. You never felt tired when you were doing them, only when you got back to the locker room. Back in high school, I'd always held back on expending energy running [sprints] so I could do the drills. Wooden would get you into great shape without you even noticing it." For this reason, former players say that there never was heard on the UCLA practice court any moaning or groaning.

The tremendous conditioning of his team would prove to be a deciding factor in Wooden's final championship game.

"There were no secrets to his approach to teaching basketball or life," offers Gary Cunningham, one of Wooden's two assistants in '75 and perhaps his closest professional confidant and most loyal acolyte. "He taught fundamentals, reinforced through simple everyday repetition and execution. There was nothing fancy about any of it. Just consistent principles that were easy to grasp."

That was John Wooden, basketball coach nonpareil. Off the court, as a human being, he was less consistent and harder to grasp.

Though humble in most respects—Wooden's salary never exceeded $35,000 in any year, and he lived out his days in a modest two-bedroom condo in the valley, where he kept his Presidential Medal of Freedom buried under a coat rack—his competitive nature at times clashed with his image as the clean-living family man and role model of gentlemanly behavior. The dichotomy between the man and the image rankled more than a few of his fellow coaches, who referred derisively to Wooden in private as "St. John." And the US Olympic Committee seemed to have it in for the guy, as well, never tapping him, despite his unparalleled record of success, to coach his country's team. To be sure, the green monster was behind a lot of this cynicism, but Wooden gave his staunchest critics enough reasons to seriously question the reverence with which he was held in most basketball circles.

For one thing, Wooden was a notorious baiter of referees, a habit he is said to have fallen into because it was easier to taunt refs than harangue his own players. According to some of those players, Wooden was adept at timing his ref-induced outbursts to catch the attention of the TV cameras, an indication that he was not totally without vanity. Also, Wooden's relationships with most of his players were not of the warm and fuzzy variety, and he could come off more times than not as aloof and indifferent to their personal concerns. Nevertheless, the accusation that Wooden cared nothing about the lives of his players beyond the confines of the basketball court is refuted by members of the 1975 championship team, who say that the coach managed to touch their inner lives in some profound ways.

Drollinger says Wooden encouraged his ambition to enter the Christian ministry—today Drollinger ministers to the spiritual needs of 100 Christian members of the US Congress—and Washington says Wooden was a big influence in teaching him how to walk humbly.

"I remember one day strutting around the airport with the team and feeling like a great, big, important man, and Wooden just looks at me and says, 'You know, most of the people in this terminal don't know who you are and don't care.' I think that was one of the most important things he ever said to me. It woke me up."

But, by far the biggest personal knock against John Wooden's reputation for honesty and integrity concerns the activity of a UCLA booster and benefactor named Sam Gilbert, an LA businessman with reported ties to the Mob who, throughout Wooden's reign, was extremely active in procuring benefits for UCLA players—the kind of benefits that in today's climate would have put the UCLA basketball program squarely in the NCAA investigative crosshairs and would most certainly have resulted in severe penalties and immense damage to the image of the vaunted program.

According to exhaustive articles in the *Los Angeles Times*, Gilbert provided Wooden's kids with discounts on automobiles, stereos, meals, clothing, and even cash for an abortion for the girlfriend of a player.

Wooden, for his part, insisted right up until his death that at no time during his coaching tenure was he aware of these extracurricular shenanigans.

On this issue, "my conscience is clear," Wooden said. He did acknowledge feeling uneasy about Gilbert's close relationships with the players and asserted that he and the UCLA athletic director had both advised players to steer clear of this booster.

There is no credible evidence that Wooden was being deceitful in his denials. Still, at the very least, he turned a blind eye to what was going on in his program for a long time. Actually, it was more like two blind eyes, because Gilbert was pretty open about his beneficence and his ties to the players.

For a man internationally renowned for his probity, how do we account for Wooden's abject failure to keep his program as morally spotless as he was? We grant that he was not St. John, but just a flawed individual, like the rest of us.

"At a certain point," writes Seth Davis of Wooden, "he had to make a choice," and that choice was that it was better for his beloved program, and for himself, if he didn't dig too deeply into this sticky Gilbert situation and just went with the flow.

Nevertheless, according to *The Sons of Westwood: John Wooden, UCLA, and the Dynasty That Changed College Basketball*, by John Matthew Smith, Wooden was plagued by his inaction and having "knowingly allowed an outsider to undermine his authority, tarnish his reputation, and jeopardize the integrity of his program." The manner in which Wooden "enforced rules for everything" during his final season at UCLA was, according to Smith, in direct proportion to the shame Wooden experienced from the long-running Gilbert scandal.

All his personal compromises, big and small, aside, the bottom line is that John Wooden was a marvelous educator and a fundamentally decent man, whose legacy, unlike, say, that of the legendary Penn State football coach Joe Paterno, remains firmly intact. And, it should be added, deservedly so.

The Short Goodbye

The overwhelming favorite entering the thirty-two team 1975 NCAA tournament was Indiana University, coached by the indomitable and controversial Bobby Knight. The Hoosiers came into the Mideast regional final with a 34-game win streak. That team, which would go on to the win the NCAAs (with an undefeated record) the following year and be named by *USA Today* as the all-time greatest college basketball team, featured a lineup of future NBAers, including Scott May, Kent Benson, Quinn Buckner, Tom Abernethy, and Bobby Wilkerson. Their opponent, Kentucky, which came into the game ranked fifth in the country with a 24–4 record and was coached by Joe B. Hall in his third year as head man in Bluegrass-land, was likewise loaded with superior talent. Six players off that team—Rick Robey, Jack Givens, Kevin Grevey, Bob Guyette, Jimmy Dan Conner, and Mike Flynn—were eventually drafted into the NBA.

But, while Kentucky did not appear to be quite in Indiana's league—the Hoosiers had blown them out by 24 the previous December—the Wildcats had the edge in motivation (revenge) and in luck. Indiana's best player and leading scorer, Scott May, started the game with a cast over his left forearm, having broken his wrist four weeks earlier. May played only seven insignificant minutes, taking just four shots and making one. While the 6-foot-11 Benson had a tremendous game, with 33 points and 23 rebounds, Kentucky was able to match him with a parade of big, muscled frontcourt bulls, who ultimately roughed him up and wore him down. Final score: 92–90, Kentucky, which now entered the 1975 Final Four as the presumptive favorite to take the crown. At least you would think they would be. But to some of the younger Kentucky guys, specifically their four freshmen studs, such was not necessarily the case.

"The thing is, we weren't expected to be in the Final Four at all . . . the team was 13–13 the year before," explains Rick Robey, the freshman starting center who went on to a lengthy NBA career. "There was this feeling that we didn't belong there. So, no, to my mind we were not brimming with confidence at all."

Jack Givens, another freshman star who would go on to become the Most Outstanding Player in the 1978 NCAA final, concurs with Robey's assessment, but puts it a bit differently.

"I think the whole thing, frankly, was probably more important to our senior leaders than it was to us. We were kings of the world after beating Indiana. Even now, I think to myself that the Indiana game was bigger than the final. Part of it comes from being freshmen. You think it's going to be like this every year, so you don't take it [so seriously]."

Joe B. Hall, Kentucky's coach, when apprised now of the comments of his two top freshmen, just shakes his head and sighs. "They were freshmen, what did they know? But, overall, we had a mostly veteran team that year, and I believe that most of our guys didn't feel that way."

In any case, Kentucky, gliding into the Final Four on the fumes of their Indiana euphoria, dispatched Syracuse with minimal trouble in the semifinal. The Orangemen, who were making their first-ever appearance in the Final Four under coach Roy Danforth (they would make many more in the years to come under Jim Boeheim), were overmatched against the much deeper and stronger Wildcats.

Wooden's Bruins had a somewhat easier path into the Final Four that year, coming into the tourney 23–3 and beating Michigan and Arizona State by double-digits, sandwiched around a surprisingly close three-point win over Montana. But standing in their way in San Diego was a much greater challenge—a very talented Louisville team, helmed by Wooden disciple Denny Crum, who knew something about matching up against the UCLA high-post offense and exploiting the full-court zone press.

The Louisville semifinal was an instant Final Four classic, razor-close and tense throughout. UCLA closed a four-point deficit near the end of regulation, and Louisville's number one star, Junior Bridgeman, missed a jumper at the buzzer that would have won it for the Cardinals. In OT, the teams went back and forth. Terry Howard, one of the best foul shooters in the country, who had made 28 straight free throws, missed two that would have iced the game with under a minute left. This allowed Richard Washington, who had played brilliantly all evening, to nail a midrange jumper with three seconds left to give UCLA a 75–74 lead. Louisville botched the ensuing inbounds pass, and that was it.

After the final horn had sounded on Louisville, the fireworks went off. John Wooden, after twenty-seven years in the surrealistic hothouse of UCLA basketball, up and quit coaching forever.

But, according to *Wooden: A Lifetime of Observations and Reflections On and Off the Court*, one of the former coach's autobiographical tomes, the decision to call it quits that night was no slam dunk. "If I had gone to the media room first [to make the announcement], perhaps I wouldn't have announced it then. But, instead, I turned and headed to the locker room where all our youngsters were." After telling his celebrating players how much they'd meant to him and how proud he was of their effort all season, Wooden advised them that they would be the last team he would ever coach. "I'm bowing out," Wooden said, before getting out of his chair and walking into the press room to deliver this shocking news to the rest of the basketball world.

To be sure, there had been published rumors that this would be Wooden's last year and another rumor had surfaced that UCLA had gone so far as to interview his future replacement, Gene Bartow, earlier in the season. More than the retirement itself, it was the timing of Wooden's announcement that had everyone sleepless in San Diego. The UCLA players, for the most part, remained in stunned silence well into the following day, when they got together to engage in some light stretching exercises. "The tension in the workout room was huge," says one player. They knew, as it was hardly a deep secret, that their coach was dog-tired, stressed out, and bitterly angry at the spoiled alumni who had made his life miserable over the past decade.

"The alumni disgusted him," states Ralph Drollinger. "Maybe that's what happens when you've had the success he had, but it was very hard on him. After the final game in 1975, one major alum came up to coach and said, 'You owed us this one for last year' (UCLA had been beaten in the Final Four semis in 1974) ... I think these ridiculous expectations wore the man down." Pete Trgovich references the famous Wooden quote on the price of success: "For all the coaches I like, I wish they would win one [championship], and for all those I don't like, I wish they would win one."

The seniors on the 1975 team, roommates Dave Meyers (since passed away) and Trgovich, sensed early in the season that something might be up, as Wooden hadn't told this group, as he had other groups in the past, that he would be sticking around through all their years of eligibility. But they never guessed he'd bow out like this. Gary Cunningham says Wooden advised him at the beginning of the season of his plan to retire at its conclusion, owing to his being emotionally exhausted by the demands of coaching at UCLA and a heart attack Wooden had suffered two years earlier. Cunningham adds that at age sixty-four, "coach's enthusiasm never flagged, but he just couldn't maintain the energy it takes to coach in this environment every day." Still, even Cunningham was taken aback by the timing of the announcement.

But if the news of Wooden's imminent departure stunned the UCLA community, it positively floored the opposition—and not at all in a good way.

"It knocked me right out of my chair," says Joe B. Hall. "I remember feeling awful about all the sentiment that I knew was now going to be in his favor, and I knew this announcement would be very bad for us." Hall says his worst fears were borne out before the tip-off, when the head of officials advised the referees to be careful "not to let the game get out of hand."

"We were a very physical team, and having the game called closely would change the way we matched up with UCLA. It would change our tempo. It would kill us." Indeed, it is Hall's firm belief that Wooden's retirement announcement was but another of his sneaky competitive ploys, like tightening the nets.

Kevin Grevey, the leading scorer on the Kentucky team, says he didn't hear the news about Wooden until the next day when the press approached the Kentucky team for comment. The team at the time was relaxing and communing with the animals at the San Diego Zoo.

"Now here we are playing in San Diego, a stone's throw from LA, and the great John Wooden has just announced his retirement. Are you kidding me? I was like a deer in the headlights. I remember Coach Hall kind of stepped in and helped me get through the interviews with the press . . . I just felt that everything we had all worked for all year was coming down on us."

The Game

Coach Wooden, according to his players, was not half as concerned with Kentucky as they were with his last-minute machinations.

"He felt we were in better shape, we were faster and quicker and that would negate their size advantage," says Drollinger. "We didn't talk about Kentucky at all, as I remember."

Dave Meyers and Pete Trgovich, the seniors, came into John Wooden's last game with a mind-set grounded in a winning tradition. "When you come to UCLA," explains Trgovich, "you buy into the idea of *never* losing and a belief that you've got to keep that tradition alive. The loss we had in the 1974 Final Four [against North Carolina State] was devastating to Dave and me. We thought that if we could come back after that, without Bill [Walton] and Jamaal [Wilkes], and win, when everybody was saying our dynasty was over ... well, that would be the greatest thing we could imagine."

Irv Brown, a veteran college referee who called three of John Wooden's championship finals in the late '60s and early '70s, says this is just how they rolled during the glory years at UCLA.

"I remember during the Sidney Wicks/Curtis Rowe era, in the '60s, I'd hear the guys on the floor of the championship game saying to one another, 'We can't be the first ones to lose!' That was the UCLA mentality. The legacy of winning all the time got passed from class to class."

But tradition can get you just so far. UCLA was seriously undermanned going into the final. While Kentucky had a deep bench with no less than five talented big men they could shuffle in and out and afford to give fouls galore, UCLA was down to only six go-to players, and one of them, forward Marques Johnson, had been debilitated by hepatitis all season and couldn't go very hard for very long, particularly in a fast-paced, run-and-gun style contest like the one they were expecting against the Wildcats. Dave Meyers, for his part, had a pair of seriously banged-up legs and by season's end was pretty much running on sheer desire and a wad of confidence.

"That was our advantage," argues Washington. "We'd all practiced against Bill Walton the year before. Of course, we couldn't match Kentucky's muscle, but after Walton, no way that was going to intimidate us. I thought it would be our guards who would control the tempo for us and take away their press, and that's what happened. Andre [McCarter, the point guard] and Trgovich played great."

Over on the Kentucky side, Coach Hall was advising his team that what had worked so well against Indiana and Syracuse, "freelancing a lot, clearing sides, penetrating and kicking," was not the ideal way to attack UCLA's man-to-man defense, for which he had limited respect. The key to winning this championship, Hall cautioned his players, was a virtue with which they had little familiarity—patience.

"Above all, I didn't want the guys taking the first open shot," explains Hall. "I felt strongly that if we were to just make that extra pass, we'd get a much better shot, and we'd be okay."

So what happened? Naturally, says Hall, "we came out firing up everything right away, and I wound up having to waste all my timeouts to get everybody calmed down."

Kevin Grevey and Jack Givens, among others, pleaded guilty to the charge of impatience under fire.

"I was trying to do too much," admits Grevey, who scored 34 points in the final but shot an unimpressive and uncharacteristic 13-for-30 in doing so. "I saw our guys struggling, having fouls piled up on them. I should have trusted my teammates more, but instead I just kept shooting. I was wide open all night long, their defense was soft. I remember thinking throughout the game, *Is this all they've got?* But coach was right, I needed to be more patient. It's a lesson I took with me to the pros."

Givens, another scoring machine, shot just 3-for-10 in the final. "I didn't play well at all. I think the freshman in me showed up that night," he confesses. "We all should have listened to Coach Hall."

In military parlance, such impulsive-style behavior is said to stem from a desire to be "at the tip of the spear." Elite combat troops and great ballplayers, according to recent scientific research into peak performance, do not stop to analyze and ponder their environments. They act and adjust as they go.

"That's it," continues Givens. "We're ballplayers, and we just want to go out and play basketball . . . forget about running plays and let it all go. There was no shot clock back then, no way of judging our offensive tempo."

The 1975 championship matchup, as advertised, was up-tempo and aggressively (and raggedly) played from the opening tip-off, until both teams settled down a few minutes into the game. Kentucky, with Grevey and Givens hitting some early jumpers, went up by six, but at 25–25, Wooden made a key substitution, Drollinger for the ailing Marques Johnson, that shifted the entire story line in UCLA's favor. Drollinger, a wiry seven-footer seemingly at a distinct physical disadvantage among all those hefty Kentucky bodies, somehow found himself in a sweet zone that night. He started asserting himself down low, clearing rebounds, blocking shots, drawing fouls from Kentucky's mountain men, and otherwise creating havoc for the Wildcats.

"It was the game of my life," Drollinger says. Billy Packer, doing the color commentary that night on NBC TV, could hardly believe the quality of play he was witnessing from Drollinger.

"That kid, Drollinger, probably hurt us the most," seconds Hall. "He just worked the weakside on offense and cleaned up on the glass, putting back those missed shots."

UCLA's guards, McCarter and Trgovich, neither known for shooting, ran the high-post fluidly, and with aplomb. McCarter racked up 10 assists in the first half alone (14 overall) and Trgovich made a few key baskets in the first 20 minutes, which ended with UCLA up, 43–40. But, on the down side, the Bruins by the end of the half looked totally gassed.

"UCLA's fatigue will be key to whether they can withstand Kentucky's pressure," intoned Billy Packer.

"We definitely were gassed," confirms Drollinger. It seems that UCLA's trainer, Ducky Drake, had not yet discovered the benefits of carbo-loading, and UCLA's pregame diet that season consisted almost entirely of protein-rich foods. "If you looked really closely at us during that game," remarks Drollinger. "You'd notice that those custom-fitted uniforms from early in the season were now hanging off our bodies. We looked like malnourished string beans. I wasn't large to begin with, and I'd lost twenty pounds that season. We were lucky that our conditioning and experience got us through."

Kentucky, to counter the smooth flow of UCLA's offense in the first half, at one point switched to a 1-3-1 zone to take away UCLA's speed and quickness advantage, and it bothered the Bruins for a while. But on the offensive end, Kentucky was much too prone to standing around, waiting for Kevin Grevey to make something happen. For one key period in the first half, UCLA was able take Kentucky's most potent scorer completely out of the offensive flow.

Kentucky, a 50 percent-shooting team throughout the season, shot just 33 percent in the first half, to UCLA's 47. It was to be expected that Kentucky's superior shooting, size, and depth would ultimately assert themselves in the second half, which began with Grevey taking a flying leap into the stands in pursuit of a loose ball. But while Kentucky's shooting accuracy did improve somewhat as the game wore on, once the Wildcats had cut UCLA's lead to one early in the second half, they could not get any closer the rest of the way. Their big men kept picking up fouls, and Drollinger continued to have a gay old time playing put-back on the offensive boards.

UCLA's lead remained fairly steady in the low to mid-single digits throughout most of the second half. Keeping Kentucky close in the early going was junior forward Bob Guyette, who scored eight points in the first five minutes of the half. At 56–52, Kentucky again went to the 1-3-1 zone to counter the speed gap. UCLA, remarked Billy Packer ominously, was still looking like a "tired ballclub," but somehow the Bruins just kept grinding away.

Meanwhile, Wooden, sitting stiffly on the sideline, his rolled-up program, as always, wrapped tightly in his left hand, was trying to mix and match his players to compensate for a severe shortage in manpower. Drollinger's strong play gave him some leeway to rest Marques Johnson until later in a close game, when his explosive offensive talents would be most needed. And Wooden handled the injured Dave Meyers with just the right degree of caution, taking him off his tough defensive assignment, Kevin Grevey, for an extended period so as to rest Meyers's battered legs and keep his senior star out of foul trouble.

Nearing the midpoint of the second half, UCLA had grown its lead to 66–56. Then Richard Washington, who scored 28 points that night on the way to the MOP trophy, picked up his fourth foul, severely limiting his defensive effectiveness, and Grevey's shooting touch began heating up again. Four Grevey jumpers, a pair of foul shots and a drive to the hoop by Mike Flynn, another bucket by Guyette, and pretty quickly it was a one-point game again at 76–75.

And then came the moment that, for both teams, may have determined the course of NCAA history.

With 6:23 left, Meyers was called for an offensive foul on Grevey. Meyers overreacted in the heat of that moment by banging his hand on the court and drawing a technical foul. Precisely what happened next is a function of which side you believe. According to Joe B. Hall, it was Wooden, himself, who turned around the whole game right then and there with antics that befitted his exalted status and his sense of entitlement.

"He comes all the way out to the foul line to argue, and the refs, they were intimidated out of their minds. Wooden should have had a technical on the spot. I thought of going out there, too, but I knew if I did, they'd have slapped a T on me ... meanwhile, the refs are saying, 'Oh, please, Mr. Wooden, won't you go back to the bench?' I finally go over to the scorer's table to complain, and the ref points at me and tells me to get back to the bench now or he'll hit *me* with a technical."

In Hall's version of events, Wooden stayed out there on the court just long enough to thoroughly mess up Grevey's shooting rhythm. Grevey, one of the team's best foul shooters at close to 80 percent for the season, not only missed the front end of the one-on-one, but also the technical. And, compounding the impact of Wooden's alleged misbehavior, on the inbounds play that followed, the ref called an offensive foul on Kentucky's freshman big man, James Lee. That's a total of five potential points lost on that one sequence.

"And that, to me, was the game in a nutshell," sums up Hall. "The legend of John Wooden, playing his last game in his own backyard, and he's got it all going his way."

Adds Grevey, "I can't recall missing two foul shots in a row in my entire career at Kentucky. I can't say for certain that this episode cost us the game, but it was a huge turnaround sequence in UCLA's favor."

The Bruins' side of the story goes something like this: Coach Hall was the one who had been violating the referee's edict not to cross over the line from the bench. The officials, says Gary Cunningham, had clearly instructed both coaches before the tip-off that they were going to strictly enforce the boundaries. "Coach Hall repeatedly crossed the line and was never called for it. At one point, I had to restrain Coach Wooden, actually grab him. He was justifiably angry at the refs about that all night."

In any case, from that point on, things only got worse for the Wildcats. With 4:35 remaining and Kentucky still down by only three, at 80–77, Rick Robey, their most skilled big man, fouled out. Robey's loss was a big hit to the Wildcats.

Kentucky got as close as 88–85 on another Grevey basket, but with 38 seconds left, Andre McCarter sealed the win with a drive in the lane, and UCLA coasted home from there.

In the postgame Kentucky locker room, the seniors were morose. The four freshmen were disappointed, too, but looking toward a brighter tomorrow.

"I have been trying to put 1975 behind me my whole life," says Kevin Grevey, still grieving the loss forty-two years later in his restaurant in Virginia. "The game haunts me still. I feel I got cheated out of my one chance at a [college] championship." Grevey ultimately got his championship ring, in the NBA, with Elvin Hayes and the Washington Bullets in 1978.

The freshmen POV is expressed by Rick Robey: "We learned something that night, and we knew that lesson would be useful when we got back to the Final Four."

And, indeed, Robey and Co. did return to the Final Four as seniors and grab the crown behind 41 points from Jack Givens in the 1978 title game against Duke.

The Bruins, suffice it to say, left San Diego exhausted, but

John Wooden's wan postgame victory smile spells it out: R-E-L-I-E-F.

sporting deep smiles of satisfaction, having sent their esteemed coach into retirement on a cloud of glory (but still steaming about Joe B. Hall and the incompetent referees).

"Truth is," notes Pete Trgovich, "as much as we admired our coach and wanted to give him [this parting gift], we didn't need him for motivation. If you need the retirement of John Wooden to inspire you to play your best in a championship game, then there is something seriously wrong with you."

Aftermath

John Wooden most certainly did not expect his retirement to last thirty-five years. Nevertheless, say those who remained close to him after '75, he made the most of that time, befriending a new generation of admirers and indulging his passions for family, baseball, and the poetry of his former player Swen Nater. He loved being a UCLA basketball fan.

"Coach had his own way of watching a game from his seat at Pauley," says Gary Green, a former team physician at UCLA who got to know Wooden well in the last ten years of his life. "Two things he focused on; the UCLA defense, and on the offensive end, he'd follow everything that took place away from the ball. Coach would say that this is where the game is most interesting, if one knows where to look."

John Wooden remained an upright citizen to the end. But the air of chilly detachment that had also been his trademark as a coach ultimately gave way to a more thoughtful and caring presence. Coupled with his lifelong attention to detail, it was a potent combination.

"The medical staff used to throw a party for Coach Wooden every year at the Valley Inn," recalls Gary Green. "One year, one of the fellas brought along a basketball for him to autograph, which he did with a borrowed pen. At the end of the night, we're all putting on our coats and walking out the door, and coach stops me and hands me the pen. 'Now you be sure to bring this pen back to Sophia,' he says. 'It belongs to her.'"

Chapter 8

What Price, Glory?:
Texas Western vs. Kentucky, 1966

"When the legend becomes fact, print the legend."
Spoken by a frontier journalist in John Ford's film, *The Man Who Shot Liberty Valance*.

Let us, for a moment, reverse the course of basketball history, with regards to the legendary 1966 NCAA championship game, played at Cole Field House in College Park, Maryland, on March 19 of that year and won by Texas Western University over Kentucky by the score of 72–65. Let's imagine that Kentucky's all-white Wildcats did not play one of their worst games of the season (which they did that night) and that two or three of their many misfired open jump shots or missed tip-ins, instead, fell gently into the basket. Or, just as validly, that the seven black Texas Western players who saw action in that game executed their 34 foul shots (compared with 13 for Kentucky) with slightly less accuracy.

So instead of nursing a fairly comfortable seven-point lead as the seconds ticked down, Texas Western is only up by a point, with, say, three seconds remaining in regulation, and Kentucky is in possession of the ball under its own basket. And, finally, let's imagine that the ensuing Hail Mary inbounds pass lands in the hands of Kentucky's star player, Pat Riley, who, while falling out of bounds, heaves the ball over his shoulder toward the basket and watches it swish through the net as the final buzzer sounds, thus immortalizing "Rupp's Runts"— as that undersized Kentucky team was known—as the 1966 national collegiate basketball champions.

Hardly a far-fetched notion.

What would it all have meant back then, and now? Would the long and bitter struggle for the equal rights of millions of African-American citizens have taken even a small step backwards? Would the highly talented and super-disciplined Texas Western team have exited the arena that night in ignominy, rather than trailing glory in which the university (now called the University of Texas at El Paso) has bathed for more than five decades?

One thing is certain. Such an alternate ending would have put the kibosh on fifty-one years of national media hype that has been extravagant even by media hype standards. What was at the time, by most accounts, just a basketball game, has since morphed into a watershed event in the history of the American civil rights movement.

And there is something not quite right about laying the enormous weight of our sad racial history on a bunch of young men barely on the threshold of adulthood.

"I just wish all this would stop," sighs the 6-foot-3 Larry Conley, one of those five Kentucky runts, coached by the venerable Adolph Rupp, aka the "Baron," who listed four national titles on his résumé.

In advance of the fifty-year anniversary celebration, Conley says he was approached by an Atlanta newspaperman seeking Conley's umpteenth comment on the events of '66. "How does it feel," the reporter asked Conley, "to have been on the wrong side of history?"

It's a question one might legitimately ask of a former Confederate soldier. But not of a good-natured youngster, now a grandfather, who long ago played in a basketball game.

"I wonder all the time how it came to be this giant thing," concludes Conley, still smarting from another thoughtless remark. "It seems crazy to me after all these years. I really thought once I did all the twenty-fifth anniversary game interviews, that it would finally be over. But it's never over for us."

Cliff Berger, a reserve teammate of Conley on that Kentucky team, says he'd be more comfortable being thought of as a "small part of history." By society's measure, he adds, "it would actually have been the wrong side of history if we had won, wouldn't it? Whatever the case, none of us should have to deal with questions like that."

Put yet another way, if those seven black Texas Western players were on the side of the angels on that fateful Maryland evening in 1966, on which side were Conley and his all-white teammates? When did ending up on the wrong side of a score translate into being on the wrong side of history?

It is not an easy thing to determine with any exactitude how one basketball game, a rather mundane contest played on late-night syndicated TV long before the NCAA tournament was a media Goliath, came to stand with the Birmingham march and the resistance of Rosa Parks as landmarks in the most important social justice movement of the twentieth century. A movement, we might add, that's still moving, and not anywhere near fast enough.

"College basketball needed its symbol, its iconic equivalent of a Jackie Robinson, its *aha!* moment," argues Charles Martin, a sports and civil rights history professor at UTEP and author of *Benching Jim Crow: The Rise and Fall of the Color Line in Southern College Sports, 1890–1980*. "The '66 final was the closest thing they could get to that level of symbolism."

For sure, the canonization of the 1966 final had a lot to do with it being the first-ever championship match pitting all-whites against all-blacks (five white Texas Western players rode the bench that night). Heightening the dramatic impact of a black-on-white hardcourt confrontation was the fact that the all-white team came from an all-white conference—the Southeast Conference—one of a number of major lily-white southern conferences (ACC, Southwest) that had yet to recruit a single black scholarship athlete. It's a statistic that all these years later seems almost incomprehensible, until you factor in that some coaches and athletic administrators, and a great many more alumni boosters at those southern schools, were prisoners of racial assumptions that caused their rational intellects to cease functioning.

By 1966, it would seem like anyone who truly believed that blacks were incapable of playing good, solid fundamental basketball had to be either a Klan sympathizer or legally blind. Along the route to '66, several major Midwestern and Western universities sporting mostly-black lineups had already copped NCAA championships. The great University of San Francisco teams of the mid-'50s, led by Bill Russell and K. C. Jones, won consecutive titles with three black players in its starting lineup. The champion Cincinnati Bearcats of the early '60s and Loyola of Chicago in '63 (see Chapter 9) each started four blacks. And that's not to mention what had been going on for more than a decade in the National Basketball Association, where black superstars were solidly ensconced by 1966 and the league well on its way to becoming the African American-dominated entity it is today. The NBA's Boston Celtics in the mid-'60s were smack in the midst of an unprecedented streak of eight straight NBA titles with an all-black starting lineup. Hadn't anyone in the southland bothered to check out the bodies of work of Bill Russell, Wilt Chamberlain, Oscar Robertson, Lenny Wilkens, Walt Hazzard, Wayne Embry, Elgin Baylor, and Sam Jones, to name just a few of the many African-American professional stars of that period?

How to explain broadcaster Rod Hundley, who said of the Texas Western players back then that they could do "everything with a basketball but sign it?" Or the southern scribe who wrote of the Miners of Texas Western that they were a "running, gunning quintet that does more things with a basketball than a monkey on a 50-foot jungle wire." Quite apart from a strong racial bias implicit in these old quotes, these expert observers had clearly never observed Texas Western play basketball. "We were the most disciplined, boring team in the Final Four," points out the 5-foot-8 Texas Western guard Willie Worsley, nicknamed the "Little One." "We played a whiter [brand of] basketball than Duke or Kentucky."

Indeed, they did. That's the basketball irony underlying this extraordinary story.

Smarter Than the Average Bear

Joe B. Hall, an assistant on Adolph Rupp's staff that season and later Kentucky's head coach for 13 years, asked what he thought of Texas Western entering the final game, notes that Kentucky's players and coaches were well-apprised of TW's disciplined, yet fierce, man-to-man defense and its outstanding point guard, Bobby Joe Hill. But what most garnered Kentucky's respect, adds Hall, was simply this: "They were coached by an 'Iba Man.'"

What, you may ask, is an Iba Man?

Not some Paleolithic being, but rather a protégé and devotee of the legendary Oklahoma A&M (later Oklahoma State) coach Henry Iba. Texas Western coach Don Haskins, a gentleman of substantial proportions who wore the nickname "Bear" with pride, was *the* archetypal Iba Man. Haskins had played for Iba as an undergraduate from 1949 to 1952 and soaked up life lessons and basketball lessons straight from the Iba School of Hard Knocks. Iba men learned early on that basketball, in its basic form, is a lot like life; life as it's lived on a subsistence dirt farm in rural Oklahoma. Simply stated, in Haskins's own words, his time at A&M was "four years of hell."

"Back then, it wasn't supposed to be fun," Haskins explained to reporter Alexander Wolff in a deeply moving 1999 profile in *Sports Illustrated*. "Over Christmas break, [Iba] would have us go from nine to noon, two to five, and seven to ten. Seven to ten would be three one-hour scrimmages. No water. No sitting. One night by the end, the skin on the ball of my foot had come off . . . [the] school president was at practice and he asked if I was tired when I came off the floor."

"No sir," replied Haskins, who passed away in 2008.

"Sure shouldn't be," shot back the president, "'cause you haven't done a damn thing all day."

The echoes of Stillwater, Oklahoma, resounded in the Texas Western gym fifteen years later.

"We hit the floor every day at 3:30," remembers Nevil Shed, one of Haskins's two "whipping boys" in that championship season (Bobby Joe Hill being the other). "Many times he'd have [assistant coach and Henry's son] Moe Iba call the cafeteria to tell them we wouldn't be on time for dinner at 5:30. No water breaks, no sitting . . . end of the day, my feet were burning and blistered. I hated the SOB back then." While Haskins may have been especially tough at times with Shed and Hill, for a variety of reasons, his players roundly agree that the Iba Man was, if nothing else, an equal-opportunity SOB.

Still, some unpleasant memories grow faint over a half century, even when it comes to dehydration and blistering feet. Jerry Armstrong, one of the five white players on the 1965–66 team, recalls practices regularly grinding on for as long as four hours. Others, including David Lattin, the 6-foot-7 big man known as "Big Daddy D," remember the daily practice regimen as particularly harsh, but not extremely protracted. "Practices never ran more than two hours," insists Lattin, still wearing a little of his "Daddy" persona a half-century later. "Haskins was a smoker. He couldn't go for more than that even if he wanted to."

Whether the practice lasted two hours or into the night, Haskins made the time count. He preached and demanded DEFENSE played the Iba way—straight man-to-man, with one overarching, ironclad rule: no switching. Ever. A defender could offer "help" to another, but the man you were assigned to guard was your responsibility and no one else's. And woe to you if you weren't up to the job.

And woe be to him who fancied himself a hotshot, even in the moment.

Orsten Artis, a 6-foot-2 guard and the team's best pure shooter, recalls dribbling behind his back one day in practice and getting reamed out like he had just stolen his coach's wallet.

"For some reason, I was probably the only guy on the team who didn't get yelled at all the time," relates Artis. "But when Haskins saw me go behind my back that day, it really set him off. He hated when you did any showboating."

"Coach's major focus was all about defense," reiterates Lattin.

"You never switched or went under a pick. You went over it, or through it, and you picked up your man well outside the basket."

"You did whatever Haskins told you to do," adds Armstrong. "And you didn't ask questions. If you did, coach was there in your face and gettin' all red in his face. White or black, it didn't matter to him. I was always yessir and no-sir with him. Coach was the boss, and this was work."

Haskins ran a lot of two-on-two and four-on-four defensive drills, getting his players to focus on maintaining eye contact with their man and the ball at all times, taking away the cutters, and pressuring the men they were guarding into moving in the direction desired by the defense. Haskins also was fond of "suicides," or "killer" drills, as the TW players called them, which consisted of countless mad dashes from half-court to the foul line and back. One of Haskins's most insidious concoctions was gleaned from Utah basketball coach Jack Gardner, who Haskins once saw running a five-on-two fast break drill. Haskins, given his defense-oriented mind-set, simply flipped it to run as a defensive drill, with two defenders scrambling all over the court trying to contain a five-man break. "That drill alone would break you," quips Armstrong.

Strangely enough, players on the Texas Western '66 championship team can't recall ever running the notorious "Iba drill," named for Haskins's mentor. The Iba drill entails a player diving on the court for a loose ball, throwing it back to an assistant coach, getting a return pass and heading to the basket for a layup. There, he is met by more assistant coaches wielding football pads and banging away mercilessly at his arms, chest, and legs until that player has put the ball in the basket not once, not twice, but three times a layup. These types of extreme measures fall into a general category commonly referred to by coaches as "GATA"—Get After Their Asses—drills. An Iba Man is, by definition, a GATA man.

The elevation of the 1966 Miners into a symbol of racial equality and pride did not occur overnight. The legend grew gradually through frequent team reunions, biographies and autobiographies, newspaper and magazine articles, many TV documentaries, and shout-outs from 1600 Pennsylvania Ave. The twenty-fifth anniversary celebration, according to Charles Martin, got the propaganda machine really pumped up, with a visit to the first President Bush in the White House and a ream of testimonials in mainstream media.

But, by far, the biggest boost to the legend of '66 came from the 2006 release of *Glory Road*, a Disney-produced Hollywood hagiography based on Haskins's book of the same name. The movie is entertaining and inspiring in the manner of many a sports biopic, but is rife with historical inaccuracies. Playing fast and loose with the facts may be par for the course in dramatized sports films such as *Pride of the Yankees* or *Hoosiers*, but to those who view Texas Western's triumph as part and parcel of a much more important human struggle, the facts matter a great deal.

Among the film's more significant inaccuracies:

- Don Haskins did not arrive at Texas Western that season, after a stint coaching a girls high school team. The 1965–66 season was Haskins's fifth at TW, and the championship squad he put together was a product of five years of diligent teaching and recruiting. Haskins had spent the previous six years prior to coming to El Paso coaching boys basketball at three tiny rural high schools in west Texas. His duties there included driving the school bus through the dusty country roads and keeping the rattlesnakes on his front porch out of the family living room. Haskins's initial experience at TW was not all that far removed from those high school outposts. Texas Western in 1961 was primarily a football school, and the administration was more interested in having a guy who would live in the athletic dorm and keep the place clean. Irv Brown, a former college referee and a longtime Haskins confidant and drinking buddy, says the new coach "cleaned that disgusting place out in a week."
- Black players were nothing new on the TW campus. Over his first four years, Haskins coached and recruited a fair number of highly-skilled black athletes, including Jim "Bad News"

Barnes (the first player chosen in the 1964 NBA draft), Nolan Richardson, and Willie Brown. Brown, a New Yorker, was influential in the recruitment of three key pieces of the '66 championship team—Shed, Worsley, and Willie Cager, all schoolyard players from the Bronx.

- There was no racial divide between the white and black players on the '66 team, as depicted in the movie.
- Many of the most dramatic episodes portrayed in the film never happened, most notably the savage beating of Nevil Shed by a couple of white thugs in a public restroom. There were a few death threats phoned into players before games and a report that vandals splattered some blood in the coach's room. But the players report no actual racial violence occurring during the season.
- Haskins was no civil rights crusader and never spoke to his players before the championship game about making a social statement by playing only the black guys. Haskins was all about playing the guys who would give him the best chance to win. Indeed, he had started five blacks in nearly every game that season. Moreover, Haskins never issued a blanket apology to the white players for leaving them out of the final game. In fact, no one on the team back then can remember Haskins apologizing for anything. Jerry Armstrong says it took the man forty years to personally apologize to him. "Coach came up to me at one of our reunions and said, 'Jerry, I did you wrong that night. I'm sorry.'"
- The Don Haskins portrayed in the film was a martinet virtually without humor. The coach, in fact, had a wonderful, droll sense of humor. One night he approached a referee after a loss at home. "You called a helluva game tonight," he said. And then, pointing to the only door out of the gym, he added with a sly grin, "Now, let's see you get out of here."
- And, finally, on a lighter note, casting Josh Lucas, with his matinee idol looks, as Don Haskins, was, with all due respect to Haskins's appearance, something of a stretch.

But, fictionalized aspects aside, the movie did get much of Haskins's story right. It captured his mental toughness, his ultra-competitive nature, his nuanced relationships with some of his players, and his loving and supportive marriage to his wife, Mary. Those who knew the man intimately off the court say they were particularly gratified by the tender scenes of an enduring marital union.

Irv Brown, who spoke at Haskins's funeral, remembers his friend as a "hard living, hard drinking bear of a man, who liked challenges, loved getting up in people's faces, and was the biggest sucker I ever knew."

By sucker, Brown means a man of enormous kindness and generosity who invariably wound up on the wrong side of a debt.

"Haskins would help out anybody and he rarely got anything back," says Brown. "One morning we're having breakfast in a restaurant and he says to me, 'Irv, do me a favor... if you see so-and-so, could you ask him for my money. He owes me five hundred bucks, and I can't get the guy to pay me.' He'd leave twenty dollar tips for countermen. I remember once he was in his car and he passed a family in a beat-up truck that had broken down. He paid to have the truck towed and repaired. Never said a word about it to anyone."

There are dozens of similar stories of Haskins's gruff, but generous nature, including rumors that he gave money to his players (which his players vehemently deny). But once they became former players, Haskins was the softest touch in the west. One notable example was when Willie Cager needed heart surgery and could not afford it, Haskins not only had him transferred to a better hospital, but arranged and paid for the services of a world-class cardiac surgeon.

Somewhat countering Haskins's well-earned reputation as a "sucker" and contributing to an equally strong reputation for guile is the fact that Haskins was known to hustle pool on occasion. He was pretty good at it, so the story goes. Haskins's hustling skills even extended to his own players. He got Orsten Artis, a prized high school recruit from Gary, Indiana, to agree to come to Texas

Western by hustling him in a foul shooting contest. Artis shot 9 of 10 from the line. Haskins hit all 10.

Nevertheless, the coach's generous instincts, combined with some extremely poor business decisions (including a lettuce-growing scheme) and a family tragedy (large, uncovered medical expenses for the care of his son, Mark, who died in 1994), would prove to be his financial undoing in his later years. In that 1999 *Sports Illustrated* interview, done during his final year at UTEP, Haskins confessed that his financial misfortunes had forced him to supplement his relatively-meager coaching salary by killing coyotes and selling their pelts for $75 each. Having turned down numerous offers over the years to coach at better-endowed Division I programs paying several times the UTEP salary, Haskins had to face up to the reality of having to coach college basketball past the time when he might have preferred to retire and hunt varmints for pleasure, not eating money.

The Road to Glory

Coming off a good, but not great 1964–65 season (16–9 record and a trip to the NIT), Haskins and his team came into the new season with more questions than answers. It was, to be sure, his most talented bunch, wrote Haskins, but he had to play GATA with them every day in practice. Bobby Joe Hill, the team's star point guard, on-court leader and a kid who most enjoyed partying with a girlfriend who would later become his wife, "would rather take a punch in the face" than practice hard. The good news was that the Miners' schedule was relatively easy, as it was next to impossible to find top teams willing to travel to El Paso. "Defense always wins," notes Daddy D, "Just read my book. In it, Abe Lemons [the legendary Texas coach] says if he had twenty open games on his schedule, he wouldn't schedule Texas Western. We were murder to play. Not very exciting, just murder."

The first major sign that this year could be something special came in late December at the annual Sun Carnival tournament held in El Paso. Iowa, ranked No. 4 in the nation, was somehow persuaded to make the trek to the Texas Panhandle. In the final tourney game against the Hawkeyes, Texas Western came out of the locker room on a mission, exploding to an insurmountable 34–4 lead. They ultimately relaxed a bit and cruised to an 18-point win. That convincing effort got TW into the Top 10 national rankings, and pretty soon the excitement began to build among its students and the El Paso citizenry.

"The players began to feel that they weren't just playing for themselves or their school, but for an entire city," Haskins wrote in his book. "My problem was [still] getting them to play for me." Case in point was Arizona State, a team that Texas Western should have handled with relative ease. "We were screwing around, just like always," Haskins said. Play hard one minute, take off the next minute. It got so bad, recalled Haskins, that he took the unprecedented step of calling for a zone defense, which, for Haskins, was the coaching equivalent of holding an orgy in the Vatican. This switch finally woke up his team. Instead of going into a zone, they went out and played the toughest man-to-man defense they had played all year.

"I was trying to piss them off [by putting them in a zone]," concluded Haskins, "so they tried to piss me off by not playing that zone."

This back-and-forth pissing contest pretty much defined the entire season, up to and including the NCAA Final Four.

Texas Western made its last regular season road trip to Seattle, carrying a 23–0 record. Seattle was good, and had several very adept black players of their own. But Haskins says what did Texas Western in was the hometown ref. "He took care of them [Seattle] pretty good ... we didn't get a damned call all night. I got called for a technical before the game even started."

According to Nevil Shed, looking back fifty years, the solitary loss to Seattle was a godsend. "It took the monkey off our backs," he says. "I don't think we'd have won the championship if we'd gone into the tournament undefeated."

Texas Western entered the NCAAs ranked third in the country. After a 15-point regional quarterfinal win over Oklahoma City in Wichita, they moved on to the next regional in the friendlier confines of Lubbock, Texas. There they eked out a two-point overtime win vs. unranked but always dangerous Cincinnati, and then took on fourth-ranked Kansas in what was, by all accounts, the most exciting game in the tournament. In the end, the double-overtime, 81–80 win came down to one angry inch of Jo Jo White's heel. The Kansas guard tossed in a corner jumper with the clock running out in double OT, seemingly giving the Jayhawks the victory. But the ref called off the shot. White's shoe was a smidgen over the sideline. No basket, game to Texas Western. That moment in time, dramatically presented in *Glory Road* the movie, remains an extremely touchy subject among Jayhawks fans. Was his foot really on the line, or was it just the shadow cast by his shoe? Only the shadow knows for sure, but it was enough to propel Texas Western to the Final Four.

In the semifinal, TW faced Utah and its All-American wunderkind Jerry Chambers (who wound up the Most Outstanding Player in the Final Four despite having lost in the semi). Chambers dumped a big bucket of points on Texas Western's beleaguered big men, who simply couldn't contend with his amazing offensive prowess. With most of his big men in deep foul trouble in the second half and pretty much out of available options, Haskins turned to the Caucasian side of the bench and put in Jerry Armstrong to try his best to contain Chambers.

"Chambers was kicking my ass all night," acknowledges Shed. "Man had me jumping up and down like a piss-ass punk. Nobody could stop that guy. Armstrong didn't exactly stop him, either, but Jerry did a terrific job of at least slowing him down. We would not have been in the final game if not for Jerry."

Quite naturally, for Armstrong, the second half going belly-to-belly with Chambers was *his* championship. "Of course, I wanted to play in the final more than anything," he says, "but I understood why coach did what he did that night. He always went with what he thought would work on the court, and in the Utah game, that was me."

In contrast to Haskins's "pain-in-the-ass" Miners, the 1965–66 Kentucky Wildcats, Rupp's Runts, were a coach's dream. While Rupp was more prone to huffing and puffing than to actual coaching—increasingly so in his final years at Kentucky—his assistant, Hall, recalls the Runts as "a great group, probably the most unselfish group of kids I've ever been around. Someone would go up for a short jumper and give up the ball to a guy standing a little closer to the basket. They loved playing together, and all season long, those guys made us proud."

Kentucky's march to the Final Four—led by All-Americans Pat Riley, Louie Dampier, and Thad Jaracz—was smoother than Texas Western's. With the exception of a double-OT win at Georgia, a four-point victory at Mississippi State, and a lone, late-season loss at Tennessee, the 24–1 Wildcats had not been seriously tested heading into the tournament. After fairly routine seven-point wins in the regional against Dayton and Michigan, they traveled to the Final Four in Maryland to play archrival Duke, another all-white squad, from the Atlantic Coast Conference. The two teams had been ranked first and second since January.

"We played great against Duke." says Coach Hall. It is perhaps not too presumptuous to believe that Kentucky was more enamored of Duke's talent than it was of Texas Western and that the 83–79 semifinal win over the Blue Devils may have created overconfidence among the Wildcats going into the final.

Cliff Berger, the 6-foot-8 Kentucky reserve, who played a key role in the Duke win, remembers that semifinal in much the same context.

"We did play really well, and Duke was incredibly loaded with talent. Bob Verga, Jack Marin, Steve Vacendak. It was a close back and forth game all the way. Marin killed us in the beginning. But we somehow managed to get through it."

"That semifinal," sums up Hall, "was our championship."

The Game

"Oddly enough," wrote Don Haskins of the '66 final, "the most memorable thing about the actual game was the lack of memorable moments." Haskins describes it in his book as a good, clean, and hard-fought game, but one could just as easily describe it as something less than that. Kentucky, for its part, seemed out of sync all evening, especially on offense. How much of that was Texas Western's rugged man-to-man and how much could be blamed on illness (Conley had the flu, and Riley an infected toe), the refs, or just an off night, depends entirely on who you talk to.

The game kicked off at about 10 p.m. EST. The crowd was decidedly pro-Wildcats, and there was a lone Confederate flag unfurled behind the Kentucky bench, which some Texas Western players noticed during the game, to their obvious dismay. But the crowd, with few exceptions, did not go in for racial epithets. During the pregame introductions, Claude Sullivan, the announcer who called the radio play-by-play for Kentucky, gave the Miners very little chance of winning. Thereafter, his call focused almost entirely on Kentucky's numerous failures throughout the game—its poor shooting and shot selection, turnovers, and, on the defensive side, its marked tendency to commit needless fouls.

"I wish I could tell you what went wrong out there," says Larry Conley. "We were terrible. There are just some nights when you don't show up, and this was one of them. Everything we tried to do offensively didn't work. We had all kinds of good looks [at the basket] and couldn't knock them down."

Conley, nevertheless, credits the little man who guarded him much of the evening, the 5-foot-8 dynamo Willie Worsley, who was giving up seven or eight inches to his opponent.

"I told Rupp in the huddle, just get me the ball. I can shoot right over this guy ... well, the first time we come downcourt, I face the little guy up from the foul line and he hits my elbow hard. The ball goes over the backboard. No call. I look at the ref. 'Hey,' I said to him. 'I may not be the world's greatest shooter but I'm not that bad!' Next time I face up Worsley, he hits me again, and the shot goes off the side of the backboard and again, no call. It was just that kind of night."

Responds Worsley, speaking in the lingua franca of the New York City schoolyard, "If the ref don't call it, it ain't no foul." Worsley dismisses all Wildcat complaints with the following aphorism: "If a bird had a square butt, he'd shit bricks."

Worsley, who played all 40 minutes that night, was a last-minute, unexpected addition to the starting lineup. Haskins, anxious to slow down Kentucky's vaunted high-speed, fast-break offense, advised Worsley just before tip-off that he was going to be the third guard on the floor. Worsley himself was floored, but ready to go. Maybe not for 40 minutes, but he was hyped up as never before in his playing career. Despite his lack of height, he somehow managed to grab four rebounds to add to his eight points.

"The greatest day of my life," he says. "My whole world opened up out there. Not just playing and winning the game, but having my folks and all our friends and family back east seeing us on TV for the first time. That was maybe the biggest deal of all for me, Nevil, and Cager . . . man, I was eighteen or nineteen. I'd never played in a college game close to home."

Before the team stepped out on the court that night, Haskins also had some final words for Big Daddy D.

"He told me to go out and get a dunk right away," recalls Lattin. "He wanted to send a message."

Lattin complied, getting two early dunks that, along with two Bobby Joe Hill steals in the first half, were the turning points, according to Texas Western lore. Pat Riley of Kentucky has been oft-quoted as confirming that Lattin's monster dunks shook up the whole team, but not all Riley's teammates buy into that narrative.

"That is total bullshit," argues Conley. "You think Lattin was the first guy who ever dunked on us? We were runts, for God's sake, we got dunked on all the time that year. Hill's two steals (which occurred at the midpoint of the first half and put TW up by 14–9, a lead they never relinquished), now that *did* get our attention. I never saw either of the steals; I was up the court facing the other way. But, again, it wasn't like nobody had ever stolen the ball and made a layup on us." Conley, for his part, considers the key to the game to be the decision by Haskins to go with Worsley and a quick, agile three-guard lineup.

"That was a brilliant move. It gave them a very different look, and that caught us off-guard."

Nevertheless, if Conley and his teammates were not driven to distraction by Bobby Joe's steals, the Baron certainly was. According to Eddie Mullens, the TW sports information director at the time, Rupp could be heard during a timeout screaming at Tommy Kron and Louie Dampier for getting their pockets picked. "You stupid sons of bitches," the Baron is quoted as exclaiming. A *Sports Illustrated* reporter quoted Rupp using the word *coons* when addressing the matter in the locker room at halftime. Cliff Berger has a strong recollection of the coach screaming all matter of expletives at his two veteran guards, but "I never heard him say 'coon.'"

Conley says his head coach was his "usual blustering self" on the bench during timeouts. "He used colorful language all the time. And after he would unleash all that bluster, his assistant, Harry Lancaster, would come in and tell us what to do out there. It was your classic macro/micromanagement. One coach looking at the big picture, the other guiding us through the game."

The first half ended 34–31, Texas Western, with the Miners maintaining a small lead throughout, but just not quite managing to leverage their size advantage into a sizeable lead. The team had adjusted beautifully to losing star forward Harry Flournoy, who crashed to the floor in the first six minutes and never went back in the game.

The second half played out much as the first, only with more on the line. Kentucky kept trying desperately, and fruitlessly, to get its fast-break going, with TW jamming them up at nearly every turn. With about three-and-a-half minutes to go, TW finally was able to open up a 10-point lead and hung on from there for a seven-point win.

Haskins and most other observers attribute the victory to TW's staunch man-to-man defense, which held one of the best pure shooting teams in the country—close to 50 percent for the season—to just 39 percent from the field. But another curious stat may have had even more to do with the final outcome. TW's 28-for-34 performance from the foul line, versus only 11 foul shots on 13 attempts by Kentucky. Kentucky, in fact, made five more field goals than Texas Western in that game, but that wasn't enough to overcome a whopping 17-point free throw differential.

"Free throws were the difference," insists Jerry Armstrong.

"We were bigger and stronger and faster, and Bobby Joe was running all through their 1-3-1 zone all night," says Nevil Shed. "How do I explain the free throw [disparity] . . . Well, it sure as hell wasn't the referees. They weren't about to give us anything where we were playing. Truth is, Kentucky players were reaching in and fouling us all night, and the refs were calling it."

Whatever went on that night at the foul line, it is unlikely that Don Haskins experienced it. Among his many coaching quirks was a bizarre inability to watch his team shoot free throws during a game.

"He couldn't bear it," says Irv Brown. "He'd even stick a tablet over his face so he couldn't see the court."

Moe Iba, deeply grateful to Haskins for having given him his first coaching job right out of college (where he, of course, played for his old man), watched a film of the entire 1966 final on ESPN in 2016.

His assessment at game's end: "We were better athletically. We jumped higher and ran faster. We deserved to win."

"But, you know," concluded Texas Western's junior Iba Man, "if Jo Jo White's foot doesn't nick that sideline, we're not having this conversation. And that's how history works."

Aftermath

Texas Western got its championship trophy that night in Maryland, but according to the players, not much else, aside from some

WHAT PRICE, GLORY?

The Texas Western Miners celebrate their victory (over Kentucky, not racism). A half-century later, they're still celebrating.

gracious congratulatory greetings from Kentucky's Runts. "You know how the winners always get the ladder to cut down the nets," says Shed. "We never got the ladder. Willie Worsley stood on my head to cut down the net. No favorite treatment for us . . . this wasn't our crowd." In fact, back then no championship teams got ladder boosts, but that doesn't change the eerie postgame feelings experienced by the TW players.

David Lattin recalls how the members of the press hung out on the court after the game, reluctant, for whatever reason, to come into the winning locker room. "I don't think these guys knew what to write. This wasn't supposed to happen. They just stood out there on the court, stunned."

Similarly, the immediate aftermath of the game did not offer a preview of the glory that was to come. There was no invitation to visit with Lyndon Johnson in the White House (those presidential praises and invitations would come many years later). Within the black community as a whole, according to Dr. Martin, the immediate reaction to the events of March 19, 1966, was muted, at best. However, among sports-minded African Americans, particularly those in the Deep South, there was some postgame celebration.

In the southern precincts of the SEC, ACC, and Southwest Conferences, the near-term reaction was more pronounced. The following fall, Perry Wallace enrolled at Vanderbilt, becoming the first black player in the SEC (although his recruitment had clearly begun before the final buzzer went off in Cole Field House). The other southern dominoes quickly fell into line, as coaches, a number of whom had long known what they were missing on the cement courts of New York, Detroit, Philly, and Washington, DC, finally had the imprimatur from their administrations and alumni to head north and start colorizing their rosters. The sole exception to this immediate sea change in recruiting was the Baron himself, who didn't bring in a black player until 1969. But even here, the history is muddled, because Coach Rupp had been looking to bring in African Americans for years. Among the players he attempted to recruit were guard Butch Beard and the great Wes Unseld, later a star center with the NBA's Baltimore Bullets. But Rupp, who was admittedly less than enthusiastic about this recruiting exercise, had a habit of advising all his potential black recruits of what they could expect as the first African Americans in the SEC. And that note of caution was enough to scare them away from Kentucky and from every other major southern university.

And lastly, with respect to Rupp's racial views, it ought to be noted that he played against blacks while in college in Kansas and coached black players in high school in Illinois before coming to Kentucky and gaining a reputation as the consummate bluegrass bigot. The reality, as regards the Baron and his relationship with black America, appears to be more nuanced than popularly thought.

As for Don Haskins, Moe Iba, and their '66 TW players, none did, or has ever, thought of himself as a hero in the civil rights struggle.

"Look, let's face it," says Shed. "If we'd lost that game, the integration of college basketball in the South would have happened anyway, just maybe not quite as fast."

David Lattin, who gave an interview to ESPN for their fiftieth anniversary special and was thanked by the sports network's hosts for "paving the way" for racial equality, says he takes those kinds of compliments with a grain of salt. "We were youngsters, and it was a game. But, hey, I'm proud we helped a lot of black kids get recruited by southern schools. It changed their lives. I wouldn't ever compare us to [the Birmingham march], but what we did do in that game went beyond the court. And I will carry that with me forever."

"Let me tell you something," concludes Willie Worsley. "Anyone who was out there who says he don't appreciate folks asking him about that game fifty years later is a damn fool. I'll be talking about 1966 the rest of my life."

In what was clearly a form of homage to their old coach, at least seven members of the 1966 Miners team went into teaching and/or coaching at the high school or college level. Nearly all Haskins's former players, before and after 1966, who once thought of their rough-hewn leader as an SOB, have come to truly, madly, and deeply love the man.

Only Willie Cager from the championship team, while sincerely thankful for Haskins's life-saving assistance, has some doubts, believing that Haskins's innate "prejudices" led Cager's son to transfer out of UTEP some years back. Cager says his son's relationship with a white woman was a "no-no" for Haskins. That idea is dismissed, with extreme prejudice, by the rest of Cager's teammates, who can't figure why Cager would want to smear the man who once threw a Bronx kid a lifeline and then dipped deep into his pocket to save his life.

David Lattin says that in the gloaming of Haskins's life, he got a call from his former coach at home. Haskins was suffering from a severe case of diabetes and starting to go downhill. "Coach said, 'Hey, Lattin, they cut off my toes!' So I got right on a plane, flew down to El Paso, spent three hours visiting with him and flew back to Houston. That is how I felt, and still feel, about Coach."

Nevil Shed, who served briefly under Haskins as an assistant, feels the same way.

"He treated me like crap back then, and then he gave me a job on his staff, got me another assistant job at the University of Wyoming, and then another job with University of Texas-San Antonio. This man changed my life, gave me a purpose. I visited him a lot when I left El Paso. We'd sit around at breakfast and he'd tell these great, big funny stories. I just loved being around him."

After Haskins died in 2008, Shed drove back to El Paso one more time to view the body with Nolan Richardson.

Standing over Don Haskins in death, they reflected on the many twists and turns on that long road to basketball glory and wondered about the appropriate way to bid goodbye to an Iba Man.

Chapter 9

The Contrast Contest:
Loyola vs. Cincinnati, 1963

"The lid is closed on the basket for the Ramblers."
—Red Rush, radio announcer, WCFL, Chicago

The Loyola University of Chicago Ramblers were the highest scoring team in the country during the 1962–63 season, averaging 92 points a game. They played a wide-open, fast-paced game, racing down the court on fast breaks and almost constantly pressing their opponents on defense, looking to force turnovers. The Ramblers excelled in whipping the ball around the court until someone had an open shot.

"We go out and run and shoot and press," coach George Ireland said at the time, describing Loyola's style as "organized chaos."

Loyola had lost only twice during the regular season and had breezed through the tournament. In the play-in game to get to the Mideast regional, Loyola annihilated Tennessee Tech, 111–42, a margin of victory that remains an NCAA tournament record. They went on to beat Mississippi State and Illinois to advance to the Final Four in Louisville, and then turned back Duke to get to the title game.

But in the championship game against the University of Cincinnati, the Ramblers missed 13 of their first 14 shots. After eight minutes of play they had four points. Cincinnati controlled the boards, sweeping up nearly every rebound. Loyola's leading scorer, All-American Jerry Harkness, didn't score at all in the first half. His teammates picked up some of the slack, but the Ramblers' offense never jelled, and Loyola trailed Cincinnati the entire first half. They were down by eight points at halftime, 29–21, but the score was deceptive. Cincinnati was dominating the game, which was hardly shocking. The University of Cincinnati was the defending national champion—two-time defending champion, in fact. The Bearcats had four starters—Tom Thacker, Ron Bonham, George Wilson, and Tom Yates—returning from the team that had defeated powerhouse Ohio State, led by future NBA Hall of Famers John Havlicek and Jerry Lucas, in the 1962 championship game.

Thacker and Bonham were All-Americans. Cincinnati had the country's best defense, which had given up a miserly 53 points a game. The Bearcats had been ranked number one in the polls all season and had lost only one game, by one point, to a Wichita State team featuring future New York Knick Dave Stallworth, who in that game scored 46 of his team's 65 points.

Cincinnati dispatched Texas and Colorado in the Midwest Regional and crushed Oregon State in the opening Final Four game, 80–46.

The championship game couldn't have been better scripted:

The number one-ranked team, a major public university with a big-time program that had featured one of the games' greatest players, Oscar Robertson, against the number two-ranked team, a small Catholic school that had, until now, languished in basketball obscurity.

The best offense in the men's game against the best defense. Teams with starkly contrasting styles of play: Loyola's hard-charging, high scoring offense and Cincinnati's deliberate, slowed down, controlled tempo. A journeyman coach who had never been to the NCAA tournament before (Ireland) and a high-profile coach (Cincinnati's Ed Jucker) who had just been named Coach of the Year and was on the verge of becoming the first coach in NCAA history to win three consecutive titles.

Plus, both teams had bona fide stars: Harkness, Loyola's take charge small forward; Thacker, Cincinnati's agile and athletic forward; and Bonham, the Bearcats' sharpshooting guard. All three of them were All-Americans that year.

Breaking New Ground

When the two teams lined up to face each other on March 23, 1963, at Louisville's Freedom Hall, there was something else. Something that had never happened before in the twenty-five-year history of the tournament: most of the players on the court, seven out of ten, were African Americans.

To be sure, there had already been prominent black college basketball players. Bill Russell and K. C. Jones starred as the University of San Francisco won consecutive titles in 1955 and 1956. Wilt Chamberlain of Kansas and Seattle's Elgin Baylor were the tournament's Outstanding Players in 1957 and 1958, respectively. Oscar Robertson was a consensus All-America at Cincinnati for three years in a row, from 1958 to 1960.

But college teams below the Mason-Dixon Line, reflecting a society that was still legally segregated, remained all white. And even outside the South, black players were subject to an unspoken but powerful "gentlemen's agreement." One interpretation, according to Ireland, was "two blacks at home, if you had to play them, and one on the road." The other interpretation was "two [blacks] at home, three on the road, and four if you're in trouble."

But things were changing—and not only in college basketball.

The Civil Rights movement was in full swing. The Reverend Dr. Martin Luther King was leading demonstrations—and getting arrested—in cities across the South. The Freedom Riders were organizing black people in the South to vote—and meeting fierce and violent resistance from white racists.

Just before the basketball season began, in early October 1962, riots broke out on the campus of the University of Mississippi when James Meredith—who had to be protected by Federal marshals—became the first black student to enroll in the school. Three thousand troops had to be called in to stop the rioting.

"You could hear 'We Shall Overcome' everywhere," says Jerry Harkness. "We were well aware of what was going on."

In a twist of fate, Harkness, an African American from Harlem, wouldn't have been at the forefront of an historic event in US race relations if it had not been for a chance encounter with Jackie Robinson, the man who broke the color line in Major League Baseball in 1947 when he played for the Brooklyn Dodgers.

Harkness was a star track and cross country runner for DeWitt Clinton High School in the Bronx. He liked playing basketball, but didn't think he was good enough to make his high school team. One afternoon before his senior year, he was shooting around at a YMCA gym near his home in Harlem. Robinson happened to be there that day and complimented Harkness after watching him play, telling him that he was good enough to get a scholarship.

"Nobody ever mentioned that in my life," Harkness told author Michael Lenehan in *Ramblers*, his book about Loyola's championship season. "I never thought of college or a scholarship . . . I said, well, if he thinks I'm pretty good, I'm gonna try out."

Harkness made the team and helped lead DeWitt Clinton to the public school city title over heavily favored Boys High of Brooklyn. He was offered a track scholarship to St. John's University in New York but couldn't meet the school's academic requirements.

Texas Western (which, in another twist of fate, would go on to become the first NCAA championship team to start five black players in 1966), offered Harkness a basketball scholarship, but the dorm he was going to live in burned down and he didn't go. Instead of going to college, Harkness found himself stuck in the projects, working odd jobs.

Making Adjustments

Enter George Ireland.

Ireland had been Loyola's basketball coach for 11 years and none of his teams had gotten to the tournament. Basketball wasn't a priority at Loyola, a small, academically rigorous Jesuit college on Chicago's North Side. The team played in a bandbox gym, and Ireland's recruiting budget was miniscule.

But basketball was a city game, and Chicagoans took their basketball seriously. Loyola's fans were losing patience with the underachieving basketball team, and after consecutive losing seasons at the end of the 1950s, Ireland was hung in effigy on campus. His job was in danger, and he needed to win.

Ireland realized he would have an advantage over other schools if he did something they wouldn't, or couldn't, do—recruit talented black players. He also knew they had to be the right kind of players: not just good athletes, but young men who could fit into the orderly environment at Loyola and accept the school's emphasis on academics over athletics.

"He didn't care if someone was black or green, he just wanted players who could play and stay in school," says John Egan, the point guard on the 1963 team and a pallbearer at Ireland's funeral. "He sold black parents by telling them their kids would graduate—and they usually would."

Harkness's mother liked what she heard, and so did Harkness. He could go to a very good college for free, play basketball, and come out with a degree. But when Harkness arrived in Chicago in the fall of 1959, he discovered that the Loyola campus was more urban enclave than the bucolic environment depicted in the photos that Ireland showed him back in New York. And it was very, very white.

Not only was the student body mostly white, so was the surrounding North Side neighborhood.

"There wasn't much we could do on the North Side," Harkness says. "I didn't have much of a social life. Blacks had to go to the South Side."

He recalled going to a party near campus with other black players. "The girls were scared of us. They didn't know how to act around black guys. We felt we weren't wanted, so we left."

Despite some initial misgivings, Harkness eventually came to terms with the situation and grew to appreciate Loyola. He also had to adjust to Ireland.

"We had a disagreement early on," he says. "I was a very sensitive kid. He yelled at me, and I got really upset. I left practice, and I told him I wasn't coming back. Later we had a long talk, and I told him yelling at me wouldn't work. I told him if I made mistakes he could tell me and I would acknowledge them. We made an agreement, and he never yelled at me again."

By all accounts, Ireland was not a particularly sociable man.

"He was respected, but not necessarily well-liked," Egan says. "He told us he wasn't there to make friends; that he had four friends already and they were all relatives."

While describing Ireland as somewhat of a loner and "set in his ways," Harkness says he and most of the other black players held their coach in high regard.

"He was an excellent guy," says Harkness. "He didn't get along with everybody but he played to win. And he took a lot of pressure for playing four blacks. It was not that popular."

While at local games scouting players for Ireland, Harkness would hear people say that Ireland wasn't there because he "was in Africa, recruiting."

Ireland didn't care. By the time Harkness was a senior in 1962, Ireland had brought in three other black players who were ideal matches for his criteria of combining athletic talent with academic discipline: Ron Miller, a shooting guard from New York; and Vic Rouse and Les Hunter, skilled big men from Nashville, Tennessee. All three—as well as Harkness—graduated from Loyola and Rouse went on to earn four graduate degrees.

Harkness, Miller, Rouse, Hunter, and Egan were eager for the 1962–63 season to begin. They played together the previous season and had done well, winning 23 games, finishing third at the prestigious National Invitation Tournament in New York, and getting ranked as high as 10th in national polls.

"I thought we were really good," Egan says. "We were experienced, we played within a team concept, and we knew what it takes to win."

"It was a perfect setup," Harkness says. "We knew each other so well and our press was really effective."

Egan and Harkness were right. The team's experience, talent, and personalities meshed perfectly.

At 5-foot-10, Egan was considered a bit stocky for a point guard. But Egan started for one of the best high school teams in Chicago, knew how to find the open man, had a good shot, and was a very aggressive player, driving fearlessly to the basket and not afraid to go nose to nose with his man on defense or dive after loose balls.

Harkness wasn't the most talented player on the team, Egan says. But he was considered the best. He was the captain, the only senior, the top scorer—and the leader. Harkness was the type of player who made clutch shots and whom the rest of the team counted on. And he had incredible stamina, his own natural ability as a long-distance runner bolstered by Ireland's relentless training drills.

Like Harkness, Ron Miller, a solid shooting guard with a deadly jump shot, was from Harlem and learned his moves on New York City playgrounds. Les Hunter, the team's 6-foot-7 center, probably had the most natural talent on the team and Vic Rouse, his high school teammate in Nashville, a 6-foot-6 forward with good hands and phenomenal jumping ability, wasn't far behind.

Ireland rarely used his bench players but didn't have to. His "Iron Men" starters were in great shape thanks to his exhausting drills in practice and often played the entire game without a substitution.

The Ramblers scored over 100 points in each of their first six games, thrashing their opponents by an average of more than 40 points a game. Keeping his starters in the game, Ireland didn't hesitate to roll up the score, sometimes to settle a grudge, sometimes to make sure Loyola was getting the attention it needed to rank high in the polls and be tapped for a coveted bid to the NCAA tournament.

Slow Motion

The defending national champion University of Cincinnati didn't need to seek out national attention, having defeated the powerful Ohio State Buckeyes two years in a row for the title.

Instead of running up the score, they slowed the ball down offensively. This "keep away" style of play, as it was called then, was hardly popular when Jucker introduced it in 1960. But Oscar Robertson had graduated, leaving a high octane offense without an engine. A methodical offense and a suffocating defense were the keys to winning in Robertson's aftermath, Jucker reckoned, and he was right.

To be sure, the Cincinnati players had no difficulty putting the ball in the basket, but Jucker correctly ascertained that by using their athleticism to concentrate on defense and stifle the other team's offense, his team would have an advantage.

"We could flat out score," says George Wilson, the team's 6-foot-8 center, "but that's not the style we played."

Controlling the ball, discipline, and teamwork were the keys to Cincinnati's game, according to Wilson.

"The main thing was, we played together, and when you play together, you win together," he says. "Turnovers will kill you, and we had very few turnovers. On defense, we boxed out every time the other team shot the ball, and we led the country in team rebounding."

Wilson came from Chicago, and was well known to Egan, who played against him in high school, and to Harkness, who scouted Cincinnati for Ireland when they played games at Chicago Stadium.

"George Wilson played in the middle," Harkness recalls, "and he stopped everything that went in there."

Flanking Wilson in the frontcourt were Thacker and Bonham, both All-Americans in 1962–63. Larry Shingleton was the 5-foot-10 point guard and Tony Yates, the 6-foot-1 shooting guard.

Everyone except Shingleton had started for the previous season's championship team, and the 1962–63 team picked up where they left off, reeling off 19 straight wins (37 straight going back to the previous season) before the one-point loss to Wichita State.

As Loyola and Cincinnati kept winning, the world around them in the early 1960s kept changing.

A new rock and roll band from England named The Beatles released their first single. A graphic designer from New York named Andy Warhol exhibited paintings of Campbell's soup cans in an art gallery. A young playwright named Edward Albee debuted his new play, *Who's Afraid of Virginia Woolf?*, on Broadway.

The United States was preparing for more flights into outer space, following John Glenn's orbit of the Earth. American soldiers had begun fighting Communists in an obscure country in Southeast Asia called Vietnam. Closer to home, the Cold War brought the United States and the Soviet Union to the brink of nuclear war during the Cuban Missile Crisis, when Soviet missiles aimed at the United States were found on the Caribbean island ninety miles from Florida.

And that most intractable American dilemma, relations between whites and blacks, was, a century after the country's Civil War, getting worse.

Dr. King was being arrested and jailed for demanding basic civil rights for African Americans. A white "citizens committee" in New Orleans offered blacks a one-way ticket if they moved to the North. And George Wallace was sworn in as governor of Alabama in January 1963, pledging to uphold "segregation now, segregation tomorrow, segregation forever."

When Loyola traveled down South, the basketball team saw the ugliness for themselves.

In Houston, fans threw popcorn, soda, and coins at the black players, cursed at them, called them niggers, and chanted "Our team is red hot; your team is all black."

"It was bad," says Harkness. "I was really worried that we weren't getting out of there."

The year before, the black players couldn't stay in the same New Orleans hotel with their white teammates. Outraged, Ireland got in a cab to accompany his black players—only to be told by the African-American cab driver he could be arrested if anyone saw him driving whites and blacks together.

The team kept winning and gaining confidence. "One of the reasons we were successful was that everybody was trying to prove that we really were that good," Egan says.

There was racial tension in Chicago, too. Civil rights demonstrations protesting housing discrimination and other injustices against African Americans were being led by a young preacher named Jesse Jackson, who Harkness got to know through his girlfriend.

And while the team bonded on the court and in the locker room, outside the gym, black and white players parted company.

"We got along great," Harkness says, "but socially they [the white players] would go their way, and we would go ours."

When black players went to the party where there were white girls, Ireland heard about it.

"He called us in and said that in fifteen or twenty years things will be different, but society was not ready right now," Harkness says.

As it turned out, Loyola would soon confront the issue of race in a way they had never imagined, in what came to be called the "Game of Change."

The Ramblers were cruising towards postseason play, highly ranked, leading the country in scoring, with only two losses.

Loyola was selected to go to the NCAA's Mideast Regional, where they would face an all-white team, Tennessee Tech, in a setting that was almost a home game for the Ramblers—Northwestern University's McGaw Hall, less than five miles from the Loyola campus.

Tennessee Tech was hardly a powerhouse and had gotten into the tournament by virtue of winning the Ohio Valley Conference playoff that year. But it was a segregated school, and the team was all white. And the game was being played in a Chicago suburb.

"We heard about it," Harkness says. "People from the black community were calling us and saying 'You gotta win.'"

Tennessee Tech's center, John Adams, was a high school teammate of Egan's. Before the game, Egan told him, "Don't worry. It will all be over quickly."

It was. After the opening tip-off, the teams traded baskets. Then Egan stole the ball, Miller blocked a shot, and Harkness, Miller, and Hunter made consecutive steals. Miller blocked another shot, and Harkness stole the ball again. The score was 16–2. Tennessee Tech ended up making 18 of 82 shots, had a 22 percent field goal percentage, and lost, 111–42.

"I was always accused of running up the scores," Ireland said in an interview with the *Chicago Tribune* after he retired. "I never did that . . . except against those who belittled my players."

Ireland later told *Sports Illustrated* that he deliberately ran up the score on southern teams. "Yes, I poured it to them," he said. "I was twenty years ahead of my time, and I wanted them to wake up and smell the coffee."

The Mideast regional moved to East Lansing, Michigan, where Loyola was scheduled to play—scheduled being the key word—Mississippi State.

Old South, New World

Mississippi State had never been to an NCAA tournament before, but not because their basketball team wasn't good enough. Future Hall of Famer Bailey Howell starred for the Bulldogs in the late '50s, and the team won the SEC title in 1959, 1961, and 1962.

But they didn't go to the tournament because the state of Mississippi had an unwritten, but strictly enforced, rule that its all-white athletic teams could not play against integrated teams.

Mississippi's unabashedly racist governor, Ross Barnett, an arch segregationist who had tried to prevent James Meredith from integrating Ole Miss the year before, made clear he intended to keep the no race-mixing policy in place in 1963, even though the state university had won the SEC title again, earning a trip to the Mideast Regional.

Barnett had the firm support of the state capitol's afternoon newspaper, the *Jackson Daily News*, which editorialized that breaking the state's "unwritten law [would be] diluting a principle that wise men of Mississippi made years ago . . . that a crack at a mythical national championship isn't worth subjecting young Mississippians to the switchblade knife society that integration inevitably spawns."

But Mississippi State coach James "Babe" McCarthy and his players, who had won the SEC crown, very much wanted a crack at a national championship and didn't care who they played. "Race was no issue to us," Bobby Shows, the team's center, said in *Game of Change*, a documentary about the events that culminated in the Loyola-Mississippi State game.

And Dean Colvard, an "outsider" from North Carolina who had become president of the university in 1960, risked his job by supporting them. "Some people thought it was an act of courage," Colvard later wrote. "I thought it was simply doing what needed to be done."

After informing the Southern Association of Colleges and Schools that "unless hindered by competent authority" he would send the team to the NCAA tournament, Colvard received mail informing him a contribution had been made in his name to the NAACP, along with congratulations, because he was "now an HONORARY NIGGER."

Barnett told the association that he did not think it was in the best interest of the school, the state, "or either of the races" for Mississippi State to participate in the tournament. The game in East Lansing was scheduled to be played Friday, March 15. The association's state college board met on Saturday, March 9 to decide the matter. A motion to keep the team out of the tournament was defeated, 8–3, and the board subsequently gave Colvard a vote of confidence.

Students on campus cheered the decision, and the team began to practice. They were set to leave for Michigan on Thursday, March 14. On Wednesday, state senator Billy Mitts, a Barnett ally and former Mississippi State cheerleader, obtained an injunction ordering Colvard and other university officials to refrain "from allowing any athlete enrolled in Mississippi State University to compete in any athletic contest against members of the Negro race."

Effigies of Mitts and his co-conspirator in getting the last-minute court injunction, B. W. Lawson, were strung up at a pep rally on campus. Colvard, McCarthy, athletic director Wade Walker, and a local attorney met on Wednesday afternoon.

"I knew we were in a fight and had to finish it," Colvard wrote in his diary.

By evening, Colvard and a colleague were out of the state, having driven 140 miles east, to Birmingham, Alabama. Walker and McCarthy headed north to Nashville, Tennessee, to slip beyond the reach of Mississippi's jurisdiction, as Walker drove and McCarthy hid on the floorboard of their car.

The players, scheduled to leave on a chartered plane early Thursday morning, were kept in the dark. When they woke up, they were told there was a change in plans. A decoy team of nonstarters would go to a private airport in Starkville with the trainer. If law enforcement officials stopped them, the starters and the first three substitutes would drive to a nearby town where a second plane was waiting to fly them to Michigan.

The second plane wasn't needed. Local law enforcement officials sympathetic to the players didn't overly exert themselves trying to serve an injunction to Colvard or McCarthy, who weren't at the airport anyway. Told the coast was clear, the first team joined the scrubs and flew to Nashville, where they picked up McCarthy and Walker.

In East Lansing, no one was sure if Mississippi State was coming. Rumors abounded: the team had been prevented from leaving the state; the plane had been turned back; the game was cancelled.

But the Bulldogs did make it to East Lansing, arriving to a flurry of publicity that would cascade as the teams stepped on the court to play the "Game of Change."

For some, however, it was unwelcome change.

Hate mail poured into Loyola.

You're not good enough to beat white boys.

Don't show up unless you want your neck in a noose.

Ireland intercepted as many letters as he could, but some got through to the players.

"They knew our names, they knew where we lived," Harkness recalls. "It was a little nerve-racking."

But the Mississippi State basketball players just wanted to play basketball.

At the time, the game itself loomed much larger than the social implications of the off the court publicity, according to Egan. "They were the best team we faced so far," he says. "If we lost, the season was over."

But the rest of the country was riveted by the shattering of a once insurmountable racial barrier: an all-white team from one of the country's most segregated states—Mississippi would not ratify the Thirteenth Amendment ending slavery for another thirty years—playing an integrated (and then some) team for the first time.

Indeed, when Harkness stepped on to center court to shake hands with Mississippi State captain Joe Dan Gold, the arena lit up from the popping flashbulbs of the unusually large contingent of photographers.

"It wasn't until those flashbulbs went off when we shook hands that I realized this was more than just a game," Harkness says. "I knew this was special."

Mississippi State jumped out to a 7–0 lead, which may have been the worst thing that could have happened for them. Like Cincinnati's Ed Jucker, Babe McCarthy believed in slowing the game down when his team had a lead. "They can't score when we have the ball," he told his players.

But Loyola "was quicker with better athletes," MSU's play-by-play announcer Jack Cristil recalled afterwards. Loyola gambled on defense, stole the ball, and quickly ran off ten points to tie the game, and they pulled ahead 26–19 at halftime.

Loyola opened up 10-point leads in the second half, but Mississippi State kept coming back, twice pulling within three points. Then Ron Miller stole a pass at half-court, raced to the basket, soared above the rim, and slam-dunked the ball with a two hand flush.

That was not, as MSU's Don Posey told author Michael Lenehan, "the kind of stuff that we were used to seeing." Soon afterwards, Egan jumped in front of MSU star Leland Mitchell, drew a foul, and Mitchell was out of the game with his fifth foul.

The final score was 61–51—Loyola's lowest scoring game of the season.

When Mississippi State returned home to Starkville, "the cars were lined up for 20 miles with thousands and thousands of kids there to see us," Bobby Shows told the Associated Press thirty-five years later. "The KKK boys were a nasty, ugly minority. Most people weren't like that. And even though we lost, we came home as winners."

As one resident put it in a letter to Colvard, "the state had lived in the past for too long."

Led by Harkness's 33 points, Loyola went on to beat Illinois, 79–64, in the Midcast regional final to advance to the Final Four in Louisville.

Although the Final Four was not the national phenomenon then that we know now, it was clearly a major sporting event. The first national TV contract had just been signed to syndicate the game across the country and Louisville's Freedom Hall was sold out to watch Loyola, Duke, Oregon State, and Ohio State compete for the national championship.

Oregon State was the dark horse, having upset fourth-ranked Arizona State in the West Regional to get to Louisville. The team's stars were seven-footer Mel Counts and Terry Baker, who also was the quarterback for the school's football team and the only Heisman Trophy winner to ever play in a Final Four game.

Duke was not then the national power it is now, but had made two previous appearances in the tournament and was riding a

20-game win streak. The Blue Devils were led by two outstanding players: Jeff Mullins, a future NBA All-Star, and Art Heyman, who averaged 25 points a game and was named National Player of the Year that season by the Associated Press.

Despite being in the NCAA tournament for only the first time, Loyola, boasting the nation's most potent offense, was not being taken lightly. "For all its madcap, undisciplined ways," *Sports Illustrated* wrote in its Final Four preview, "[Loyola] has looked hotter than anybody in the regionals."

But the clear favorite was the defending champion, Cincinnati, going for a record third straight title and playing in their fifth straight Final Four.

Sure enough, Cincinnati proceeded to destroy Oregon State in the semifinal, 80–46.

Meanwhile, Loyola took control over Duke quickly in the first half and cruised to a 13-point lead at halftime. Led by Heyman, who was later named the Most Outstanding Player in the tournament, the Blue Devils stormed back to within three points with four and a half minutes to go.

Undaunted, Loyola's well-conditioned starters, despite having played the whole game, went into another gear, harassing Duke, stealing the ball, snatching away rebounds, and racing down court to score on fast breaks for ten quick unanswered points.

Loyola went on to outscore Duke, 20–4, for the rest of the game to win, 94–75.

Once again, Loyola had spanked an all-white team from the South, and Les Hunter, who led the Ramblers with 29 points and 18 rebounds, admitted it felt good.

"I wanted to run it up on those guys," he told *Sports Illustrated*'s Ron Fimrite years later. "We weren't just beating players. We were beating a student body, a system, the Klan. We weren't just playing a team, we were playing an ideology."

Race was also an issue in the next game, but for a very different reason—for the first time in the history of the Final Four, a majority of the players in the championship game were African American.

It was also the only championship where one team (Loyola) never substituted and Cincinnati only played one sub for a few minutes.

Clashing Styles

Above all, it was a great matchup of two excellent teams that couldn't have been more different: the nation's best offense vs. the best defense. A fast, up-tempo offense vs. a slow, deliberate one. One coach (Ireland) who hated to spend time going over opponents' plays before a game vs. another (Jucker) who couldn't spend enough time running through the other team's plays in practice and poring over scouting reports.

George Ireland and his players wanted respect; Ed Jucker and his team wanted to make history.

At first, the country's highest scoring team could hardly score at all. Loyola kept missing, while Cincinnati controlled the backboards and worked the ball around on offense to get good shots, maintaining a comfortable lead throughout the first half, which ended 29–21 in their favor.

The country's best defense played like it, not allowing Jerry Harkness, Loyola's best player, to score a single point. "It was the first time I realized I could be stopped," Harkness said later.

Cincinnati extended its lead in the second half as Tom Thacker kept the clamps on Harkness, battled for rebounds (Thacker would eventually get 15, George Wilson 13), and scored with precision.

With 12 minutes to go, Cincinnati led by 15 points, 45–30. Jerry Harkness still hadn't scored.

"Come on, come on," Ireland told his players. "You know we can score in bunches. Let's get that ball."

"It is called keep-away. Come out and get me if you can."

Loyola began a full-court press, forced turnovers, and chipped away at the lead. Instead of trying to pull away from Loyola, Jucker opted for the conservative strategy that had brought him success in the past. As fans in Louisville booed, the Bearcats slowed the game down, playing "keep away" on offense, holding the ball instead of looking for an open shot.

But instead of maintaining their lead, the Bearcats saw it diminish, as Ron Miller, Vic Rouse, and John Egan hit consecutive shots to cut the deficit to nine, while Cincinnati turned the ball over, committed fouls, and missed free throws.

"Oh, is this a ball game now."

With less than five minutes to go, Harkness hit a turnaround jump shot for his first basket of the game and then intercepted a pass by Thacker, sped downcourt, and scored on a layup to bring Loyola within three points.

Stubbornly, Cincinnati continued to stall and hold the ball on offense. After trading free throws, Harkness snaked his way through a crowd underneath the basket to score again and cut the lead to two with just two and half minutes to play.

The slowdown strategy clearly seemed to be backfiring, but George Wilson says Cincinnati had no regrets. "It didn't hurt us—that had been our style for three years."

Wilson does think the referees hurt the Bearcats, pointing to what Cincinnati loyalists described as questionable calls leaving Thacker, Wilson, and Yates all with four fouls in the final minutes, hampering them on offense and defense.

One particularly egregious travel call on Ron Miller very late in the game was indisputably missed. But Cincinnati was up by one point with 12 seconds left when Larry Shingleton was deliberately fouled by Harkness and stepped to the free throw line for a one-and-one.

The left-handed Shingleton smoothly swished the first free throw, putting the Bearcats up by two. In an era before the three-point shot, one more and the game would almost certainly be out of reach for Loyola. But Shingleton looked surprisingly awkward as he shot the second free throw, which bounced off the front rim of the basket.

Hunter grabbed the rebound and whipped the ball upcourt to Miller, who took at least one extra step before he hit Harkness, who quickly nailed a mid-range jump shot on the left side of the key, tying the game and sending it into overtime.

"It's a dilly. It's a great one."

Harkness made the first basket in overtime to give Loyola its first lead of the game. The Loyola captain's legendary stamina was paying off, and he ended up with 14 points in less than ten minutes. "I wasn't tired," Harkness recalls. "I was just getting started."

Thacker and Wilson responded with a picture perfect pick-and-roll to tie the game. Miller intercepted a Cincinnati pass, dribbled to get open, and drained a 20-foot jump shot, putting Loyola back on top. But after a Loyola miss, Thacker grabbed a rebound and launched a full-court bomb to Shingleton, who scored his only basket of the night to tie the game up again.

"Oh, this is action!"

With 1:49 left to play, it was Loyola's turn to stall and the Ramblers appeared to be playing for the last shot with the score tied. But Shingleton tied up Egan, and the two 5-foot-10 guards faced each other for a jump ball. Although about 20 pounds heavier, Egan timed his jump perfectly to tap the ball to Miller in the backcourt.

Cincinnati, the masters of the stall, got a taste of their own medicine as supposedly undisciplined Loyola expertly weaved the ball between Hunter, Miller, and Rouse with the Bearcats watching as if mesmerized.

"They were frustrated," Egan says. "It was the first time I could see they were frightened."

As the seconds ticked off the clock, Miller passed the ball to Harkness on the left side of the basket. Harkness dribbled into the corner and went up to shoot, but Bonham got a hand on the ball at the last second, forcing Harkness to pass to Hunter on the foul line.

Time was running out and Hunter shot a high, arching jump shot that landed on the right side of the rim and bounced into the air. "We all just seemed to freeze in place," Yates told *Sports Illustrated* years later. "It was as if we were frozen in time."

George Wilson figured Cincinnati, who had 12 more rebounds in the game at that point than Loyola, would get this one too. But

The biggest shot in the history of Loyola University of Chicago basketball: Vic Rouse (40) jumps over Cincinnati's Tom Thacker (25) to put in the winning basket with time running out in overtime in the 1963 championship game as Jerry Harkness (15) looks on.

the 6-foot-8 center had been pulled away from the basket to guard Hunter.

That left the 6-foot-2 Thacker under the basket with the 6-foot-6 Vic Rouse. Egan watched from the other side of the basket. "I knew Rouse could jump very well from a standstill position," he recalls.

"I've played with Les a long time and I know how he shoots," Rouse said in interviews afterward, "so I was able to get in position for the rebound."

With the ball above the rim, Rouse extended his arms straight up, soared above Thacker, caught the ball with both hands, and gently banked it against the backboard and through the hoop as time ran out.

"I felt suspended in air—you could almost say it was an out-of-body experience—and I was totally focused," Rouse said later. "I shot that ball, and it went in."

"It's over. We won. We won. We won. Loyola won the ball game."

Chapter 10

The Slickers vs. the Hicks . . . and Wilt: North Carolina vs. Kansas, 1957

The 1957 championship game taps into a rich, deep vein in basketball history.

James Naismith, Phog Allen, Red Auerbach, Louie Carnesecca, Dean Smith, Frank McGuire, and Wilt Chamberlain were all, in one way or another, connected with the game.

And the matchup between The University of North Carolina and The University of Kansas pitted two schools now nearly unrivaled in the pantheon of elite college basketball programs.

After inventing the game of "basket ball" by putting up two peach baskets and giving a scrum of young men a leather ball at a YMCA gymnasium in Springfield, Massachusetts, in December 1891, Naismith acquired a medical degree and joined the Kansas faculty in 1898, where he became the school's first men's basketball coach.

Naismith developed a close relationship with one of his former players and assistants, Forrest "Phog" Allen, who succeeded Naismith when he retired and went on to win nearly 600 games at Kansas over almost forty years, including a national championship in 1952.

Allen was known as the "Father of Basketball Coaching" and helped found the coaches association which went on to create the NCAA Tournament. Allen's basketball lineage was impeccable, and unrivaled. His program was one of the very best. If you knew anything about college basketball in the 1950s, you knew about Phog Allen.

In 1954, a very tall and very talented young basketball player named Wilton Norman Chamberlain was attracting national attention.

A senior at Overbrook High School in Philadelphia, Chamberlain was close to seven feet tall and dominated the city's basketball scene.

He was a superb athlete who seemed to score and rebound at will; he also excelled on the school's track and field team. In Chamberlain's three years on the varsity, Overbrook only lost three games and won two city championships. During the summer, he was already playing against pros in the Catskill Mountains of New York.

Chamberlain could easily have become a professional after he graduated. But he wanted to get a college education, and he wanted to become a better player before he entered the NBA. Not surprisingly, he was the most highly sought-after recruit in the country.

Allen was determined to bring Chamberlain to Kansas. He was nearing the end of his career and desperately wanted to go out with another national championship—or two or three. He went to Philadelphia and charmed the young man's parents. Wilt was impressed by Allen's pedigree and seduced by his vision of competing for national titles under the tutelage of a legendary coach at an idyllic campus free—he thought—from racial segregation.

He signed on to become a Jayhawk.

(The approximately $15,000 to $20,000 in cash Chamberlain later claimed to have received from Kansas alums while he was there was also presumably a factor.)

The Turnaround

In the early and mid-1950s, the big basketball school in North Carolina was located in Raleigh, not Chapel Hill. Under Everett Case, North Carolina State routinely won conference championships, went to national tournaments—and during one stretch beat North Carolina in 15 straight games.

Although UNC was considered a football school, there was a contingent of alumni and school officials who wanted to turn the basketball program around. They seized their opportunity in 1952.

Frank McGuire, a brash, confident, streetwise New Yorker who dressed like a million bucks and knew everyone who mattered in the city's thriving playground and scholastic basketball scene, had just coached St. John's University to the national championship game against Kansas.

Losing to Phog Allen in 1952 was no mark of shame. McGuire had gotten the Redmen to their first Big Dance and was riding high. But despite his success and deep roots in New York City—he grew up the son of an Irish cop in Greenwich Village with twelve siblings—McGuire was open to a possible change of scenery.

His son had cerebral palsy and could be treated at Chapel Hill, and the family could live in a big house and not in a cramped apartment. Plus McGuire had ties to Carolina from his days in the Navy.

UNC offered the thirty-nine-year-old McGuire a salary of $12,000, and he accepted.

Now all he needed was players—and Frank McGuire knew where to get them.

"I believe we know more about basketball in New York," he once told the *New York Times*. "Even the players are better. A kid has to dodge and fake just to get on the subway. It makes him a good feinter just to walk on the streets."

The centerpiece of McGuire's grand plan to establish North Carolina as a basketball power was Lennie Rosenbluth, a 6-foot-5 scoring machine from the Bronx who had an uncanny ability to put the ball in the basket with a deft assortment of hook shots, jump shots, and layups.

Like Wilt, Rosenbluth was good enough to play against college stars and professionals in the Catskills in the prestigious summer league the Borscht Belt hotels sponsored to attract and entertain the New Yorkers, many of them Jewish, who patronized these summer havens in the mountains to escape the oppressive city heat before the advent of air-conditioning.

"That's really where I developed the most," Rosenbluth says. "I was still in high school and I was playing against college ballplayers, more experienced guys who were bigger and stronger. Everything came together for me. I could see the court better, and the game slowed down. I became a much better player in the mountains."

Red Auerbach coached the Kutsher's Hotel summer league team and thought Rosenbluth was good enough to work out with the Boston Celtics before school started. Not surprisingly, Rosenbluth also caught the eye of college coaches and the New York scouts who worked for them, notably "Uncle Harry" Gotkin, a sideline fixture on the city's courts.

Gotkin steered Rosenbluth to Everett Case at North Carolina State, who offered him a scholarship. When he went down to Raleigh to visit the school in late spring and sign the papers, he was surprised to find dozens of players assembled in the gym for a tryout to make the team.

Rosenbluth told Case he hadn't been expecting to play competitively and wasn't in shape. Case told him not to worry about it and just go out and play.

"I got blisters, got tired, and my legs were hurting," Rosenbluth says. "I looked terrible. The next day I couldn't move."

Case summoned Rosenbluth to his office.

"Son, we only have one scholarship left, and we don't want to waste it," Case said.

Big mistake.

When Auerbach invited Rosenbluth to Madison Square Garden for a Celtics game, he sat next to McGuire. The prodigy and the coach took an immediate liking to each other. After being rejected from NC State, Gotkin told Rosenbluth that Frank McGuire wanted to recruit him.

"But I don't want to go to St. John's," Rosenbluth said.

When they met again, McGuire told Rosenbluth he was leaving St. John's. "I told him, 'Coach, wherever you go, I'm going with you.'"

Rosenbluth enrolled as a freshman at UNC in the fall of 1953. McGuire had his star. Now he needed a supporting cast.

Building the Underground Railroad

Using his Gotham connections, coaching bona fides, authenticity as a no-bullshit New Yorker, and considerable powers of persuasion, in 1954 McGuire lured a bumper crop of first-rate prospects from the cacophony of the city streets to the slower tempo of Tobacco Road.

The fabled "underground railroad" that shuttled top players from New York City to Chapel Hill, North Carolina, and forever altered the school's basketball history had officially opened for business.

Tommy Kearns, a cocky playmaking guard from the Bronx who also liked to shoot and played for future St. John's coach Lou Carnesecca in Manhattan (even though his family had moved to New Jersey), was the catalyst on the court.

Two Brooklyn boys, Pete Brennan, a rugged forward with a nice touch, and Joe Quigg, a 6-foot-9 center who could rebound, pass, and shoot, provided height and muscle underneath. Bob Cunningham, a taller than average guard at 6-foot-3 and a hustling defensive specialist, doing whatever dirty work needed to be done, accompanied Kearns in the backcourt.

This talented quartet attracted considerable attention while playing, as required at the time, on the freshman team. As sophomores, they joined fellow New Yorkers Rosenbluth and Bob Young, a 6-foot-6 forward from Queens who came off the bench to back up McGuire's big men.

Although the New Yorkers didn't know each other well back in the city, they shared a common playground ethos, cultivated by McGuire, characterized by aggressive play, cuts to the basket, and passing the ball around while looking for the open man.

Just as important, they became familiar with each other on the court and knew who liked to do what and when. And the more they played together, the more they played against the other teams in the Atlantic Coast Conference (then only a few years old), the more they realized they could win.

Before the 1956–57 season began, Rosenbluth, as captain, called a team meeting.

"We looked at the schedule," he says. "We all bought into the idea that no one could beat us and the only way we could lose was if there was dissension. I was the go-to guy, but I told them if I was shooting too much, let me know. We had five guys who could take the last shot. We were aggressive, we could run, we had great shooters, and we out-rebounded every team we played. We were super, super confident."

Surprises at Kansas

One thousand miles away in Lawrence, Kansas, the KU Jayhawks were hardly filled with doubt about the upcoming season. When Chamberlain enrolled, Allen was exuberant.

"Wilt Chamberlain's the greatest basketball player I ever saw," he said. "With him, we'll never lose a game. We could win the national championship with Wilt, two sorority girls, and two Phi Beta Kappas."

Wilt's spectacular freshman year only heightened expectations. His arrival on the varsity couldn't come fast enough for Kansas basketball fans.

With Phog "Doc" Allen coaching (Allen was also a practicing osteopath) and Wilt Chamberlain playing, how could Kansas lose?

But Allen wouldn't be on the bench. Contrary to his—and Chamberlain's—expectation, the university didn't waive the school's mandatory retirement age of seventy, even for the Hall of Fame coach.

The basketball gods had thrown Wilt the first of many curves he would see in his career.

Dick Harp, Allen's assistant and one of his former players, stepped into the great man's shoes.

"He was a good coach, technically very sound," says Harp's assistant coach Jerry Waugh. "But at times he was a little uptight with the kids. He put a lot of pressure on himself."

To be sure, there *was* a lot of pressure on Harp. He had Wilt, didn't he? And he was filling in for a local legend, who many—including one of Allen's sons—felt should still be coaching and would be doing a better job than his replacement.

The team respected Harp, according to Waugh. In his autobiography, Wilt described Harp as a "good, decent, moral man." But, he added, "I sure as hell don't think he was much of a basketball coach."

At the time, however, Wilt kept his feelings to himself.

By all accounts, Chamberlain was an easygoing guy who liked people but who also had a very healthy ego.

"He was special, and he knew it," Waugh says.

Nonetheless, "The team had great *esprit de corps*," Waugh recalls. "They liked each other and played well together."

Most of the starters had in fact played together for the past two years and had local roots. Senior forward Maurice King, the team's only other African American besides Chamberlain, was from Kansas City, Missouri; Senior co-captains John Parker and Gene Elstun, a guard and forward respectively, were from Shawnee-Mission; and center/forward Lew Johnson, a 6-foot-6 senior, was from Kansas City, Kansas.

Ron Loneski, a sturdy 6-foot-5 forward from the Midwest, replaced Johnson in the starting lineup as the season progressed.

Wilt, Waugh says, "kind of fit in. The other players accepted him, there wasn't any jealousy. All the players knew Wilt was important and that they had to play through him. That part of it was easy. The fact that he was a good person helped as well."

Chamberlain's college debut in the season opener against Northwestern was nothing if not auspicious: he scored 52 points and hauled down 31 rebounds. Both statistics remain school records more than six decades later.

In the next game against Marquette, Wilt blocked 14 shots and held Marquette's center to four points while scoring 39 points and getting 22 rebounds. The Jayhawks reeled off ten more wins before finally losing to Iowa State on a last-second shot at the buzzer.

Chamberlain was everything Phog Allen hoped he would be.

"He was an exceptional athlete," Waugh says. "He was tall and graceful, with good balance and jumping ability. Wilt was also very strong. He lifted weights and worked out with the shot putters. And people didn't realize how quick he was."

Chamberlain was also a savvy player, Waugh says.

"He had a good sense of where the ball was, a natural feel for that kind of thing. He could get off his man and help out without fouling. The other team didn't know when to put it up. They were afraid if they shot the ball Wilt would get it—and he did."

Opposing teams responded with near continual physical harassment and occasional verbal taunts.

Coaches would position players in front and back of Chamberlain and have players run down the court in front of him, hoping he would run into them.

"A lot of their strategy was to try and [get] Wilt fouled out," Waugh says. "But he was a patient person and didn't lose his temper."

Some teams, such as Iowa State, simply froze the ball when they had possession. But Kansas only lost one other game the entire season and cruised into the championship tournament as the team to beat.

Tobacco Road to Tournament

North Carolina, meanwhile, didn't quite cruise, but they weren't losing either.

After reeling off three early wins, Rosenbluth made a declaration that he would keep repeating throughout the season, much to McGuire's consternation: "Coach, we're going to win them all!"

After surviving an overtime scare from South Carolina, the Tar Heels' confidence got a further boost when the team traveled to Raleigh and won its first Dixie Classic, a prestigious holiday tournament hosted by NC State that always included fellow ACC powerhouses Duke and Wake Forest.

Despite being undefeated, Rosenbluth says the team stayed loose, even when games got tight.

Not only were the New York kids used to playing with each other in college after a season and half, they—and their coach—

shared an almost telepathic schoolyard mentality that relied on instinctive ball movement, not set plays.

"We never had a play, except for taking the ball out of bounds," says Rosenbluth. "It was just like the schoolyard, that's exactly what it was. We did practice situations; like what to do, or not to do, if the game was tied with a minute left. And McGuire had a rule: the ball is like gold, and you never throw gold away."

North Carolina also had a secret weapon.

Assistant coach James "Buck" Freeman was yet another New Yorker, but he was the ying to McGuire's yang. McGuire was dapper, smooth, and outgoing; Freeman was rumpled, harried, and introspective. McGuire excelled at game psychology, motivation, and grasping the Big Picture; Freeman was the master tactician, sweating every little detail, the classic Xs & Os guy.

Freeman had in fact been McGuire's coach when he played for St. John's as part of the famous "Wonder Five" in the early 1930s. His battles with alcoholism had derailed his major college head coaching career, but his love for the game never faltered, nor did his encyclopedic knowledge of it.

McGuire had insisted that Freeman accompany him to Chapel Hill, where Freeman's tiny apartment, appropriately enough, was practically adjacent to the gym.

"He had us sit at the foul line at the end of practice and wouldn't let us go into the locker room until we made ten free throws," says Bob Young. "We had to be seated with our legs extended because he wanted us to learn to extend our arms and finish in front of the rim."

During a game, Kearns told author Adam Lucas in *The Best Game Ever*, "Freeman might pull you aside and say, 'That guy who's guarding you crosses legs defensively. When he does that, that's when you can beat him and take him to the hoop.' You'd go back out on the court and that's exactly what would happen."

North Carolina's unbeaten streak appeared to be in jeopardy in February in College Park, Maryland, when the Tar Heels found themselves trailing the Terrapins by two points with two minutes to go.

Ever the master manipulator, McGuire pulled his team's strings by telling them it looked like they were about to lose, which had to happen sometime, so "let's go graciously. When the horn goes off, go right over and congratulate those Maryland boys."

The players couldn't believe it. Was this the same man who spent countless hours in practice methodically "practicing with the clock" for just such situations?

It was—and it was also the same coach who always looked for an edge, even when he had to trick his own ballplayers, who he knew would react strongly to any notion of conceding.

They did and went on to eventually beat Maryland in double overtime.

North Carolina survived another scare at the ACC tournament. Meeting Wake Forest in the championship game—after three previous bruising encounters with the Demon Deacons during the regular season—North Carolina was down by a point with under a minute to go.

This time McGuire was in no mood to play psychological games. He may not have had set plays, but during the timeout, he told his team what to do: get the damn ball to Rosenbluth.

They did, and Rosenbluth swept across the lane and lofted his patented hook shot at the top of the key just as he collided with a Wake Forest defender. The shot went in, but was the contact a charge or a foul? The referee decided it was the latter, and after Rosenbluth made the free throw to put UNC up by two points, the Tar Heels were on their way to the NCAA tournament with an unblemished record.

Showdown

Nonetheless, Kansas, with only two losses—and the services of Wilt Chamberlain—was favored to win. The Jayhawks proceeded to make the prognosticators look good, taking on the fourth-ranked (and all white) Southern Methodist Mustangs before a hostile crowd in Dallas, SMU's home turf. In a rough game marred by ugly racist taunts directed at Chamberlain and King, KU prevailed in overtime in an impressive road win.

After breezing past Oklahoma City University in the regional finals, Kansas had the luxury of going back to their home state, because the national championship that year was being played in Kansas City, Missouri—a mere thirty-five miles from the KU campus in Lawrence, which meant a virtual home game for the Jayhawks.

In the semifinal game on Friday night, March 22, 1957, at the Kansas City Municipal Auditorium, Kansas took the penultimate step towards the crown they expected to claim the next night by romping past San Francisco, 80–56.

By contrast, the Tar Heels barely squeaked into the championship game. They made it to Kansas City easily enough, mowing down Yale, Canisius, and Syracuse, but the semifinal game against the Big Ten's Michigan State was a different story.

The Spartans were led by Jumpin' Johnny Green, a dynamic sophomore forward who would go on to be an All-American and star for the New York Knicks. Green, who gave Rosenbluth and North Carolina fits with eight blocked shots and 19 rebounds, got fouled with six seconds left in the second overtime and Michigan State up by two.

North Carolina was on life support and needed a miracle. They got it. The future NBA All-Star went to the line to shoot a one-and-one. Green's free throw looked good, but bounced off the rim.

Pete Brennan got the rebound. He knew there was very little time left, so he raced downcourt as fast as he could, pulled up for a jumper at the top of the key, and, as the game clock wound down, made the shot.

North Carolina had survived, and went on to outlast Michigan State in the third overtime.

The game had gone past midnight. In less than twenty hours, the exhausted Tar Heels would be back on the court to play in the national championship game.

As game time approached, the already shadowy auditorium

became enveloped in a haze of cigarette smoke as 10,000 fans filled the seats, along with an unusually large national press corps and North Carolina governor Luther Hodges, who proceeded to take a seat on the Tar Heels bench.

North Carolina was unbeaten, but Kansas was favored by at least three points.

The Jayhawks, easy victors in the semifinal game, were playing in front of friends and family.

And their star was the best college basketball player in the country.

The Tar Heels, coming off the draining triple-overtime win, would be playing far away from home in front of a decidedly inhospitable audience—and their tallest player was nearly half a foot shorter than Chamberlain.

As it happened, North Carolina wasn't particularly fazed by the lack of fans—by a scheduling quirk, they only had eight home games over the course of a grueling season.

"We were used to it," says Young.

As for Chamberlain, several of North Carolina's best players had already played against him in the Catskills.

"No big man could play like him," says Rosenbluth. "You couldn't stop him one-on-one. But the main thing was that after we played against Chamberlain, we weren't afraid of him. We weren't in awe of him. We saw that the way to beat him was to keep the ball away from him, keep him off balance, and box him out."

"When we saw Wilt in the Catskills," Young recalls, "he was a big bony kid who could do a lot of things you wouldn't expect such a big guy to do. He was agile, and he could run, shoot, and rebound. But we saw that he wasn't a banger. He didn't have an aggressive nature. That was not part of his makeup. He was not that kind of guy.

"So when we faced him in the championship game we had no fear, because we had already played against him," Young says. "We knew Wilt was a great player, but he was not the intimidating person he would have been if we hadn't played against him."

About to coach the biggest game of his life, Frank McGuire, the city slicker who "reeked of success and confidence" according to Pete Brennan, never broke character.

There was a way to beat Kansas, he was sure, and only one way: contain Chamberlain.

"We're not playing Kansas now," he told his team. "We're playing Chamberlain. Kansas can't beat you, but Chamberlain can.

"If we can concentrate on Wilt, harass him, keep the ball away from him as much as possible, and keep him away from the basket, we will win."

The players bought it.

"We felt like it was going to be our five against their one," Tommy Kearns recalled in *The Best Game Ever*, "and I liked those odds."

Having laid the strategy, McGuire wanted an edge.

Psych-Out

He asked each of the players if they were afraid of Chamberlain.

When he got to Kearns, the shortest starter, McGuire looked him right in the eye, and asked him directly: "Are you afraid of Chamberlain?"

Kearns said he wasn't. "Then you're jumping center against him," McGuire replied.

Then McGuire went to work on Kansas.

First he had his team manager commandeer the bench that had been assigned to Kansas, upsetting Jayhawks coach Dick Harp. Then McGuire didn't even appear on the floor until a few minutes before the opening whistle.

The tip-off was the coup de grâce. McGuire sent 5-foot-11 Tommy Kearns out to jump center against 7-foot-1 (or 7-foot-3, depending on who's measuring) Wilt Chamberlain. As the referee held the ball up with his arm outstretched, Kearns crouched down, as if he were going to spring up and challenge Wilt, who towered over him.

"Wilt looked down at him like a Great Dane would look down at a little dog," Rosenbluth says.

McGuire later said that he wanted Wilt to wonder if he was crazy. But he also clearly embarrassed Wilt in front of 10,000 people, made fun of him—exactly the kind of move that might get under the skin of a sensitive young man who happened to be freakishly tall.

McGuire also wanted to get under the skin of his coaching counterpart.

"The tip-off was McGuire's way of sending a message that we would do things differently," says Young. "He wanted to piss off Harp."

He succeeded.

"McGuire was a good coach, but he was also a New York gambler, a showman, and Dick Harp was the opposite," says Jerry Waugh. "Harp was a Kansas boy. When McGuire sent Kearns out to jump center and made a show of that, it bothered Dick. It was an attitude, like the New York slickers are coming to town to show up the Kansas hicks. It was orchestrated that way and it got to Harp."

Besides the psych-out factor, the tip-off gambit was extremely practical: no one on Carolina was going to outjump Wilt anyway, so why not have the big guys try and grab the ball when Wilt tipped it, or at least have a head start on getting downcourt and preventing Kansas from getting a first easy basket?

Wilt was able to tip the ball to Kansas, but as soon as he began taking his long strides to set up on offense the North Carolina game plan became clear: wherever Wilt Chamberlain went that night, he was going to have a lot of company.

Matching Up

Six-foot-nine Joe Quigg got in front of Wilt, 6-foot-5 Lennie Rosenbluth got behind him, aided by 6-foot-6 Pete Brennan—and more often than not, one of the guards also helped out.

But collapsing on Chamberlain left most of the other Kansas players open.

"If they were going to beat us," Rosenbluth remembers, "they were going to have to score from the outside."

They didn't.

Kansas looked for Wilt, but found it hard to get the ball in to him. When his teammates shot, they missed.

"They couldn't put a pea in the ocean," was the way Wilt remembered it in his autobiography. "With North Carolina surrounding me, they were all wide open, but they just couldn't buy a basket."

On defense, Kansas opted for a box–and–one, with Maurice King shadowing Rosenbluth.

It was a mistake, leaving the other North Carolina players free to shoot over the zone.

And if they did shoot, they were under orders to make sure Wilt wasn't close to the basket.

"If he was under the basket, we wouldn't shoot," Rosenbluth says.

On offense, Kansas set up for Wilt, but couldn't get the ball to him and seemed frustrated. By contrast, Carolina patiently passed the ball around the perimeter, outside the zone, until they found an open man.

The early tempo of the game was set: Carolina in rhythm, hitting their shots; Kansas out of sync, forcing shots and missing.

McGuire, fearful of Chamberlain's demoralizing (and crowd pleasing) shot-blocking ability, instructed his players not to shoot unless Wilt was drawn out away from the basket and in their line of vision.

Carolina pulled ahead, 19–7, "before we knew what hit us," Chamberlain recalled.

"I felt like they were playing into our hands," Cunningham said in *The Greatest Game Ever Played*. "Our strategy on offense was simple: stay away from the middle and stay away from Wilt, because if you challenge him, he will knock it down your throat. Take the ball to the sides and hit those corner shots. When we started hitting those shots, Kansas knew they were getting a game."

Harp began to adjust, and Kansas went to man-to-man defense while on offense Wilt began to hit some shots. The Jayhawks reeled off 10 points to pull within two.

But then Brennan blew past two defenders—including Chamberlain—and drove to the basket for a much-needed Carolina answer to the Kansas run. Rosenbluth took over, hitting several turnaround jumpers, while Kansas couldn't keep pace on offense, not being able to find Wilt inside and subsequently missing open outside jump shots.

"North Carolina had players in front and back of Wilt and kept him away from the ball," Waugh recalls. "That puts a lot of pressure on your shooters. If they go ahead and shoot and miss, that's when the collar tightens. It took us awhile to get back into the game."

Holding their lead and taking advantage of their 65 percent shooting accuracy, North Carolina went into the locker room leading, 29–22.

In the smoke-filled stands, a young man in his mid-twenties decided he needed to find another seat. Dean Smith, a former Kansas player who was on the '52 championship team and was now an assistant coach at the Air Force Academy, had been sitting with his boss, the Academy head basketball coach Bob Spear, and Spear's counterpart at the Naval Academy, Ben Carnevale.

Every year, the two old friends met up at the NCAA championship, which coincided with the national coaches' convention, to share a big hotel suite with two other old Navy pals, University of Denver head coach Hoyt Brawner and Frank McGuire. Smith slept in the living room that year, but the price of the inconvenience was well worth it—he soaked up invaluable basketball wisdom from the veteran coaches, and he was able to meet and get to know McGuire in an intimate setting.

But while Spear and Carnevale were vociferously rooting for McGuire, Smith remained true to his alma mater. To preserve goodwill—and future relationships—with his roommates, Smith concluded that discretion was called for, and his dissenting presence with them was not.

Smith certainly had more to cheer about as the second half unfolded.

Kansas stayed in a match-up zone and their jump shots were finally falling. Wilt made some baskets, but to prevent him from getting his high volume of usual shots off, North Carolina had instructions to foul him. But that meant the Tar Heels picked up fouls and it gave Chamberlain an opportunity to score anyway, which he did, going 11-for-16 from the free throw line that night.

And the effects of the previous night's late-ending three-overtime game were beginning to take a toll. North Carolina was fading, just when Kansas was surging.

After an impressive 10-2 run, Kansas had a 40-37 lead with ten minutes left in the game.

"We were in a precarious position," McGuire admitted in interviews afterwards. "The boys were tired, and we were in a bad foul situation."

High Stakes Strategy

Instead of pressing his advantage, Waugh decided that a three-point lead was enough breathing room, and decided to play it safe, ordering the Jayhawks to freeze the ball.

"It was a strategic mistake," says Bob Young. "He shouldn't have done that."

Maybe not—but it almost worked.

Kansas held on to that lead for the next eight minutes. With 1:43 left, Rosenbluth picked up his fifth foul. The score was 46-43.

"It looked like we had the championship in the bag," Chamberlain recalled in his autobiography. "I remember looking up in the stands at some friends and thinking how groovy it was going to be to celebrate with them later."

North Carolina coach Frank McGuire (left) wanted a psychological edge over favored Kansas in the 1957 championship game. He rattled Jayhawks coach Dick Harp and referees had to separate the two men.

Gene Elstun, one of Kansas's best free-throw shooters, stepped to the line. He missed the first shot, then the next. North Carolina got the rebound and set up downcourt. They swung the ball around to Bob Young, Rosenbluth's replacement.

Young had missed the first half of the season because of a disciplinary suspension. McGuire preferred to stick with his starters as long as he could, so Young didn't see a lot of action when he rejoined the team, and he was completely off Kansas's radar.

But Young had been a highly recruited high school star in New York City. His teammates knew how good he was and trusted him. Wilt Chamberlain had no idea who Bob Young was.

"Chamberlain didn't anticipate that I would shoot, so I drove to the basket," Young recalls. "He was the only guy that I was worried about, but I got around him and made the basket."

Kansas failed to score to extend their slim one-point lead and North Carolina's Kearns made a free throw to tie the game. When time ran out, the score was tied at 46.

As overtime began, both teams were tight and each managed to score only one basket each.

The stalemate continued in the second overtime, but tensions boiled over when Chamberlain took exception to a hard foul, emptying both benches and bringing McGuire and Harp nose to nose. Things eventually cooled down, but neither team could get out of its scoreless funk and found themselves in a third overtime, North Carolina's second in two nights.

Kearns was able to penetrate the Kansas defense for a layup to give North Carolina a two-point lead. Elstun tried to answer with a 17-foot jump shot but missed. Kearns got inside Kansas's interior again and was fouled. He made both free throws, putting the Tar Heels up by four.

But Kansas got the ball back and threw the ball high in the air for Wilt. He soared high above everyone else and glided to the basket to deposit a graceful scoop shot, was fouled in the process, and made the free throw. Kansas trailed by one.

North Carolina couldn't convert on successive trips downcourt, while Kansas took advantage of fouls to King and Elstun, who each made a foul shot to put Kansas up by one with just 31 seconds to play.

McGuire called a play for Kearns, who beat his man as he drove the lane for what appeared to be a game-winning layup—until Wilt Chamberlain came over and cleanly swatted the ball away from the basket and out of bounds.

North Carolina had 15 seconds left to salvage their season, remain undefeated, and win a national championship. No time-outs. The ball was inbounded to Bob Young, who took two dribbles, thought about going to the basket but then saw Joe Quigg open on the side of the key.

"He was in perfect position, the perfect spot to get the ball," Young recalls.

Quigg gave Wilt a head fake, and the big man went for it. Quigg went past him and up for the shot. But with perfect timing, Wilt extended his long arm to flick the ball away. At the same moment, however, Maurice King, who had been watching the play from the weak side, had rushed over to prevent a game-winning shot and made contact with Quigg as the ball left his hand.

A two-shot foul.

Counterintuitively, McGuire called time-out. That's what the other coach is supposed to do, to rattle the guy going to the free throw line. But McGuire knew his players, and even though Quigg was a 72 percent free-throw shooter, he had missed his last foul shot.

"McGuire took the pressure off us," Young says. "He knew how to talk to us and he was always composed. There was never a sense of urgency from him. He told us to get the job done and we'll win."

In the huddle, McGuire gave his orders calmly. "Now when Joe makes these two shots," he said, "this is what we're going to do..." and went on to instruct Quigg and reserve forward Danny Lotz to get in front of and behind Chamberlain when Kansas came down for the final play.

Before the players went back on the court, Buck Freeman, always attentive to the smallest detail that could make a difference, pulled Quigg aside.

"Get up on your toes when you shoot, Joe," he told him.

Quigg made sure to lift off his toes as he brought his arms up to shoot. The ball rotated cleanly as it spun through the air to plop into the net and tie the game. The next shot was a duplicate of the first.

North Carolina was up by a point. Six seconds to go.

Kansas called timeout. Harp called for the obvious play: get the ball into Wilt.

Five seconds to go.

The rules of the day allowed Kansas to take the ball in at midcourt. Ron Loneski flashed to the top of the key and received the inbounds pass. He turned to look for Chamberlain, who had backed Quigg to within a few feet of the basket. Lotz, who had come in for Young, had blown his assignment and wasn't in front of Wilt. Loneski threw the ball in to Chamberlain. Quigg gambled, snaking around Wilt to prevent the giant center from catching the ball and converting the pass into a game-winning dunk.

Quigg jumped as high as he could and was able, barely, to tap the ball away from Chamberlain. Kearns beat Parker to the loose ball. With time running out, Kearns gripped the ball in both hands and threw it straight up in the air as high as he could.

When the ball came down, North Carolina was the national champion.

The victory marked the beginning of North Carolina's rise to prominence in the college basketball pantheon, the first of the Tar Heels' record 20 Final Four appearances, 11 appearances in championship games, and six titles.

The happenstance encounter of Dean Smith and Frank McGuire as roommates in the Kansas City hotel room led to McGuire offering Smith a job as his assistant coach a year later when Freeman retired.

The intense interest in the game and the Tar Heels' undefeated season led to the weekly broadcast of the ACC Game of the Week the following season, and the growth of the conference's phenomenal regional popularity and outsized national influence.

Legacy Questions

The game was also the beginning of a legacy that Wilt Chamberlain hated and arguably didn't deserve: loser.

It was his first conspicuous failure on the national stage with a championship at stake. In the NBA, he went up against his nemesis Bill Russell and the Boston Celtics in six championship series (five in the Eastern Conference finals, once in league finals) and won only once.

Against the New York Knicks, Wilt's Lakers team lost two out of three NBA Finals series.

Wilt did win two championships in his 14-year NBA career. And, to be sure, he is without question one of the all–time greats, the only man to score 100 points in a professional basketball game, the only player to average 50 points and 26 rebounds in a season, and the only Hall of Famer who, more than forty years after his retirement, still holds a slew of league records and is in the top ten of many more categories, including scoring and rebounding.

But there were those who thought Wilt liked to set records as much, if not more, than winning. That he was a selfish, spoiled, uncoachable, chronic underachiever who always had an excuse for losing. That he wasn't determined enough to win, totally committed to winning, or willing to do whatever it took to make sure his team won.

Chamberlain openly quarreled with one of his coaches in the NBA who would only shake a player's hand after the team won. "There are more important things than winning," Wilt snapped at the coach in front of the whole team. "You have to learn how to lose in life." By only shaking hands after a victory, he argued, the coach wasn't taking into account the individual effort of a player whose team happened to lose.

Maybe losing so many championships has even been to his advantage, Chamberlain rationalized to Frank Deford. "I think, in the long run, it gave me more insight. If you're a winner all the time, you'll never see the other side of the coin, you'll never understand other people's troubles."

Indeed, when you lose, Wilt wrote in his autobiography, "you're forced to confront yourself as you really are, way deep down inside. You gain insights and a perspective on yourself and others—and life in general—that a guy who always wins just never gets."

Still, the loss to North Carolina was one he didn't want and couldn't let go of.

"I've always been more bitter about that loss than almost any other single game in my whole college and professional career," Chamberlain wrote.

That was the game, he explained, "that started the whole 'Wilt's a loser thing.'"

But Kansas assistant coach Jerry Waugh insists Chamberlain was hardly to blame for the team's loss.

Wilt was the game's high scorer with 23 points. North Carolina limited his shot attempts by fouling him all game long, and he responded by hitting 11 of 16 free throws. He had a game-high 14 rebounds. He was named the tournament's Most Outstanding Player. His teammates missed nearly 75 percent of the shots they took that night; Wilt made almost half of his.

"Wilt didn't underachieve at all," Waugh said. "He followed the coach's directions. If he was going to be part of the team, we didn't want him dominating. That's how he was coached."

The men who played against Chamberlain that night remain his staunchest defenders sixty years later.

"It's not fair to call Wilt a loser," says Lennie Rosenbluth. "We just boxed him out and Kansas had to make their outside shots but they didn't. Wilt was frustrated. If they had made those shots, we would have had to change our defense and it would have been a different game. And they should not have held the ball when they had the lead in the second half."

Bob Young, who shadowed Wilt inch for inch for most of the grueling three overtimes, says Chamberlain "couldn't do more" than he did, which was plenty. "When you have three guys on you, it's tough to score."

In the final twist of fate, both Frank McGuire and Tommy Kearns entered Chamberlain's life again, this time with very different outcomes than in 1957.

After being forced out of North Carolina in 1961 as the result of an NCAA recruiting investigation that resulted in sanctions against the university, McGuire was hired by the Philadelphia Warriors that year and found himself coaching Wilt Chamberlain. They got along famously (a rarity in Wilt's pro career) and took Boston to seven games in the Eastern Division finals.

The Warriors moved to San Francisco the following season but McGuire didn't want to move his family west. He became coach of the South Carolina Gamecocks in 1964, won 283 games in 16 years, went to the NCAA tournament four more times, and entered the Basketball Hall of Fame in 1977.

Kearns, who went on to work on Wall Street, became Wilt's friend and financial adviser.

As for Joe Quigg, who faked Wilt out to get to the basket and made the game-winning free throws in 1957, he never played another minute of college basketball.

After breaking his leg badly the following fall, he couldn't play his senior year or in the pros and became a dentist.

Chapter 11

The Consolation Games

The following five NCAA championship games are all classics of the genre—thrilling, hard-fought, magical, pick your adjectives. You can make a reasonable case that any of these five could have been included in our Memorable 10.

As we said, our selection process was subjective.

Villanova 77, North Carolina 74
NRG Stadium, Houston, Texas
April 5, 2016

This one was stamped an instant classic the moment it ended.

It didn't have much of a back story; no legendary personalities took part, save perhaps Rollie Massimino, who was in the audience that night with some of his 1985 Villanova championship players to inspire the '16 Wildcats to turn the clock back thirty-one years.

And it wasn't what you would call a brilliantly played game. On the contrary, Carolina coach Roy Williams says, "We didn't play anywhere near our best game and usually you have to do that to win a national championship." Williams notes that Carolina missed too many open shots close to the basket and displayed less than optimal shot selection throughout the game.

Moreover, the refereeing was, to put it politely, questionable.

What marks the 2016 final as one for the ages is largely what occurred as the clock wound down in the second half.

First, Carolina's Marcus Paige threw in an unbelievable, double-pump jumper from well behind the three-point arc to tie the game at 74 with 4.7 seconds left. This capped an impressive comeback for Carolina from 10 points down with less than six minutes to go. But Villanova had the last word. Nova's Ryan Arcidiacono took off with the inbounds pass and brought it all the way to the top of the key before hitting a trailing Kris Jenkins for another miraculous three-pointer to win it at the buzzer.

Villanova coach Jay Wright says this was not the preferred option on that inbounds play. It was actually option number four. Not too shabby for a fourth option, acknowledges Williams.

"We'd seen in previous games that they had thrown a length-of-the-court pass, and we wanted to cover it," Williams explains. In lieu of that, Williams (and nearly everyone else) figured Arcidiacono to take the ball all the way to the hoop for a layup or foul, and in that event, Williams instructed his guys to try to get the ball out of his hands, figuring there would not be near enough time for him to dribble all the way up the court and make a backwards pass to a trailer for a long jumper.

Williams laments that the player guarding the inbounds pass, who was supposed to pick up Jenkins, didn't.

"In looking back, it was the only thing we didn't do [right] on that play."

The 39-plus minutes preceding this frenetic action were extremely entertaining, too, albeit sloppy at times.

Villanova, coming off one of the all-time great Final Four performances, where it shot 71.4 percent in a semifinal annihilation of Oklahoma, controlled the tempo through most of the first half, its trapping defense keeping UNC out of its preferred up-tempo, transition style of play. What kept UNC close were its' remarkable three-point shooting (not generally a Carolina strong suit) and the stellar play of Joel Berry II, who ran off 12 straight Carolina points late in the half to put them up by four. The low point for Villanova in the first half, if not the whole game, occurred on a Berry drive in the lane with just under two minutes left that saw the Villanova defenders part like the Red Sea opening up to the Israelites. This necessitated a timeout and some harsh words from Jay Wright.

In the closing 10 seconds of the half, Villanova's Josh Hart blocked a driving layup by Justin Jackson that would have put Carolina up by nine, and Villanova's Phil Booth scored at the other end with three seconds remaining to cut UNC's halftime lead to 39–34. Williams says this four-point swing was critical, as a nine-point lead would have sent his team into the locker room with a healthy jolt of momentum.

Instead, Carolina came out of the locker room flat. They continued to commit uncharacteristic turnovers, their long jumpers had stopped falling, and, on the defensive end, they were giving up too many easy underneath baskets. Villanova went on a 17–5 run to take a 51–46 lead at the 10-minute mark. The never-at-a-loss-for-words TV analyst Dick Vitale opined that "Uncle 'Mo has rotated over to Villanova's side." Meanwhile, Ryan Arcidiacono, held scoreless for more than 25 minutes, finally came out of his offensive cocoon to hit several big baskets to help stretch the 'Nova advantage to 67–57 with 5:29 left.

And then, a bad Arcidiacono pass, some tougher interior Carolina defense, and Berry coming out of his second-half scoring funk to drill yet another three-pointer, in just two minutes reduced the 'Nova lead to 67–64. 'Nova stretched it to 70–64 before Marcus Paige's baseline three-pointer and a Brice Johnson mid-range bank shot with one minute left brought the score to 70–69. By now, the joint was rocking, echoes of '85 resounding over the Villanova bench.

A questionable foul call on Carolina's Isaiah Hicks under the basket resulted in two Booth free throws with 36 seconds left to make it 72–69. On the other end, Paige made still another incredible play, ripping a rebound of his own missed layup away from a 'Nova defender and putting it back in the hoop to cut the lead back to one. Carolina intentionally fouled Hart in the frontcourt with 13.5 seconds left, and he hit both free throws to restore Villanova's advantage to three.

Ball to Carolina.
And the rest you know.

Kansas 75, Memphis 68
Alamodome, San Antonio, Texas
April 7, 2008

"Mario's Miracle."

That's what they call this game in Lawrence. They have other names for it in Memphis.

It was a tight game throughout, until Memphis went on a 10–0 run to take a seven-point lead with a little over five minutes left. They stretched the lead to nine with only 2:12 on the clock, at which point Kansas went on a frenzied 12–3 tear of its own, aided by very poor foul shooting on Memphis' part and capped by a Mario Chalmers jumper that tied the game at 63 with 2.1 seconds remaining. In overtime, Kansas, still amped up, got off the blocks first with six straight points and never trailed en route to its first NCAA title in twenty years.

It was the first for coach Bill Self, who had replaced Roy Williams as head coach a few years earlier. John Calipari, Memphis's coach, didn't have to wait too long for his first crown, which he won with Kentucky in 2012.

For the record, Memphis's appearance in the Final Four was ultimately vacated due to NCAA rules violations.

Syracuse 81, Kansas 78
Louisiana Superdome, New Orleans, Louisiana
April 7, 2003

What the 1982 final was to Dean Smith, this game was to Jim Boeheim. Despite his consistent record of success over 27 years, which included two trips to the championship final and his uncanny ability to persuade some of the best high school players in America to spend their winters in frigid Syracuse, New York,

Boeheim wasn't feeling the love. The fans' lack of affection—and respect—went deeper than Boeheim's failure to win them a coveted title. Boeheim's personality could be diffident and even prickly at times. To the more disgruntled Orange fans and alums, he was "F—king Boeheim."

But all those bad feelings disappeared in a matter of moments in the Superdome.

With under 15 seconds left in the game and Syracuse up by three, the Orangemen's Hakim Warrick missed a pair of free throws that would have cemented the victory. Down at the other end, Kansas's Mike Lee found himself all alone on the baseline for an open three-pointer that would have sent the game into overtime. That is, until Warrick, on condor's wings, soared to block the shot with less than a second on the clock. A desperate Kansas heave on the inbounds play flew over the basket, and F—king Boeheim was now Champion Boeheim. Just like that.

On the frozen tundra of upstate New York, this game is celebrated today as "The Block."

Meanwhile, on the opposing bench was another coach, Roy Williams, who was under pressure of his own to win the big one, which he had failed to do in his 15 years at Kansas. But Williams, too, would soon put that part of his past behind him, moving on to North Carolina the following season and capturing his first NCAA title in 2005.

North Carolina 77, Michigan 71
Louisiana Superdome, New Orleans, Louisiana
April 5, 1993

Just as UNC's 1982 championship came down to a shocking mistake by an opposition player in the closing seconds, so, too, did Dean Smith's second NCAA title. Michigan's star forward, Chris Webber, bringing the ball upcourt (he had clearly traveled in the backcourt, but the refs whiffed on that call), ran smack into Carolina's half-court zone trap which pinned him up against the

Michigan bench and gave him absolutely nowhere to go with the ball. With Michigan down, 73–71, 11 seconds remaining, and all other options shut off, Webber signaled for a timeout when his team had none to call. The resulting technical foul and free throws salted the game away for the Tar Heels.

Nevertheless, it's tough to pin this loss solely on Webber's mental miscue. Coach Steve Fisher has taken responsibility for not having adequately informed his players about the timeout situation. And you've got to give Carolina credit for some superb half-court team defense.

The '93 final was the second to feature Michigan's heralded "Fab Five." As freshmen starters the previous year, they took the college basketball world by storm. Their baggy shorts and low black socks, as well as their youthful swagger, helped create a hip-hop style of basketball (and fashion) that has since been emulated by countless teams. The Fab Five had been scalded by Duke in the '92 championship game. But as sophomores, the party of Five—Webber, Jimmy King, Jalen Rose, Ray Jackson, and Juwan Howard—was ready for prime time. All that is missing from their exhilarating two-year run is an NCAA title.

As it turns out, however, there would have been no title, even in victory. In 2002, after it came to light that several former Michigan players, including Webber, had taken money from a booster, Michigan's entire 1992–93 season was wiped from the record books.

Indiana 74, Syracuse 73
Louisiana Superdome, New Orleans, Louisiana
March 30, 1987

Before "The Block" took the monkey off Jim Boeheim's back, there was "The Shot," which had the opposite effect.

After a tightly-played game, 'Cuse's Derrick Coleman missed the front end of a one-and-one with 27 seconds left and the Orange up, 73–72. At the other end, Syracuse, which had been switching defenses all night, went into a box-and-one, with Sherman Douglas dogging Steve Alford. That strategy worked to keep the ball away from Indiana's best shooter. With only 10 seconds left, the ball wound up in the hands of junior guard Keith Smart on the left side of the basket. Smart passed it to Daryl Thomas posting down low, but Thomas's head fake failed to get Derrick Coleman off his feet. Thomas returned the ball to Smart, who shook free of defender Howard Triche with a quick dribble to his left and put up a smooth 16-footer that fell cleanly through the basket with four seconds left.

Syracuse allowed three of those four precious seconds to drain away before calling timeout (although some Syracuse players later claimed they did call an immediate timeout, which the refs failed to recognize). In any event, all Syracuse could do in the final second was throw a long inbounds pass that was intercepted by Indiana.

This was the third and last NCAA championship in Bobby Knight's storied, but disputatious, coaching career. In 2000, Knight, who had a long history of bizarre and unruly behavior (especially toward the media), violated Indiana's "zero-tolerance policy" on violence, when he put his hands on a student who he believed had disrespected him. Knight refused to resign and was fired. He finished out his coaching career at Texas Tech, relatively quietly and non-violently.

Sources

Interviews

2010
Miles Plumlee, Duke player
Chris Collins and Steve Wojciechowski, Duke assistant coaches
Zach Hahn, Avery Jukes, and Shawn Vanzant, Butler players
Brad Stevens, Butler head coach
Matt Graves and Terry Johnson, Butler assistant coaches

1989
Mark Hughes and Terry Mills, Michigan players
Andrew Gaze and John Morton, Seton Hall players
Bruce Hamburger, Seton Hall assistant coach

1985
Harold Jensen, Villanova player
Steve Lappas, Villanova assistant coach
Grady Mateen, Georgetown player
Craig Esherick, Georgetown assistant coach

1983
Ernie Myers and Dereck Whittenburg, NC State players
Ray Martin, NC State assistant coach

Max Perry, NC State graduate assistant coach
Reid Gettys and Larry Micheaux, Houston players
Michael Klahr, former Sports Information Director at Metro State College

1982
Matt Doherty and Eric Montross (class of '93), North Carolina players
Roy Williams, North Carolina assistant coach
Eric Smith, Gene Smith, and Ed Spriggs, Georgetown players
Bill Stein, Georgetown assistant coach

1979
Mike Brkovich, Terry Donnelly, and Mike Longaker, Michigan State players
Jud Heathcote, Michigan State head coach
Alex Gilbert, Bob Heaton, Alex Gilbert, Brad Miley, Carl Nicks, and Leroy Staley, Indiana State players
Bill Hodges, Indiana State head coach
Ed McKee, former Indiana State Sports Information Director
Tony Ponturo and Fran Kirmser, producers of *Magic/Bird* on Broadway

1975
Ralph Drollinger, Pete Trgovich, and Richard Washington, UCLA players
Gary Cunningham, UCLA assistant coach
Jack Givens, Kevin Grevey, and Rick Robey, Kentucky players
Joe B. Hall, Kentucky head coach
Irv Brown, referee
Gary Green, UCLA team physician

1966
Jerry Armstrong, Orsten Artis, Willie Cager, David Lattin, Nevil Shed, and Willie Worsley, Texas Western players

Moe Iba, Texas Western assistant coach
Irv Brown, referee and close friend of Texas Western coach Don Haskins
Charles Martin, professor at UTEP and authority on the integration of college basketball in the South
Cliff Berger and Larry Conley, Kentucky players
Joe B. Hall, Kentucky assistant coach

1963
Jerry Harkness and John Egan, Loyola players
George Wilson, Cincinnati player

1957
Lenny Rosenbluth and Bob Young, North Carolina players
Jerry Waugh, Kansas assistant coach

Books

Beckett, John. *Mission Accomplished!: Michigan's Basketball Miracle, 1989.* Taylor Trade Publishing, 1989.
Bird, Larry and Earvin Magic Johnson (with Jackie MacMullan). *When the Game Was Ours.* Houghton Mifflin Harcourt, 2009.
Black, Jimmy (with Scott Fowler). *Jimmy Black's Tales from the Tar Heels.* Sports Publishing, 2006.
Chamberlain, Wilt and David Shaw. *Wilt: Just Like Any Other 7-Foot Black Millionaire Who Lives Next Door.* Macmillan, 1973.
Davis, Seth. *When March Went Mad: The Game That Transformed Basketball.* Times Books, 2009.
_____. *Wooden: A Coach's Life.* Times Books, 2014.
Feinstein, John. *The Legends Club: Dean Smith, Mike Krzyzewski, Jim Valvano, and an Epic College Basketball Rivalry.* Doubleday, 2016.
Fitzpatrick, Frank. *The Perfect Game: How Villanova's Shocking 1985 Upset of Georgetown Changed the Landscape of College Hoops Forever.* Thomas Dunne Books, 2013.

Golenbock, Peter. *Personal Fouls: The Broken Promises and Shattered Dreams of Big Money Basketball at Jim Valvano's North Carolina State.* Carroll & Graf, 1989.

Hager, Tom. *The Ultimate Book of March Madness: The Players, Games, and Cinderellas that Captivated a Nation.* MVP Books, 2012.

Haskins, Don. *Glory Road: My Story of the 1966 NCAA Basketball Championship and How One Team Triumphed Against the Odds and Changed America Forever.* Hachette Books, 2005.

Lenehan, Mike. *Ramblers: Chicago 1963—The Team that Changed the Color of College Basketball.* Agate Midway, 2013.

Lucas, Adam. *The Best Game Ever: How Frank McGuire's '57 Tar Heels Beat Wilt and Revolutionized College Basketball.* Lyons Press, 2006.

Menzer, Joe. *Four Corners: How UNC, NC State, Duke, and Wake Forest Made North Carolina the Crossroads of the Basketball Universe.* Simon & Schuster, 1999.

Smith, John Matthew. *The Sons of Westwood: John Wooden, UCLA, and the Dynasty That Changed College Basketball.* University of Illinois Press, 2013.

Taylor, John. *The Rivalry: Bill Russell, Wilt Chamberlain, and the Golden Age of Basketball.* Random House, 2005.

Wooden, John. *Wooden: A Lifetime of Observations and Reflections On and Off the Court.* Contemporary Books, 1997.

Film/Television

1957: Year of McGuire's Miracle, 1996, Produced by Doug Fuller, Tar Heel Sports Marketing

Game of Change: Documenting the 1963 Mississippi State vs. Loyola (Ill.) Basketball Game, 2009, Produced by Jerald Harkness, Team Marketing

Glory Road, 2006, Directed by James Gartner, Buena Vista Pictures

Hoosiers, 1986, Directed by David Anspaugh, Orion Pictures

Making History: The 1966 NCAA Championship—Texas Western vs. Kentucky, March 30, 2016, ESPN
Survive and Advance, 2013, Directed by Jonathan Hock, ESPN Films
The Blind Side, 2009, Directed by John Lee Hancock, Warner Bros.

Websites

Dukechronicle.com
Tarheelblog.com

Newspapers and Magazines

The Atlantic
News & Observer (Raleigh, North Carolina)
Newark Star-Ledger
New York Times
Proceedings of the National Academy of Sciences
Sports Illustrated
Washington Post

INDEX

Abdul-Jabbar, Kareem, 133
Alabama-Birmingham, University of, 7, 9
Allen, Phog, 199, 200, 201, 204, 205
Anders, Benny, 81, 82
Arcidiacono, Ryan, 224, 225
Arizona State University, 33, 34, 143, 166, 191
Armstrong, Jerry, 160, 161, 163, 167, 172
Artis, Orsten, 160, 164, 165
Atlantic Coast Conference, 66, 90, 168, 203
Auerbach, Red, 199, 202
Avent, Anthony, 38

Bailey, Thurl, 67, 74, 75, 80, 82
Barnes, Jim "Bad News," 162–163
Barnett, Ross, 187, 188
Bartow, Gene, 144
Benson, Kent, 141
Berger, Cliff, 156, 168, 171
Berry, Joel, 224, 225
Berry, Walter, 52
Big East Conference, 20, 23–27, 31–32, 44, 45, 47, 49, 52, 53, 101, 102

Bird, Larry, 109, 110, 113, 114, 116, 119, 120–122, 125, 129, 131
Birdcage defense, 122
Black, Jimmy, 93, 99, 100, 101, 104, 105, 107
Boeheim, Jim, 143, 226, 227, 228
Bonham, Ron, 178, 179, 184, 195
Bonk, Thomas, 77
Booth, Phil, 225
Boston Celtics, 3, 119, 158, 202, 220
Boyd, Mike, 30
Brennan, Pete, 203, 209, 211, 212, 214
Brkovich, Mike, 113, 115, 118, 123, 129
Broadnax, Horace, 58, 59
Brown, Fred, 97–99, 106, 108
Brown, Irv, 146, 162, 164, 172
Brown, Willie, 163
Bryant, Mark, 25–27
Butler University, 1–11, 14–17, 19, 20

Cager, Willie, 163, 164, 176
Cameron Crazies, 11, 21
Canaan, Isaiah, 10
Carlesimo, P. J., 24–27, 32, 37, 38, 42
Carlesimo, Peter, 24, 25

Carnesecca, Lou, 47, 51, 52, 199, 203
Case, Everett, 200, 202
CBS-TV, 46, 55, 103, 130
Chamberlain, Wilt, 133, 158, 179, 199, 204–206, 208–215, 217–222
Chambers, Jerry, 167
Charles, Lorenzo, 71, 73, 76, 82
Charles, Ron, 118, 125
Cincinnati, University of, 123, 158, 167, 177–179, 184, 185, 190, 192–196
Cleveland State University, 62
Coleman, Derrick, 28, 228, 229
Collins, Chris, 3, 12, 13, 15
Colvard, Dean, 188, 189, 191
Conley, Larry, 156, 157, 169–171
Conner, Jimmy Dan, 141
Crum, Denny, 143
Cunningham, Billy, 92
Cunningham, Bob, 203
Cunningham, Gary, 138, 144, 145, 151

Dalton, Ralph, 52
Dampier, Louie, 168, 171
Davies, Bob, 23
Deford, Frank, 92, 221
DePaul University, 51, 123
Detroit Mercy, 8
Disco Bird, 114
Dixie Classic, 206
Doherty, Matt, 91, 93, 96, 100, 103, 105
Donnelly, Terry, 113, 117, 123, 125, 128, 129
Douglas, Sherman, 28, 228
Drake, Ducky, 148
Drexler, Clyde, 77, 78, 80, 81, 101
Driesell, Lefty, 66

Drollinger, Ralph, 136, 137, 139, 144, 145, 148, 149
Duke Chronicle, 12
Duke University, 1–3, 11–17, 21, 22, 37–39, 67, 90, 93, 100, 103, 151, 158, 168, 177, 191, 192, 206
Duke, sexual abuse scandal, 21

Egan, John, 181–184, 186, 187, 190, 191, 194, 195, 197
Elstun, Gene, 205, 217, 218
Esherick, Craig, 50–52, 55, 56, 61
ESPN "ESPY" Award, 87
Everson, Chuck, 58
Ewing, Patrick, 45, 48, 52, 55–59, 61, 94, 103–105

Fenlon, Bill, 7
Fisher, Steve, 34–36, 41, 42, 228
Flournoy, Harry, 171
Floyd, Eric "Sleepy," 102, 104–106
Flynn, Mike, 141, 150
Franklin, Alvin, 80, 81
Freeman, James "Buck," 207, 219
Frieder, Bill, 26, 28–30, 33, 34, 42

Game of Change, 188
Gannon, Terry, 71, 74, 80, 82
Gardner, Jack, 161
GATA drills, 161, 165
Gaze, Andrew, 27, 28, 31, 32, 37–40
Gentlemen's Agreement, 179
Georgetown University, 13, 14, 20, 25, 28, 31, 43–61, 90, 93, 94, 97–99, 101–106
Georgia Tech, 13, 52
Gettys, Reid, 78, 79
Gilbert, Alex, 120, 124, 130

Gilbert, Sam, 140, 141
Givens, Jack, 141, 142, 147, 148, 151
Glory Road (book), 162
Glory Road (movie), 167
Golenbock, Peter, 86
Grant, Gary, 27
Graves, Matt, 5, 8–11, 19, 20
Green, "Jumpin' Johnny," 209
Green, Gary, 153
Green, Sidney, 75
Greene, Gerald, 26, 27, 38, 41
Grevey, Kevin, 141, 145, 147, 151
Griffin, Mike, 39
Guthridge, Bill, 7, 65
Guyette, Bob, 141, 149, 150

Hackman, Gene, 2, 76
Hahn, Zach, 7, 8, 10, 15, 19, 20
Hall, Joe B., 141, 142, 145, 147, 150, 151, 153, 159, 168
Hamburger, Bruce, 25, 26, 32, 37, 42
Harkness, Jerry, 177, 178, 180–187, 190, 191, 193–196
Harp, Dick, 204, 205, 211, 212, 214, 216, 217, 219
Haskins, Don, 159–172, 175, 176
Havlicek, John, 178
Hayward, Gordon, 1, 2, 4, 9, 10, 17–20
Heathcote, Jud, 112, 113, 115–119, 123, 124, 129
Heaton, Bob, 120–123, 129
Hicks, Isaiah, 225
Higgins, Sean, 27, 30, 35, 41
Hill, Bobby Joe, 159, 160, 165, 170
Hinkle, Tony, 4
Hodges, Bill, 119, 120, 127, 129

Holland, Terry, 100
Holmes, Baskerville, 54
Hoosiers, 2, 3, 17, 76, 162
Horizon League, 2, 7–9, 20
Houston, University of, 65, 76–82, 92, 101, 106, 131, 176, 185
Howard, Matt, 4, 9, 10, 16, 17
Hughes, Mark, 27, 28, 31, 33–35, 39, 41
Hundley, Rod, 158
Hunter, Les, 182, 183, 192, 194, 195, 197

Iba, Henry, 159
Iba, Moe, 160, 172, 175
Illinois, University of, 31, 34, 37, 38, 117, 120, 177, 191
Indiana State University, 111, 114, 116, 119, 120, 122, 123
Iona College, 68, 69
Ireland, George, 177–187, 190, 193
Izzo, Tom, 10

Jackson, Justin, 225
Jackson, Michael, 45, 59
Jaracz, Thad, 168
Jenkins, Kris, 224
Jensen, Harold, 48, 49, 53, 54, 58, 59, 61, 62
Johnson, Earvin "Magic," 109, 115, 116, 121, 125, 131
Johnson, Lew, 205
Johnson, Marques, 146, 148, 149
Johnson, Terry, 6, 8–10, 15, 20
Jordan, Michael, 74, 94, 104, 105, 127, 131
Jucker, Ed, 178, 184, 190, 193
Jukes, Avery, 3–5, 7, 16, 20

Kansas State University, 10
Kansas, University of, 31, 89, 167, 175, 199–201, 204–206, 208–219, 221, 226, 227
Kearns, Tommy, 203, 207, 211, 212, 217–219, 222
Kelser, Greg, 111, 113, 116, 117, 125, 127–129
Kennedy, Doc, 94, 95
King, Bob, 120
King, Maurice, 205, 213, 218
Kirmser, Fran, 109, 110
Klahr, Michael, 69
Knight, Bobby, 12, 36, 141, 229
Kron, Tommy, 171
Krzyzewski, Mickie, 67
Krzyzewski, Mike, 2, 11–15, 67

Lancaster, Harry, 171
Lappas, Steve, 48, 53, 61, 62
Lattin, David, 160, 170, 174–176
Layden, Frank, 131
Lee, Keith, 54
Lee, Mike, 227
Lewis, Guy, 77–82
Loneski, Ron, 205, 219
Longaker, Mike, 117–119
Los Angeles Times, 140
Lowe, Sidney, 67, 70, 73, 81, 82
Loyola University of Chicago, 52, 158, 177–197
Lucas, Jerry, 178

Mack, Shelvin, 8, 10, 16
MacMullan, Jackie, 115
Madison Square Garden, 25, 51, 101, 102, 202
Magic/Bird, 109, 111

Man and a half zone, 123–124
Martin, Billy, 59
Martin, Charles, 157, 162
Martin, Ray, 67, 68, 70, 73, 84, 85, 87
Maryland, University of, 14, 53, 66, 73, 78, 155, 157, 168, 207, 208
Massimino, Rollie, 44, 47–49, 54–58, 61–63, 223
Mateen, Grady, 50, 52, 61
Maui Classic, 29
McCarter, Andre, 146, 148, 151
McCarthy, Jack "Babe," 188–190
McClain, Dwayne, 47, 48, 52, 57, 59–61
McGuire, Al, 112, 127–130
McGuire, Frank, 92, 199–203, 206–208, 211–219, 222
McKee, Ed, 122, 129
McLain, Gary, 43, 44, 53, 54, 58, 61, 62
McQueen, Cozell, 71, 75
Memphis State University, 29, 43, 54, 73 *see also* University of Memphis
Memphis, University of, 78, 226 *see also* Memphis State University
Meyers, Dave, 144, 146, 149, 150
Micheaux, Larry, 77, 78, 84, 87
Michigan State University, 10, 11, 72, 109, 111–113, 116, 117, 119, 121, 123–125, 128, 129, 209
Michigan, University of, 23, 24, 26, 28–42, 53, 108, 143, 168, 187–189, 227, 228
Milan High School, 2
Miley, Brad, 120, 121, 125
Miller, Ron, 182, 183, 187, 191, 194, 195

Mills, Terry, 27, 29–31, 34, 35, 38, 39, 42
Mississippi State University, 168, 177, 187–191
Montross, Eric, 95, 96
Morton, John, 26–28, 32, 36–39, 41
Mullens, Eddie, 171
Mullin, Chris, 52
Murray State, 9, 10
Myers, Ernie, 68, 72

Naismith, James, 199
National Invitation Tournament (NIT), 23, 25, 26, 69, 93, 119, 182
NCAA Selection Committee, 45
Nevin, Jake, 46
New Mexico State, 121–123
New York Times, 92, 201
Nicks, Carl, 120, 122, 124, 125, 127, 128, 130
Nored, Ronald, 9, 10, 16
North Carolina State University, 13, 47, 65, 68, 82, 146, 200, 202
Northwood/Keiser University, 62, 63

Ohio State University, 6, 7, 50, 101, 119, 178, 184, 191
Olajuwon, Akeem, 77–82, 101
Orr, Johnny, 24, 26

Packer, Billy, 55, 57, 81, 103, 148, 149
Paige, Marcus, 224, 225
Parker, John, 205
Pepperdine University, 74, 77
Perkins, Sam, 74, 94, 100, 101, 104
Perry, Max, 68, 71, 72, 85
Peterson, Buzz, 104
Phi Slama Jamma (PSJ), 76–80

Pinckney, Ed, 52, 53, 55, 57–59
Pittsburgh, University of, 44, 45, 53
Plumlee, Mason, 13, 14
Plumlee, Miles, 13, 14
Plump, Bobby, 2, 3
Ponturo, Tony, 109, 111
Possession-based analytics, 91
Pressley, Harold, 53, 58, 59

Quigg, Joe, 203, 212, 218, 219, 222

Ramblers, 180
Ramos, Ramon, 26, 27, 39
Reed, Steve, 122, 129
Rice, Glen, 27, 29, 31, 35, 39, 41
Richardson, Nolan, 163, 176
Riley, Pat, 155, 168, 170
Robertson, Oscar, 158, 178, 179, 184
Robey, Rick, 141, 142, 151
Robinson, Lynwood, 100
Robinson, Rumeal, 27, 31, 39–42
Rosenbluth, Lennie, 201–203, 206–210, 212–215, 217, 221
Rouse, Vic, 182, 183, 194–197
Ruland, Jeff, 69
Rupp, Adolph, 21, 90, 156, 159
Russell, John "Honey," 23
Rutledge, Ron, 102

Sampson, Ralph, 74, 100
Schembechler, Bo, 24, 28, 29, 33–35, 42
Scheyer, Jon, 13, 16
Seattle University, 36, 166
Seton Hall University, 23–28, 31, 32, 36–42, 102
Severance, Al, 46, 54
Shackleford, Charles, 86

Shed, Nevil, 159, 160, 163, 166, 167, 172, 174–176
Shingleton, Larry, 184, 194, 195
Singler, Kyle, 16, 17
Sloan, Norm, 67, 69
Smart, Keith, 229
Smith, Dean, 3–4, 65, 66, 78, 89–98, 103, 105–108, 199, 214, 215, 219, 226, 227
Smith, Eric, 102, 105
Smith, Gene, 98, 106
Smith, Linnea, 66, 67
Snyder, Quin, 38
Sports Illustrated, 43, 45, 53, 61, 92, 159, 165, 171, 187, 192, 195
Spriggs, Ed, 98, 99
St. John's University, 23, 25, 44, 45, 47, 51–53, 102, 139, 140, 180, 201, 202, 207
Staley, Leroy, 127
Stein, Bill, 98, 101–103, 106, 108
Stevens, Brad, 2–11, 15–17, 19, 20
Sun Carnival Tournament, 165
Survive and Advance, 73
Suttle, Dane, 74, 75

Tarkanian, Jerry, 36, 37, 62
Texas-El Paso, University of (UTEP), 9, 156 *see also* Texas Western University
Texas Western University, 155–159, 161, 162, 165–173, 180 *see also* Texas-El Paso, University of (UTEP)
Thacker, Tom, 178, 184, 193–197
The Legends Club, 67
The Tar Heel Blog, 94
Thomas, Lance, 14

Thompson, David, 69
Thompson, John, 45, 46, 49–52, 56, 58, 90, 94, 96–99, 101–103, 106
Tobacco Road, 66, 67, 92, 203, 206–208
Trgovich, Pete, 137, 144, 146, 148, 153
Trimble, Joe, 43

Utah, University of, 31, 75, 161, 167, 168

V Foundation, 87
Valvano, Jimmy, 47, 48, 65–76, 78, 79, 81–87
Vanderbilt University, 9, 29, 174
Vanzant, Shawn, 5, 6
Vaught, Loy, 27
Veasley, Willie, 16, 20
Versace, Dick, 122, 123
Villanova University, 43–48, 51–62, 78, 101, 102, 223–225
Vincent, Jay, 125

Wake Forest University, 73, 92, 100, 206, 208
Walker, Daryll, 26, 27, 40, 42
Walker, Wade, 189
Wallace, Perry, 174
Walton, Bill, 133, 135, 136, 138, 146
Warrick, Hakim, 227
Washburn, Chris, 86
Washington, Richard, 137–139, 143, 150
Washington, Rudy, 102
Waugh, Jerry, 204–206, 212, 214, 215, 221
Webber, Chris, 108, 227, 228
Weidenbach, Jack, 33

When March Went Mad, 112
When the Game Was Ours, 115
White, Jo Jo, 167, 172
Whittenburg, Dereck, 67, 70, 72–75, 79–82, 85
Williams, Reggie, 57, 58
Williams, Roy, 101, 223–227
Wilson, George, 178, 184, 193–195
Wilson, Othell, 75, 76
Wingate, David, 58, 59
Wojciechowski, Steve "Wojo," 13
Wooden, John, 21, 78, 90, 91, 133–153

Wootten, Morgan, 67
Worsley, Willie, 158, 163, 169–171, 174, 175
Worthy, James, 94, 99, 103–106

Yates, Tom, 178
Young, Bob, 203, 207, 210, 212, 215, 217, 218, 222
Young, Dick, 43
Young, Michael, 79, 81

Zoubek, Brian, 13, 14, 16, 17, 19